currently a freelance sports writer for a number of publications, including the *Sunday Times* and *The Golf Paper*.

CAN I CARRY YOUR BAGS?

A SPORTS' HACK ABROAD

Martin Johnson

070.449796

Constable • London

CONSTABLE

First published in Great Britain in 2015 by Constable

This paperback edition published in 2016 by Constable

A CIP catalogue record for this book
is available from the British Library.

ISBN: 978-1-47211-984-1 (paperback)

Typeset in Bembo by Initial Typesetting Services, Edinburgh
Printed and bound in Great Britain by CPI Group (UK) Ltd, Croydon CR0 4YY

Papers used by Constable are from well-managed forests
and other responsible sources

MIX
Paper from
responsible sources
FSC® C104740

Constable
is an imprint of
Little, Brown Book Group
Carmelite House
50 Victoria Embankment
London EC4Y 0DZ

An Hachette UK Company
www.hachette.co.uk

www.littlebrown.co.uk

Acknowledgements

My thanks to Charlie Burgess, for bravely taking a punt on an unknown cricket correspondent when *The Independent* launched in 1986; David Norrie, for filling in some of the blanks with his dangerously infallible memory; David 'Toff' Lloyd, for the generosity of his nature – not least in supplying the facts to the lazier scribblers in cricket press boxes around the world; and Harold Harry Ian Haywood 'Doc' Gibbons, the old Worcestershire batsman, for giving his name (albeit unwittingly and posthumously) to the world's finest website, www.gibbonsgolf.com.

To Bridget

A much-loved mother and an extraordinary person.

Thanks for everything.

AND

In memory of David Welch.

Colleague, boss and friend.

CONTENTS

PREFACE

'Let me know if you need someone to carry your bags.'

If I'd had a fiver for every time I'd heard that, I'd have been up there on the Forbes Rich List, sandwiched somewhere between Bill Gates and Tiger Woods. It was a familiar pattern. One of my chums would enquire about my next assignment, I'd say something like 'Augusta, US Masters', and back would come the offer to become my unpaid personal porter for a week.

I felt it no more than my duty, on such occasions, to assure this deluded individual that I'd actually prefer to mix it with the 7am traffic on the M25, would gladly run the risk of asphyxiation while hanging from a strap on the Northern Line, and would positively welcome sitting through a turgid meeting while some pin-striped bore from head office kept droning on about projections and targets. Not to put too fine a point on it, anything at all compared to the living hell I was about to put myself through.

'Have you ever been to Augusta?' I'd say. 'Er, no', they'd reply. 'Well, this time next week I'll be standing in the immigration queue at Atlanta Airport – an experience, incidentally, that they are now offering to prisoners on Death Row as an alternative to a lethal injection – and should I survive it, I will then find myself in another queue at the rental car office, bracing myself to stand firm against the remorseless attempts to persuade me to upgrade my mid-sized sedan to a stretch Cadillac convertible for only a modest additional outlay of $2,000 plus tax.

'Eventually, having triumphantly parted with only half that for the privilege of sitting behind the wheel of a compromise vehicle which, when stationary, still leaves the boot and bonnet in different postal districts, I will find myself trying to stay awake on the Interstate 20 to Augusta – a two-and-a-half-hour journey which, in terms of jaw-dropping scenery, makes Australia's Nullarbor Plain look like the Swiss Alps. Finally, I will arrive at one of America's ghastliest towns, whose main thoroughfare is littered with signs inviting me in for a "Dunkin' Donut" or an even more tantalizing culinary experience at the "Waffle House". Or, this being a town where – in more senses than one – you will certainly find religion, I can avail myself of the "free lemonade" offer blinking out from the neon sign outside the Christian Bookstore as a reward for attending Sunday Service.

'Then I will check into a motel, which a week ago was offering rooms for $40, but which now sports a giant sign reading: "The Cockroach Inn & Suites Welcomes Masters' Fans!" and requires more like $500 per night (paid six months in advance) in return for accommodation that you'd think twice about housing your dog in. With, mark you, no bar or restaurant, and a serve-yourself breakfast which consists of grits, more grits, maple syrup, four-day-old muffins, and a jug of liquid (for pouring into polystyrene beakers) which – in both looks and taste – is difficult to differentiate from engine oil.

'Next morning, I will set off for the course, and as the tournament has not yet started, try and find something to write about when nothing is happening. Apart, that is, from players being interviewed underneath the big oak tree outside the clubhouse, which generally involves some ole-aginous representative from the Golf Channel thrusting a microphone at everyone wearing a golf hat, with the single exception of Tiger Woods. Woods doesn't do casual inter-views, although, as we'll see later, this doesn't stop the Golf Channel man asking all the other players about him. Most of the players try to keep their heads down and keep walking when running the media gauntlet between clubhouse and practice ground, although with some of them – like Gary Player, as we'll again see later – it's the media that hopes he won't notice them rather than the other way around.

'Then, notebook full of dietary advice and trembling testimonials to the God-like status of the world's No. 1 golfer, you head back to the press room to compose your story. This would be a good bit easier if you were not sur-rounded by Americans, who have never been known to simply talk to their next-door neighbour when they have the chance to shout instead. Directly behind you are the radio commentators, who all have voices like oxyacetylene torches. "Hi there Dan!! Breaking noos!! Tiger will tee it up at 2.05 in tomorrow's first round, and who's gonna bet against the guy!! They've lengthened the course, and you know he's just gonna bomb it out there!! Live from the Augusta National!! This is Mike Motormouth, for WX2BY Detroit!!"'

Why do Americans routinely converse at decibel levels equivalent to a Formula One pit lane? My own theory is that the first pioneers parked the wagons too far apart when they were relocating to the Wild West, and, consequently, when someone ran out of provisions, they were forced to yell at each other across the campsite. 'Hey buddy!! I'm fresh outta beans!!' 'Okay fellah!! Be right there!!' Whatever, it's rare to come back from a trip to America without a matching pair of perforated eardrums.

Somehow, though, this stark insight into the cruel and gruelling world of the travelling sports hack rarely seems to strike the intended chord, and people still want to carry your bags. The only time, in fact, when I didn't get the offer was when the bags consisted of a single rucksack, and some bright spark on the *Daily Telegraph* decided it would make a nice story for me to yomp across Europe to the Champions League Cup final in Moscow on a shoestring budget that did not so much involve the usual routine of four-star hotels, as arming yourself with a travellers' guide to soup kitchens and park benches. It was, as I hope to illustrate later, not an experience to recall with great fondness, although at least it didn't involve interviewing people. Into every life a little rain must fall, but there are times when it falls so hard on the travelling sports hack you don't so much need to carry an umbrella, as start building an ark.

IT'S A DIRTY JOB BUT SOMEONE'S GOTTA DO IT

But if I've really got to report from a beach, I suppose Copacabana just shades it over Clacton

I'd just returned from South Africa with a January suntan, and a chum down at the local clearly wasn't having it when I took issue with his assertion that I had the world's most enviable job. 'Ok then, name me a cushier one,' he demanded. 'Easy,' I replied. 'The TV weather forecaster in Darwin.' I've been to Australia pretty often, sometimes for months on end on an England cricket tour, and while anyone who's been to Melbourne will tell you that you can be reaching for the sun cream one minute and an overcoat the next, not only does the temperature in Darwin never change by so much as a single degree, it also rains every day at precisely the same time. Consequently, I have this picture of the weatherman turning up at his studio in Darwin every morning, pinning: '34°C, Late Storm' onto his map, and then taking himself off to the beach or the golf course. '*That's* what I call a cushy number,' I said. 'Believe me, you wouldn't want my job. You spend half your life emptying your pockets and getting frisked at airports, lying in bed all night with your brain trying to work out what time zone it's in, and having the Wifi go down on you with a minute to go before deadline. And don't ask me when I last had a weekend off.'

I might have convinced him if the mobile hadn't started ringing. It was the office. 'Okay, when? . . . Where from? . . . Heathrow? . . . How long for? . . . Well, if you insist.' I put the phone back in my pocket, shook my head, and gave out a weary sigh. 'If I haven't already convinced you,' I said, 'you'll buy me a pint out of sympathy when I tell you what ghastly assignment they've given me now.' 'Tell me,' he said. Outside, the wind howled, and horizontal rain battered against the window. 'Beach volleyball,' I replied. Pause. 'Women's beach volleyball.' Long pause. 'In Rio de Janeiro.' Even longer pause followed by weary sigh. 'I rest my case.'

Forty-eight hours later, I was sitting in a custom-built stadium on Copacabana beach, at half past nine in the morning, with the digital temperature clock registering 91°F. The place was packed, and about every five minutes an automatic hosing system doused the crowd with cold water – partly due to the humidity, and partly, perhaps, because of what the competitors were wearing. Which wasn't a lot. The office had sent me to watch the Women's World Championships, and when the two British girls taking part were predictably eliminated on the opening morning, I spent half the afternoon lying around the hotel swimming pool, and the other half wandering around the beach bars at Ipanema. Mildly bored, I rang a friend, who was a football reporter on another newspaper, and asked him what he was up to. 'Off to Stoke versus Wolves tonight. And it's bloody freezing.' 'Lucky bugger,' I told him. 'It's too bloody hot where I am. Pardon? Sorry, hang on a minute. Er, yes please. One of those cocktails with the umbrella in it. Thanks. Now then, where were we . . . ?'

After three days of this kind of hardship, I sent over my piece, and was informed that the deputy sports editor would like a word. 'When are you due back?' he asked. 'My flight's tomorrow lunchtime,' I told him. 'Ah, you don't want to rush back here just yet. The weather's awful,' he said. 'How do you fancy a trip to the Caribbean instead?' 'What for?' I inquired. 'There's a World Cup football match in Dominica,' he said. 'But the World Cup's more than two years away,' I said. 'Isn't it?' He replied: 'Yes it is, at least the finals. But there are 635 qualifying games before then, and on Sunday it's the first of them. Dominica versus Antigua.'

'Should be of interest to at least half a dozen of our readers,' I thought on the flight over, although a football match that had no doubt bypassed the rest of the universe would at least, I reasoned, have the locals in a frenzy of anticipation. Street parties, hog roasts, non-stop Happy Hour in the rum shacks. Hey, this could be fun, I thought, and shortly after checking into my hotel, I took off in my hire car around the streets of the capital, Roseau, armed with my notebook and a single question to put to the soccer-mad populace. Which was: 'Are you looking forward to the big match on Sunday?' I was expecting pretty much the same response every time – along the lines of 'Yeah, man, can't wait', but while it was indeed the same response every time, it was more like 'Match? What match?' It was a long old day, largely because it was impossible to drive more than ten yards before coming up behind some lorry offloading bananas in the middle of the road, and while you waited your eyes were drawn to posters and billboards advertising such things as Coca Cola, Sand and Gravel Supplies, and Parish Prayer Meetings. Just about everything, in fact, bar a football match.

A telephone call to the Dominican Football Association seemed in order, but the number listed in the FIFA handbook rang out unobtainable. No matter, there were two more listed in the island telephone directory. The first gave the following message: 'I'm sorry, the number you have called is out of service. This is a recording.' And the second clicked me onto another recording, offering advice on what precautions I should take in the event of a hurricane. The only thing you could do fast in Dominica was get nowhere, so I wondered about their opponents.

I decided to phone the Antiguan Football Association office, only to discover they didn't have one, but eventually I managed to track down their secretary, a Mr Chad Green, to a shipping company, from where he handled his soccer business during tea breaks. I discovered, fairly early on in our conversation, that we had something in common, in that he too had been unable to contact any official from the home country, and still didn't know – this was on Thursday afternoon – which hotel his team was supposed to be staying in.

He was, though, 'pretty sure' the game was taking place on Sunday, but was keen to hear from someone regarding the kick-off time, and should I find out, would I be kind enough to let him know? Chad revealed – although I didn't exactly regard it as a scoop – that the secretary of FIFA, João Havelange, had been scheduled to attend the game, but Chad had now heard he wasn't coming after all. This came as no great surprise to me, given that João had probably given it up as a bad job after spending all week on the phone trying in vain to find out the date and kick-off time. Although he would at least have discovered what to do in Dominica in the event of a hurricane. Which was, for those of you planning to take a holiday on the island during the hurricane season, to 'keep some rags and cloth handy, to prevent water rushing into the house' and 'try to remain sober'.

I wondered whether trying to remain sober would have been easier while cowering under a table listening to the tiles being ripped off your roof, or when trying to get in touch with the Dominican Football Association, but just as I was about to give up and get stuck into the local grog, I tracked down the vice president of the DFA, a Mr Ferdinand Frampton, to an office at the Dominican Broadcasting Association. Ferdinand declared his surprise that the Antiguans appeared to be unaware of the time and date of their match, and while it came as less of a shock to him that nobody on the entire island knew there was a World Cup soccer match taking place at all, the publicity machine was about to spring into action and change all that.

The publicity machine, he revealed, would consist of a van with a loudspeaker driving around the streets of the capital twenty-four hours before the game – when, he said, most people would be out doing their shopping. It's an interesting marketing technique, and if ever the FA suspect that not everyone out shopping in the West End is aware that England are playing Germany at Wembley on the morrow, a van with a loudspeaker driving down Oxford Street would represent an economical method – even allowing for the congestion charge – of advertising it. Mr Frampton was certainly confident of it working in Dominica, predicting that as many as four thousand would attend the game, albeit adding that only around half of them would end up paying. The walls around the ground, he said, were 'not very high', and the police 'couldn't be everywhere' to stop people climbing over them.

Ferdinand then kindly invited me to attend that evening's team training session at the ground, which had a certain rustic charm, and a pitch that, while bumpy, had considerably less potholes than the capital's High Street. It was also impressive to see that they had no less than three groundsmen: one bloke with a lawnmower, and two goats. The team itself was made up of a few civil servants and a couple of casual labourers, but most were unemployed, said Ferdinand, who told me he would have preferred it if all his players had been unemployed. As it was, training sessions could only be squeezed in late in the afternoon.

The stadium, as it was grandly called, accommodated all sports, not just football, and looking at the two main stands, named after two fairly obscure West Indian crick-eters, made you realize that dropping the *Encyclopaedia of Dominican Sports Legends* on your foot wouldn't leave much of a bruise. Each stand had a seating capacity of around a hundred, with air conditioning supplied via holes in the corrugated roofs. I thanked Ferdinand for all his help, and wished him luck on the day, especially after hearing him making a phone call asking whether they'd found a band yet for playing the pre-match anthems. I told him to make sure they knew their stuff, as I'd just been reading about a bit of a cock-up at a Pan-American soccer game between Honduras and Brazil, when the Hondurans had returned to the dressing room in protest at being invited to stand proudly to attention for what turned out to be the national anthem of Panama.

The office wasn't interested in a match report, especially when I told them no one quite knew when the match was actually due to take place, so after sending a piece back to London about how half the island was in a lather of ignorance, I asked the deputy sports editor if he could sort out a flight back for the following day. 'Ah, yes, glad you brought that up,' he said. 'During conference this morning someone pointed out that the West Indies are playing a World Cup cricket quarter-final in Pakistan on Monday, and that there might be a good story in cricket-mad fans going crazy with excitement.' 'As crazy with excitement as they do for World Cup football matches you mean?' I replied. 'Now, now,' he answered, 'everyone knows cricket's the big thing over there. You could take one of the island hoppers to Barbados and watch it among the locals in one of the bars . . .'

Which is how I came to find myself in Bridgetown for the West Indies v South Africa in Karachi, among people, according to my deputy sports editor, who eat, breathe and sleep cricket. I soon found out that for every West Indian in Barbados eating and breathing it, there were a hundred more sleeping while the match was taking place.

It was being broadcast, given the time difference, right through the night, and the interest was such that when I drove around Bridgetown in my hire car to decide which of the island's many bars I would choose to watch it from, I found everywhere closed.

Well, almost everywhere. Only one licensed premises in the whole of the capital bothered to stay open for the night, and to describe 'Bert's Bar' as packed would have been a serious exaggeration. The audience peaked at around 1am, at roughly thirty customers, and by the time the game finished – in a surprise win for the West Indies – only three people remained: myself, Bert (the owner of Bert's Bar) and an American tourist whose complete ignorance of cricket at least provided some entertainment – more so than the one-sided game itself, that's for sure.

Already puzzled by the fact that McDonald's had just closed down on the island (rumour had it that the chain's market researchers had failed to latch onto the fact that Bajans hardly ever eat beef) our American friend was even more bemused attempting to follow what was taking place on what Bert was advertising as a 'big screen', but what was in fact so small that you couldn't see a thing from further than a yard away. A South African fielder diving to cut off a run was met with 'Hey, this guy's a short stop, right?' and when the West Indies star batsman Brian Lara hit a boundary it was: 'That's like a homer, I guess.' And so on.

Bert, a white Bajan, was either serving or glued to the screen, so he heard none of this, and was not even aware of the American leaving 'to see if there's any baseball on at the hotel'. Which was quite an achievement given that the

American had a voice so loud – albeit not quite as loud as his shirt – that it threatened to break all his optics.

As dawn broke outside Bert's, I realized that they were starting work back in London, so I phoned the office to inform them that I was walking back to my hotel, and that if the inhabitants of Bridgetown were busy lighting bonfires and dancing in the streets in celebration of victory, I had yet to locate them. I'd been walking for about ten minutes, in which time I'd spotted half a dozen early-morning commuters and a corporation dustcart. 'I'll send the piece later after I've had a bit of kip,' I said. 'Meantime, can you organize a flight back tomorrow?' A voice replied: 'You're in Barbados, right?' 'Right,' I said. 'Well, it's the start of the Cheltenham Festival today, and they're really big on their horseracing there. Did you know that Garrison Savannah (Gold Cup winner in 1992) was named after the Bridgetown racetrack?' 'No, I didn't,' I replied. 'Well, what do you think about spending the afternoon in a betting shop there, and doing us a piece about the locals watching Cheltenham on the telly, and having a bet?' 'Sure,' I replied. 'After all, you've just sent me to Dominica for a soccer frenzy story, only to find out no one even knew there was a match taking place, then to a bar in Barbados bursting with cricket fanatics – the owner, an American who hadn't a clue what was taking place, and me. So why not complete the hat-trick with a deserted betting shop?'

This time, though, the office were spot on. At the time, Barbados was grappling with a number of important topics – privatizing the shipping port, water shortages affecting tourism, and trading wrangles with their Caribbean neighbours – but the one causing the greatest amount of agitation on this particular Champion Hurdle day in March I found mildly surprising. It was snowing at Sedgefield. Up until this point, I had supposed that the weather in Sedgefield would not have caused much of a stir outside Sedgefield itself, never mind on an island in the Caribbean, but while the Champion Hurdle at Cheltenham was clearly the main attraction of the day, there were just as many punters inside the betting shop looking to have a few bob each way on some selling-platers' handicap hurdle in the frozen north of England. Bajans take their horse-racing seriously, and frontal depressions over Sedgefield (or Market Rasen and Towcester come to that) are not matters to be idly dismissed with a shrug of the shoulders and a muttered '*C'est la vie.*'

Following the horses, I discovered, was – on the evidence of the previous day at any rate – a far bigger deal than watching the cricket, and up until this point in my life I'd never have suspected that a course inspection allowing horseracing to go ahead at Sedgefield would be greeted with outpourings of joy inside the venue I was in at the time, a betting shop in Bridgetown, Barbados. The Champion Hurdle was the main event of the day, but there was just as much jostling at the betting till to hand over a slip for a race called the Monkey Puzzle Selling Handicap Hurdle at Sedgefield. And when the race began, I discovered that the locals didn't just bet on the horses, they rode them as well. Each stool in the shop doubled as a saddle, and if they'd actually been aboard real horses, the Jockey Club would have stood them down for excessive use of the whip.

What's more, even though the official language in Barbados is English, you'd have had more chance comprehending the dialogue in the Tokyo Stock Exchange than a group of Bajans watching a British horse race in a Bridgetown betting shop. They didn't even take a break when the 2.08 greyhound race from Sunderland came on, where the snowflakes blowing across the front of the traps was a mild contrast to the eighty-five-degree sunshine beaming in through the open door. It was uncomfortably hot inside, with all those sweating bodies, although it was a lot cooler for Sir Garfield Sobers inside the air-conditioned manager's office. A courtesy extended for being not only the most famous person in Barbados, but also the manager's best client.

I sent the article, phoned the secretary's extension to ask about her booking me a flight back, and heard her say: 'Just a minute. Brian would like a quick word.' It was the deputy sports editor again, who said: 'It's still snowing over here, so you won't be in any hurry to get back, and we've had another great idea.' 'Brian,' I replied, 'I only packed for three days, and I've been away three weeks. Where now?' 'Well, we were talking snooker in the pub the other day, what with the World Championship coming up, and someone said, 'Whatever became of Bill Werbeniuk?' 'You mean,' I replied, 'that enormous Canadian who looked like Doberman in Sergeant Bilko?' 'The very one,' said Brian. 'Anyway, he's apparently back in his native Vancouver, and apparently is a regular at the Jolly Coachman pub in a suburb called Pitt Meadows. If you could get hold of him and arrange an interview, it doesn't look too far to get there from Barbados.'

Every hack in the field knows that newspaper desks are notorious for misjudging distances, and the trip to Vancouver turned out to be a short hop of twelve and a half hours. Four hours to mainland USA, two hours in transit, and another six and a half hours to west coast Canada. I eventually made it to the Jolly Coachman pub in Vancouver to meet a by-then retired snooker player who never made a televised 147, but who certainly came close several times. And we're not talking points here, but pints. Wearing a tatty old tracksuit top with 'Harrogate Leisure Centre' on the front and 'Big Bill Werbeniuk' on the back, he said that he was a bit hard up and couldn't afford to go to the pub very often any more, which didn't surprise me given what it would have cost him.

As I watched fifteen pints of lager disappear in the course of our three-and-a-quarter-hour meeting it became clear that when Big Bill went out for a quiet pint, a big bill is what he ran up. All fifteen of his pints were delivered by a girl on roller skates, who operated a bit like an auctioneer at Sotheby's. She'd look over, I'd nod, and she was there thirty seconds later with a freshly topped-up glass. Each one was despatched in the same way, with one gulp removing half of the contents, and the second gulp the rest. And with only two visits to the Gents required, the 'Big' in 'Big Bill' clearly extended to his bladder as well. The receipt was a collector's item – fifteen pints and seven halves – and I only wish I'd thought to keep a copy of the bill as a souvenir before submitting it with my expenses.

Bill's biggest claim to fame as a snooker play was in managing to persuade the Inland Revenue to give him tax relief on his pints of lager, in the same way as a painter and decorator can claim for his overalls. He had some kind of ailment known as 'Familial Benign Essential Tremor', which caused his cueing arm to behave as though he was conducting the London Philharmonic. The only cure – which was prescribed by doctors and accepted as a legitimate expense by the Revenue – was a combination of alcohol and beta-blockers. However, the taxman later took the money back, and when snooker's governing body started to ban various substances to try and weed out the cocaine sniffers, Bill found that he was no longer able to take his beta-blockers. And as he couldn't play without them, at least not without ripping the cloth, he couldn't play at all.

When I met him, Bill's cue had been in mothballs for five years, although he was still on the beta-blockers, otherwise he'd have spilt more than he drank. Not even fifteen pints could make him dizzy, and if the pub hadn't eventually closed for the night, the expenses bill could have closed the paper down, but we eventually said cheerio, and he cut rather a sad figure returning home to the small apartment he shared with his mother, more or less broke, and living on state benefits. It reminded me that I hadn't seen any of my own family for quite some time, and sure enough, when I phoned the office next morning, a voice at the other end said: 'There's a big Seniors golf tournament in Arizona, and we wondered whether . . .'

I learned something from this latest assignment, which was that you can possess a plane ticket from Canada to America, but if you haven't also got a plane ticket that takes you back out of the USA, they won't let you in.

I also discovered that when an American immigration officer informs you that the absence of a plane ticket out of his country marks you out, in his eyes, as a potential illegal immigrant, the clever answer is not: 'Listen here, chum. On the dozen or so occasions I have visited America, which is, by the way, about a dozen times more than I'd care to have done, the urge to get out of the place again has seldom taken more than two minutes. Believe me.'

I had four hours to wait for the British Airways desk to open, and purchase the ticket out of America which would allow me to get in, but being a smart-arse meant that instead of passing the time enjoying a leisurely lunch in downtown Vancouver, I was obliged to remain in a detention room while various checks were made to find out whether I'd recently escaped from an asylum or was in any way related to Fidel Castro. Nowadays, every time I run into an American immigration officer, I smile and nod inanely, and call him 'Sir' about six times a sentence. It's sound advice, trust me.

It was a relief to finally get to Scottsdale, in the upper reaches of the Sonoran Desert, and it was a pleasant enough couple of days watching old people prospecting for gold in the Arizona Hills. Once upon a time they came with donkeys and panhandles, but this lot arrived in Lear Jets carting golf clubs. There was then, and still is now, a lot of money in American Seniors' golf, and the tournament was full of old timers raking in more swag than they ever did as regular pros. The first-round leader, wearing a ten-gallon hat on his head, was someone called Tom Wargo, who had earned around sixteen thousand in seventeen years before becoming eligible for the Senior Tour at the age of fifty, since when he'd trousered over three and half million in three years. They don't even have to walk – getting driven around in electric carts – and there is something about achieving senior status that makes American golf galleries even more fawning than they are at regular tournaments. Jack Nicklaus was playing, and, not surprisingly, the great man not only drew the biggest gallery, but also the most obsequious.

'You're just the nicest, Mr Nicklaus,' gushed a woman spectator as he walked onto the first tee, and this sort of thing went on almost throughout Jack's entire eighteen holes. Golfers in general, never mind golfing greats, don't have to do very much to win over a crowd, and Nicklaus more than once reduced the spectators to helpless laughter with rapier-like wisecracks such as 'Not such a great lie, huh?' or by ordering some flying beastie to stop hovering over his ball. Jack's playing partner, Larry Nelson, didn't join in the general hilarity, largely because steam was still coming out of his ears from a quadruple-bogey seven at the previous par three. His tee shot fell into a waste area, finishing behind one of several large rocks, and he only finally emerged after a series of jabs and ricochets. As happy as Larry, Nelson was not, and his mood was not improved by a comment from a lady spectator exclaiming to her husband, 'I guess he should have hit it a bit harder, huh.'

'Did you get the golf piece okay?' I asked Brian over the phone next day. 'Yes thanks. So when are you flying back?' he said. I replied: 'You mean, you don't want me to go to Vladivostok to interview some Russian ice-skater, or Tierra del Fuego for the South American trout fishing championships?' He said not. But it wasn't until I was air-borne bound for Heathrow that I felt entirely safe.

It wasn't long, though, before I was heading back to America, this time for a boxing match involving Lennox Lewis. The British heavyweight was to fight someone called Ray Mercer, who frankly I'd never heard of. It was Sunday morning, and Brian phoned me from the office. 'There's a great piece in one of the Sunday papers by Harry Mullan previewing the fight. You'll get all the background info you need from that.' So I picked up the paper, cut out the article, and put it into my jacket pocket with the view of quietly going through it, and gathering some background info, on the flight over.

The office had sent me the return plane tickets to Las Vegas, and the reservation for the 'Pink Flamingo' hotel, and although this was my first trip there it didn't take me long to discover that the American grasp of geography was as hazy in Nevada as everywhere else in the USA. 'Where you from?' asked the taxi driver as I sat in the back seat heading into town from the airport. 'England,' I replied. 'No kidding,' he said. 'I'm gonna visit England one day. I wanna see me that Eiffel Tower.' Even by American standards this startled me just a little, and I felt compelled to tell him that I had bad news to impart. That the Eiffel Tower had been moved. To Paris. Paris, France, that is, as opposed to Paris, Texas. 'They moved it?' he said. ''Fraid so,' I said. 'They moved the Eiffel Tower?' he said. 'The very same,' I said. 'They moved the Eiffel Tower to Paris?' he said. 'Paris, France.' I said. 'You don't say,' he said. 'I do say,' I said. And it was while he was digesting this clearly deflating information that I remembered the newspaper cutting in my jacket pocket and fished it out.

Harry Mullan, the author of the article, was a highly respected boxing writer, but while I had no qualms about transferring some of his observations on the fight into my own notebook, I did think it a bit odd that he could have got something so basically wrong as the venue. 'Madison Square Garden?' I thought. 'That's in New York. How can you drop a clanger like that?' Then another thought occurred. What if Harry was right and my own sports desk had somehow got it wrong. 'Don't be daft,' I thought. 'This is the biggest selling broadsheet in the country. They don't go around sending their journalists to the wrong places.' A couple of minutes later we rounded a bend and any remaining traces of doubt were emphatically removed.

There by the side of the road, as we headed into the city, was a large neon sign advertising the fight. 'Lennox Lewis Double Header!' it flashed. 'At the MGM Grand!' it added. 'Friday Night Live!' it revolved. And several more electronic signs had beamed out the same information by the time we pulled up outside the Pink Flamingo. I had a quick look at the check-in list while I was registering, and didn't see any familiar English boxing writer names, but there were hundreds of hotels in Las Vegas, and they could have been scattered all over the place. So the following morning, the day before the fight, I set off for the MGM Grand Hotel, one of Las Vegas's biggest and best-known boxing arenas, and asked at reception where I might find the press accreditation room.

'Sorry buddy, there's nothing like that here.' 'But this is where the Lennox Lewis fight is, right?' 'Sure is, buddy.

You here to watch it?' 'Yes I am,' I said. 'Which part of the hotel would it be in?' 'Follow me, bud, I'll take you right to it.' And after a while I was ushered through a door into a room about the size of Wembley Stadium, with what appeared to be several hundred television screens. 'Er, sorry,' I said. 'There's been some misunderstanding. I don't want to watch it on TV. I'm here to see it live.' 'You wanna see it live?' he said. 'Yes, live,' I said. 'You know. Ringside.' He looked at me and smiled. 'You're kidding right?' I told him that I wasn't. 'In that case, man, you're in the wrong place.' 'Blooming heck', I said. 'Where is it then? Caesar's Palace?' 'No sir, it's way out east,' he said. 'East?' I said. 'East of what? East side of town?' He smiled again. 'No sir. East as in east coast.' 'East coa . . .' A horrible thought occurred. My mind went back to the newspaper article and Harry's preview. 'Are we,' I asked, 'talking about New York by any chance?' Another smile. 'Yes sirree. The good ol' Big Apple.' I must have made some kind of gurgling noise, as he asked me if I felt okay and would I like a glass of water, but I merely thanked him for his time and trouble, and wandered back towards the Pink Flamingo to consider the situation.

It was pretty hot, so I wandered out onto the hotel pool-side terrace, ordered a beer, and phoned the office. I can't remember now exactly who picked up the phone, but the voice was a cheery one, and asked me if the trip was going well. 'Er, not bad,' I replied. 'Although, not quite as well as I'd hoped perhaps. Still, at least the weather's nice and hot.' 'Nice and hot? At this time of year? You surprise me,' he said. I replied: 'Actually, surprise you is what I'm about to do. Would you like the good news or the bad news?'

'Okay, give me the good news.' 'The good news is that I'm here in America.' 'And the bad news?' 'The bad news is that you're closer to the fight than I am.' 'Eh?' 'Well, almost.' 'Where are you then?' 'Las Vegas.' 'Las Vegas?' 'Las Vegas.' 'What on earth are you doing in Las Vegas?' 'I'm having a beer next to a hotel swimming pool.' 'But aren't you supposed to be in New York?' 'Well, that's where the fight is, but when you gave me a return plane ticket to Las Vegas I kind of assumed, and call me stupid if you like, that that's where I needed to go.' He said: 'Bloody hell. So what do we do now?' I replied: 'Well, I've been giving it some thought, and decided it might be a good idea if I flew to where I should have flown in the first place.' 'Right, I'll get someone on it.'

Eventually I got a call back saying that they'd booked me a seat on the midnight red-eye, getting into New York, with the three-hour time difference, at six o'clock in the morning. It was still only lunchtime in Vegas, and with nothing else to do I lay around the pool for most of the afternoon, shaking my head about every thirty seconds, and muttering: ' I don't believe it. I do not believe it.' A hotel employee came by offering complimentary news-papers, so I took one, and found it so full of interesting stuff it almost made coming to Las Vegas by mistake seem worthwhile. First, I discovered that they were about to start construction on a giant replica of the Eiffel Tower, which made me wonder if my taxi driver chum had seen it and realized that he would no longer have to travel to Paris (or London if they'd moved it back again) to visit it.

The best article, though, was all about a woman who'd shampooed her poodle, and then attempted to dry it off in a microwave oven, issuing a lawsuit for damages. The gist of her complaint was that the manufacturers had not put a warning on the oven door, which of course made you wonder what kind of warning the judge – when it came to the court case – might have deemed appropriate. Something like this, perhaps. 'Caution. Do not insert metal containers, tin foil, or small dogs. Otherwise, three minutes on full power might mean that your pet is substantially reduced in size, a little on the stiff side, and only fit for hanging in the back window of your Oldsmobile.'

Finally, it was time to leave for the airport, and after dropping my plastic, electronic room key into the disposal bin near reception, I hopped into a taxi to play the usual game of 'guess-where-I-come-from?' Only this time, having been born in Wales, I wasn't going to make it so easy. We went through the usual suspects, Australia, South Africa, and eventually got to England, but finally I realized the cabbie was never going to get it and that I'd have to tell him. 'Wales?' he said. 'Hey, don't tell me. Wait. I know where that is. Hang on, man. It's on the tip of my tongue. Don't tell me. Let me see now.' And a couple of traffic lights later he swivelled his head, shot me a look of triumph, and said: 'Little island in the Pacific, right?' 'Nice try,' I replied. 'You're so close I'm tempted to give it to you. It's not actually an island, nor is it in the Pacific, but it's little, so jolly well done.' 'Hey, I know Wales has some famous people, right?' 'I suppose so,' I said. 'Don't tell me,' he said.' 'I won't,' I said, and for the next ten miles or so the conversation from the front seat went something like: 'Wales . . . Wales . . . What the hell! Wake up buddy! . . . Wales . . . Wales . . . C'mon! Quit hogging the centre

lane! . . . Wales . . . Wales . . . Jeez, that was close! . . .
Wales . . . Wales . . .' and then . . .' 'Got it!' Followed by a
not very tuneful, but nonetheless impressive, rendition of
'It's Not Unusual.' 'Tom Jones right!' he exclaimed. 'I'm
impressed,' I said, and I genuinely was.

Finally, having slipped him Shirley Bassey, Ivor
Emmanuel and Barry John, none of which he'd heard
of, I arrived at the Delta Airlines desk, produced my ID,
and the girl behind the counter handed me my ticket.
'That'll be a hundred and twenty dollars please sir' she
said. 'Hasn't it been paid for?' I inquired, a tad surprised
the office hadn't sorted it. 'No sir, that'll be a hundred and
twenty dollars to pay.' I checked on how much cash I had,
which was about eighty dollars, and reached for my wallet.
Only to find that my credit card did not appear to be in it.
Puzzled, I thrust a hand into my left-hand jacket pocket
and found nothing. I tried the right-hand pocket. Bingo.
There it was. I slapped it triumphantly on the counter, and
couldn't quite work out why the airline girl was looking
a trifle puzzled. Until I looked at it, and discovered that I
was attempting to pay for my flight with one of those flat,
electronic, plastic hotel-room keys.

Strange, I thought. Strange because I remember having
disposed of it in the hotel lobby shortly after paying my
bill with the credit card. There had been a 'used key' bin
in the lobby, and I'd popped my room key in it before
leaving for the airport. Or at least I'd posted something
plastic and flat, and . . . Oh my God, I thought. Don't tell
me. It's not possible. Is it? 'Excuse me,' I said to the airline
ticket girl, 'do you think I could use your phone?' I called
the hotel, and said to someone on reception: 'I know this

sounds a bit odd, but could you check your used key bin in the lobby. I think I may have posted my credit card in it.' 'Hold on please sir, I'll check with housekeeping.' A minute went by, maybe two, and when he came back on the line he said: 'Would that be a Visa card sir?' Yes it would.' 'Mr Martin Johnson.' 'You've got it?' Yes sir, we have. We'll hold it right here for you at reception.'

I looked at my watch. The prospect of hanging around all day had been so boring that I'd left very early for the airport, and I calculated I still had time to get back there, pick up the credit card, and still make the flight. I was in no mood to play the geography game on the way back to the hotel, declining all attempts at polite conversation, and getting increasingly agitated by the fact that all the lights seemed to be on red. Finally, we got there, and I dashed inside, retrieved the credit card, and dashed back outside again. A look at my watch told me it was going to be tight, so imagine my consternation when I found that the taxi had gone. I'd simply have jumped into another one, but this one had my suitcase in the boot. Where was he? And then I realized that the Pink Flamingo actually had four different entrances, all of which led to reception via rows of fruit machines, and they all looked identical. I realized I'd gone back the wrong way, and by the time I found the cab again, I was seriously up against it.

It was a close call, but I made it, and the following morning, somewhat dishevelled and short of sleep, I found myself in the considerably colder climate of New York City, and walking from my hotel to Madison Square Garden to collect my press ticket for the evening fight. I was almost there when I spotted, coming the other way, a boxing journalist I knew very well: John Rawling. 'Jonno!' he said. ' I didn't know you were over here for the fight?' Followed by 'Blimey, what happened to your face?' Las Vegas had been hot, and I'd already discovered from the mirror in my new hotel bedroom that my skin was all red and blotchy, and starting to peel off. 'Sunburn,' I said. 'Sunburn? Where've you been to get sunburned at this time of year?' 'Las Vegas.' 'Las Vegas? What on earth have you been doing in Las Vegas?' 'John,' I said. 'Don't ask.'

2

OLYMPIC FUN AND GAMES

Sydney 2000 . . . Nagano 1998 . . . London 2012

It was during the 1996 cricket World Cup in South Africa that I slipped a disc in my back, and to this day I will give any female an argument that childbirth has got to be an absolute doddle compared to back pain. I ended up being examined by a specialist with an impressive number of letters after his name, who warned me not to attempt things like digging the garden or humping refrigerators, which I was happy to hear, and not to travel anywhere by air if I could possible help it, which was I was not so happy to hear. 'Don't fly? In my job? Sorry doc, not an option, sadly.' He asked what I did for a living, and when I told him he replied: 'Ah well, at least you'll have a reasonably comfortable seat up at the front of the plane. At least I assume you travel business class.'

It is a common misconception that all journalists travel in the front of the plane, sipping vintage champagne, nibbling canapés, wondering which wine will go best with the lobster, and finally pressing a button which turns your seat into the equivalent of a four-poster at The Dorchester. Whereas in fact you actually spend all your time flying around the world while sandwiched between a twenty-five-stone sumo wrestler and a woman with a wailing child, attempting to stave off an attack of deep vein thrombosis at 30,000 feet. Which would be a good deal easier if you were able to extricate yourself from your wholly inadequate seat and clamber your way to freedom over the sumo, whose snoring is now threatening to match the decibel level of the howling brat on your other side.

It is also assumed, every bit as falsely, that all journalists enjoy expensive five-course dinners at Michelin-star restaurants which they would then submit as 'entertaining David Beckham'. Nowadays, the meal allowances on offer almost puts McDonald's out of reach, at least unless you forgo the slice of processed cheese, or do without the McFlurry for afters. So when my back specialist said, 'Well I really don't recommend flying with what you've got,' I asked him if he wouldn't mind putting that in writing. Which he did, and which is how, for a few years at any rate, I managed to swing business-class travel on medical grounds. It was almost worth the back pain, especially when you find that your very first pampered journey is to a destination as far away as Tokyo.

All Nippon Airways might not have been my preferred choice for making my business-class debut, especially given its on-board smoking policy. While most long-haul aircraft of the time had about two smoking seats in business class, and the rest non-smoking, All Nippon did it the other way around. I had experienced smog in Calcutta before, but that was the equivalent of a perfumed spray from an eau-de-Cologne bottle by comparison with the interior of a Japanese aeroplane. I was on my way to the Winter Olympics in Nagano, and while the fact that you found your wine glass consistently full suggested that someone must have been looking after you, I never actually got to see them.

The service was equally impressive on board the train from Tokyo to Nagano, and we quickly got a flavour of the Games from the individual entertainment screens attached to the seat in front. The opening item was a video of Japanese schoolchildren engaged in such an orgy of celebration you had to assume that either double algebra had been cancelled, or the headmaster had performed a triple Salchow on a banana skin. However, it eventually became apparent that their outpouring of joy was the result of a former pupil who had just won a bronze in the ski-jumping. The way the hosts appeared to be embracing the Games was in stark contrast to the level of interest back home, which quite frankly was so close to non-existent I wondered why the office had decided to send me.

The time difference didn't help, but the BBC's decision to broadcast 100 hours of these Games – presumably in the belief that a sleeping army of curling addicts were lurking somewhere out there – was a tad surprising, and viewing figures were poor even in the USA. Four years earlier, in Lillehammer, a feud between two American girl ice-skaters, Nancy Kerrigan and Tonya Harding, had climaxed with a US TV audience bettered only by two Super Bowls and the final episode of M★A★S★H, but attempts to build up a similar rivalry between Michelle Kwan and Tara Lipinski had thus far proved beyond the American media. Much to their consternation, the two girls seemed to genuinely like each other, and by the time I got there, the American press had been reduced to in-depth revelations about the fifteen-year-old Lipinski's experiments with make-up, and her stress-relieving sessions in the Olympic village's embroidery class. Not to mention interesting features about hinged skate blades.

Personally, I found it hard to get worked up about the Winter Olympics, with so many events decided by judges. Not so much *Citius, Altius, Fortius*, as what some anonymous arbiter from Azerbaijan thought of your mid-air separation. Or, when it came to handing out the artistic impression marks, whether the sequins on Michelle's dress were more eye-catching than Tara's. By way of contrast, however, the Japanese were overdosing on Winter Olympic fever. Huge parties of locals queued enthusiastically for three-hour bus trips up into the mountains (mostly to find out that the giant slalom had been postponed again) and everywhere you went, touts were shouting 'ticketo!' Everywhere you looked there were signs promoting the official Games motto of 'Homage to Nature', the theme of which was 'caring about plant and animal life'.

They'd taken it seriously enough to move a ski-run in order not to disturb the local buzzard population, although I found it a bit of a struggle to get my head around how these laudable sentiments squared with Japan's apparent ambition to harpoon every whale in the ocean. However, after an afternoon watching the 10,000 metres speed skating, I'd definitely have chosen harpooning over ever having to repeat the experience. It began with a series of tension-building announcements involving such things as the ice temperature, followed by people dressed in Spiderman suits, who had apparently had their thighs replaced with tree trunks, skating round in circles with their hands behind their backs. On their own. For a quarter of an hour. The short-track skating was almost as tedious, although at least it involved people racing against other people, rather than a stopwatch. It was also dangerous enough for skaters to be required to wear special neck and wrist guards to protect the major arteries from flying blades – in contrast to the speed skating, where it wasn't so much the skaters who needed them as the spectators, in case they developed an overpowering urge to open a vein.

More fun to be had, perhaps, from the women's aerials, where America were winning everything, including the gold medal for the naff banner of the Games. 'We Love You Nagano – Go USA!' Unlike the speed skating, this event did turn out to be mildly entertaining, not so much for the quality of the skating, as for the antics of the spectators. A man in a Stars and Stripes anorak, who turned out to be the fiancé of the American favourite, Nikki Stone, was behaving as though his underpants had recently been invaded by a colony of wasps, and he reacted to his girl-friend's gold medal leap by letting rip with that catch-all American expression of delight, 'Waaaah-Hooo!', before clearing the fence separating the punters from the competitors' enclosure with a vault that would have earned him (at worst) a bronze in the summer Olympics high jump. His fiancée, meantime, was blubbing so hard she almost melted the snow, but finally she managed to compose herself for the TV cameras, delivering unto them the quote all America was waiting for. 'I just can't believe it' sobbed Nikki. 'It's just . . . it's just so impossible.' I quizzed those reporters with a more intimate knowledge of women's aerials than myself, and was informed that the winning jump was something called a lay full double tuck, which involves a forty-foot leap into the air, a series of backward flips, twists and somersaults, and, not least, landing the right way up. Other competitors, it appeared, had taken the wimpish option with kid's stuff called the lay tuck, and the lay, which, by comparison with Nikki's degree of difficulty, sounded like the kind of thing I could have pulled off myself merely by taking to an icy pavement wearing leather soles.

From there, I wandered over to the ice rink, where the Olympic Kissing Championships, sponsored by Interflora, were taking place. This followed a comparatively dull affair called the ladies' ice-skating short programme, which more or less confirmed my suspicion that once you've seen one triple toe loop you've seen them all, and once it was out of the way the punters were treated to a far more compelling contest to see which one of the two American girls, Michelle or Tara, would have more bouquets thrown at them. They were then required to kiss all the flower collectors, and fall tearfully into the arms of their coaches, before retiring to a booth containing even more flowers to await the judges' marks for artistic impression. Weeping uncontrollably while wiping away a small river of mascara is an important element in trying to impress the arbiters, but if you want to pick up a full set of 5.9s, and possibly the odd 6, waving at the camera while clutching a cuddly toy seems to be the way to do it. Tara got the better marks, which led to a ferocious scrum in the interview room. You wouldn't have got a glimpse of Michael Jordan, never mind a girl who stood all of 4 foot 10 with her skates on, but you could just make out a squeaky voice somewhere behind the sea of bodies. One reporter, arriving late, grabbed another as he rushed to file his copy in the media centre. 'What did she say?' he implored. 'I gotta replay this tape recorder' came the reply. 'But I think it was something about being on a cloud.'

Finally, there were the Brits, who to no one's great surprise were not uprooting many trees. They were, however, uprooting one or two obstacles on the ski course. That night I had a conversation with my boss back in London. 'How did it go today?' he asked. 'See anything interesting?' 'Well,' I said. 'Depends what you mean by interesting. I spent about two hours getting to the top of a bloody great mountain, the reward for which was all of four seconds watching the great British hope in the ladies' slalom.' 'Only four seconds?' he said. 'About that,' I replied. 'Emma Carrick-Anderson. She got through the first gate okay, but when she came to the second one, it was a terrible mess. Hard to describe it really. Carrick went one way, Anderson went the other, and the hyphen went straight through the middle.' 'Did she say anything afterwards?' he asked. 'I didn't request an interview,' I replied. 'But if I had, she might have said something like "Kibun go varui desu".' 'Eh?' said the boss. I explained that the British Olympic Association had issued their athletes with a list of helpful Japanese phrases, and that this one translated into 'I don't feel well.' 'Which is,' I said, 'as close to

"I'm as sick as a parrot" as makes no difference.' I returned to the media village determined to seek out the author of the helpful Japanese phrase list and urge upon him a vital addition. Which was: 'Can you send for an ambulance and a snow plough? That pair of skis sticking out of that snowdrift look suspiciously like those of the British No. 1.' My photographer, by the way, travelled a good deal further down the mountain than Emma did, travelling approximately two hundred and fifty yards – in what you might call the one-man luge position, only without the luge – and only coming to a halt via the intervention of some safety netting. He escaped with just a bruise or two, but his trillion-pound multi-zoom Nikon lens was, I gathered between a bout of sobbing far louder than that of a teenage skater awaiting her artistic impression marks, more or less a write-off.

The summer Olympics are much higher profile than their winter equivalent, although frankly, winter or summer, I could happily have taken myself off to Antarctica or Greenland for the entire fortnight. I couldn't understand why I appeared to be the only person in Britain who found it relatively easy to stifle a cheer when London won the vote to stage the 2012 Games, and I was even more confused when a former neighbour phoned to tell me that the Olympic torch had just passed right by the top of his street, and wasn't it exciting? I couldn't for the life of me think why. Had I still been his neighbour, and he'd knocked on the front door to inform me that the Olympic torch was about to pass by my front window, never mind at the end of the street, I'd have closed the curtains.

It's sold to us as some hugely symbolic semi-religious flame sent down from a Greek mountain, and that those who are chosen to run it with – usually about a hundred yards – can count themselves truly blessed. The way I see it is that were I to compile a list of remaining, unfulfilled ambitions, running a few yards down a pavement holding an ice cream cone would be unlikely to feature too close to the top of it, besides which the thing keeps going out. So that by the time it arrives in the stadium the flame is less likely to have been sourced from Mount Olympus as from a box of Swan Vestas from a tobacconist's shop in Luton. Then there's all the silly stuff, like Greco-Roman wrestling, and cyclo-cross. Or people with very long bendy poles using them to vault over a bar so high you almost need an oxygen pack to still remain conscious for the descent. And what, pray, is the triple jump all about? Or, as it was called when I was at school, the hop, skip and jump. None of this seemed to be any less ludicrous just because the hopping, skipping and jumping was going to take place in London.

It was, as we all know now, superbly run, but so it should have been given the obscene amount of money thrown at it. It was also a nice surprise to discover that the volunteers all knew how to direct you to where you wanted to go. But then again, what would have been the point of them if they hadn't known? The real surprise about any Olympic Games, though, is the strange power it has to turn people who normally don't watch any sport, never mind the kind of sport to which newspapers allocate smaller print than the greyhound results, into a frenzied mob of Union Jack wavers. It's hard to believe really. Organize a water polo match for ten o'clock in the morning at Brighton Municipal Baths, and you'd have to pay people to turn up. This being the Olympics, however, I sat there inside the Olympic pool watching five thousand spectators screaming themselves hoarse at the aquatic equivalent of watching paint dry. Namely, water polo.

There was a lot of spray, and thrashing around, producing much the same effect as you'd get from throwing chunks of bread into a pond full of carp. Water polo, I was surprised to know when I looked it up, was the first team sport ever in the Olympic Games, dating way back to 1900. And I could only presume that the sight of fourteen different-coloured caps bobbing up and down in the water was as turgid then as it was in 2012.

One of the things about the London Olympics which made it so impressive was that the organizers had sensibly taken on board the fact that there would be a lot of events, like water polo, that the spectators wouldn't have much of a clue about. Therefore, when the goalie made a great save, someone had come up with the terrific idea of an electronic screen flashing up: 'Great Save!' Likewise, when someone scored a goal, the spectators were able to receive confirmation of this by looking up at the screen to see – you've guessed it – 'Goal!' beaming back at them.

Watching the various athletes wandering around the Olympic Stadium in their tracksuits, and trying to guess which sport they did, was a sport in itself, and the easiest of all – not counting Bulgarian weightlifters – were the water polo players. Thanks to one of those Health and Safety edicts preventing them wearing goggles (danger of being yanked off apparently) they all had large purple plums where their eyes should have been, resulting from a combination of no goggles and all that chlorine. Almost as easy to identify were volleyball players, not so much because of how they looked, but because they were seemingly incapable of walking past anyone – spectator, crowd control volunteer, hot dog vendor, you name it – without offering them a high five. And judging from my visit to the volleyball stadium for their match against the Dominican Republic, Team GB's girls took it to a new level.

When they were introduced to the crowd before the game, they high-fived each other – one by one – and then they high-fived their coaches. All five of them. However, just when you thought that there was no conceivable combination of high-fiving left to explore, the five coaches then high-fived themselves. Rarely had I seen, in any sport, so much energy expended before a game had even started, so the British girls getting thumped in straight sets came as something other than a surprise.

Another feature of the London Games was the belief that every minor sport required non-stop music, pom-pom twirling cheerleaders, and some complete plonker blaring inanities into a microphone. Who an earth, other than somebody with the deductive reasoning of a pond hopper, wakes up in the morning wondering how to make a game of volleyball an even richer spectator experience, and suddenly says to himself: 'I know. How about inviting everyone in the crowd to join in a karaoke of "Is This the Way to Amarillo" at half-time?'

It was much the same excruciating nonsense at the handball, but if ever a sport needed something to liven it up – even some complete prat labouring under the mistaken impression that he's the next Bruce Forsyth – it's handball. It's even more boring than basketball, which is saying something, a sport with which it has certain similarities. One team runs up the court with the ball – or sometimes just walks with it – and either scores or doesn't score. Then the other team does the same. As with basketball, you can't grab the ball out of someone's hands, so you jump up and down in front of them and make a nuisance of yourself. Picture the goalmouth activity at a Premier League soccer match just before a corner kick and that's pretty much handball for you.

The beach volleyball was no different, and listening to the MC I wondered whether this comparatively minor event would produce the first positive drugs test of the Games. Whatever our man was on, he wouldn't have been able to get it over the counter at Boots. 'You guys are ex-tra-ord-inary!' he yelled to the spectators, but the most ex-tra-ord-inary thing about London's beach volleyball event was the venue. In Sydney 2000 it was Bondi Beach, in 2016 it will probably be Copacabana, but for 2012 the closest they could get to the seaside was Horse Guards Parade.

It worked though, with a custom-built stadium for nearly ten thousand people in the shadow of such iconic buildings as the Houses of Parliament, Banqueting House and the Old Admiralty Buildings. They could perhaps have saved a few quid on the playing surface by simply not cleaning up after the horses, but money clearly wasn't any object when it came to the sand. The local builders' merchant could presumably have delivered it, but this sand – all 5,000 tons of it – had been dredged from a quarry in Surrey, and specially tested to approved governing body standards in a laboratory in Canada. At least, that's what it said in the media handbook.

I would have also liked the handbook to have revealed whether the MC had been specially tested in a laboratory in Canada – or more likely on a runway at Heathrow, with the minimum requirement of being able to drown out a landing Jumbo. The first game wasn't even on court before he began warming up the crowd. 'Let's hear you practise your Olés!' 'C'mon, let's have you clapping!' 'You can do better than that!' 'That's better! Even the Queen heard that!' In the match I saw, the Russians beat the Chinese, which by all accounts constituted a shock result, and ended with the crowd on their feet. Not, mind you, because they were overcome with excitement at the enormity of the upset, but because the MC ordered them to. 'It's match point! Everyone on their feet!' he roared. And amazingly, or perhaps, this being the Olympics, not so amazingly, everyone obeyed.

My search for a sport which wasn't accompanied by the guarantee of returning home with a perforated eardrum took me to the Aquatic Centre for the synchronized swimming, although I couldn't have been the only person inside wondering quite how this qualified as sport. It certainly meets the requirement of physical exertion, unlike darts for example, which lost its single claim to providing exercise when they banned the only two activities which involved the burning of the occasional calorie. Namely, lifting a pint and lighting a fag.

Neither should it be disqualified because all the competitors wear make-up – which is, incidentally, compulsory. However, where the argument for calling it a sport falls down is that it's yet another of these events which has nothing to do with breasting a tape before anyone else, or jumping higher than the rest of the field. You end up with a medal, or miss out on one, purely on the basis of what ten men and women sitting at the poolside thought about your performance. Or your act – given that it has less in common with sport than with the Eurovision Song Contest.

If you applied the same principle to, say, cycling, it wouldn't simply be a case of whether Bradley Wiggins managed to pass the winning post ahead of everyone else, as of whether he'd come across to the judges as aerodynamically pleasing, or had finished his lap of honour up to his saddle in floral bouquets. Whichever side of the argument you sit on, there's no denying that the girls work every bit as hard for their medals as a decathlete, or a rower. The British synchronized swimming team, it said in the blurb, spent more than forty hours a week training for the London Olympics, and up to five hours at a time actually immersed in – or under – water. No wonder they needed the make-up. Underneath the Max Factor, they must all have had wrinkles like Nora Batty's stockings.

The only other summer Olympics I've attended was in Australia in 2000, which was a stroke of luck, as you'd be hard pressed to think of a more agreeable place to spend three weeks than Sydney. On top of which, the people in charge of allocating the daily assignments had decided that they'd prefer the bigger events to be covered by someone a bit more enthusiastic about the Games than me, which meant that I was spared from tiresome stuff like the opening ceremony, or Steve Redgrave winning his 300th gold medal, and instead was asked to concentrate on the really important events, like the beach volleyball and the cyclo-cross.

Just as the Brits were to do in London twelve years later, the Australians totally immersed themselves in these Olympics, as I discovered when my taxi nearly ran off the road because the driver was frantically twiddling with his radio knob in search of the archers. Not the everyday story of country folk, but the bow and arrow variety. 'Streuth mate,' said the cabbie, almost cleaning up a cyclist as he leaned over towards me in the back seat, 'Aussies on for another gold here I reckon.' I nodded, marvelling at how only the Olympic Games can make a temporary fanatic out of a Sydney cab driver.

The public interest was also reflected in the media coverage, which was like nothing I'd ever seen before. A Bulgarian weightlifter on anabolic steroids couldn't have clean and jerked one of the daily Olympic newspaper supplements, not without ending up in A&E at any rate, and I received further evidence of the Games fever gripping the city when arriving at one of the more remote suburban venues to see huge queues for the mountain biking. I arrived, still in trauma after attending a softball game, which was a bit like baseball, but with underarm pitching, and batters who swing just as lustily as they do in baseball, but without ever making contact.

After the softball, anything would have been entertaining, and the crowd certainly seemed to enjoy the cyclo-cross. The narrow track made for some spectacular crashes, and the women's races were even more brutal than the men's. An Italian girl won the race I was watching, but only by unceremoniously depositing a Spaniard into the undergrowth. The Spanish girl looked surprised as she flew over the handlebars, but as this kind of thing passes for courteous road manners in Milan and Turin, she really should have been more alert.

The course itself, carved out of a working farm, was almost as dangerous for spectators, whose admission money also entitled them to a printed guide advising on what action to take in the event of being attacked by a venomous snake, or a territorial magpie. The magpie population was in the middle of the nesting season, but alarming though it must have been for those on the receiving end of a couple of dive-bombing attacks, I was more concerned about the snakes. 'Avoid eye contact', advised the guide, 'and slowly and quietly walk the other way.' Travelling the other way was never going to be a problem, but I certainly wasn't confident of doing it either slowly or quietly.

There was no warning leaflet at the synchronized swimming the following day, although there really should have been some kind of advice along the lines of taking along a good book, or a knitting pattern. The ability to hold your breath is vital for the competitors, who are sometimes required to remain under water for five minutes, but there's not much call for spectators to hold their breath, when their own objective over a five-minute time span is to remain awake. The synchronized diving was marginally more interesting, but only in the performances of the judges. It worked like this. When the USA team dived, the USA judge awarded a maximum 10, and the Japanese judge a miserable 7.5. And when the Japanese team dived, the Japanese judge awarded a maximum 10, and the USA judge a miserable 7.5. The Japanese pair could have hit the water upside down and half a minute apart, and they'd still have got 10 from the Japanese judge. They'd probably have got 9.5 had they sunk to the bottom and drowned, which is what almost happened on my next visit to the Aquatics Centre.

You didn't have to wander too far down Bondi Beach to find a lifeguard sitting in his high chair with his binoculars trained on the water, but no one really thought there'd be much call for one at an Olympic swimming event. I was thumbing through the programme, wondering how an earth I was going to sit by a swimming pool all day and still remain sane, when three male swimmers arrived to contest a 100-metre freestyle heat. Then it was two when one of them was disqualified for jumping the gun, and then it was one when another also dived in too soon. The one that was left managed to make a legal start all right, so much so that he was still on his block about ten seconds after the gun had gone off. I wondered, in fact, whether Equatorial Guinea's Eric Moussambani was ever going to jump in. He was staring at the water like someone having second thoughts about embarking on their first bungee jump, before finally he took the plunge.

Not so much resembling a finely tuned Olympic sprint swimmer as a blubbery teenager on a package holiday in Ibiza, performing – after a lunch consisting of several bottles of beer and a jug of sangria – one of those anti-social 'hey look at me!' belly flops. We waited for Eric to surface, but there was nothing but a froth of bubbles on top of the water. It reminded me of one of those Second World War submarine movies, where the Royal Navy destroyer is waiting to see the result of its depth charges, and up floats a load of oil and various bits of debris. This time, with Eric still to appear, I waited for a pair of swimming trunks and a nose-clip to bob to the surface, but to the relief of the officials – who were just thinking about sending out for a gaff hook – Eric finally appeared. He then began to head for the other end of the pool, although it seemed to me that the stroke he was employing for the purpose was only marginally related to the freestyle advertised in the spectator programme.

This Olympics had caused something of a stir over the swimmers wearing a variety of streamlined suits rather than the pair of bathers that used to be good enough for the likes of Johnny Weismuller, but Eric was clearly more in need of a rubber ring. Finally, after some of the spectators there for the start had just returned from a long lunch, Eric finished the race – only eight seconds outside the world record. The world record for the 200 metres, as opposed to the 100, that is. With Eric's impersonation of a freshly landed North Sea tuna still vividly in mind, I wasn't about to miss the following day's swimming, which featured the other half of Equatorial Guinea's Olympic swimming squad, Paula Barila. Just like Eric, Paula's progress through the water did not so much require an electronic stopwatch as an egg timer, and while both of Eric's co-competitors had been disqualified for a false start, Paula had company in the shape of a Burmese girl. Well, she had company until it was time to leave the starting blocks, and it was a nice touch for the heat winner to wait for Paula to reach the finish before clambering out of the water. Otherwise, she could have been showered, changed and enjoying a poolside cappuccino by the time Paula arrived.

Of the two, I thought that Eric was marginally the more impressive, especially in having to swim two lengths to Paula's one. This involved the tricky business of having to turn round, and with a personal turning circle equivalent to that of the QE2 this was no mean achievement. Not surprisingly, these two became overnight superstars, and if Eric was disappointed not to have been going home with the gold medal, he was immediately signed up for an American chat show.

There was only one performance to match Eric's at the Sydney Olympics, and that took place in the final event: the marathon. In the course of my diligent research into the history of the race, I came across an unusual case in 1904, when the winner, Thomas Hicks of the USA, kept himself going on a drink made out of brandy, eggs and strychnine. However, in the Sydney marathon of 2000, I thought I'd stumbled on a case of a competitor keeping himself going on a drink made out of brandy, brandy and brandy. No one was quite sure which country he was from, although as he staggered through Sydney's Hyde Park at a pace that would have left him tailed off in the fifty-kilometre walk, you'd have taken a guess at Equatorial Guinea. There was real concern for him at one point, not so much for his health as at the fact that he was entering a zone which warned: 'No Parking. Tow Away Zone.' I never did find out whether he finished the race (if he had, it wouldn't have been in time for the closing ceremony) or had ended up being clamped, and eventually released from the police pound upon payment of the appropriate fine. Or even, like Eric, earned himself a guest appearance on an American chat show.

3

BEAM ME UP SCOTTY:
ASSIGNMENTS FROM HELL

*Tyred and emotional at F1 testing . . . McLaren and
The Spice Girls . . . and 12,000 miles for a rugby
jersey*

I was crouched under a stairwell inside some soulless concrete building on the outskirts of Barcelona, yelling into
the mobile phone in a mostly forlorn attempt to make
myself heard above the ear-perforating shriek of Formula
One racing cars outside. 'I said!' I shouted, as I just about
detected a voice at the other end saying: 'Sorry, didn't
quite catch that . . .' 'I said, get me out of here! Now!
Please!' The other voice came back: 'You're very faint. I
can barely hear you.' I said: 'If you don't get me a flight
out of here right now, and I mean right now, then that's
it. A chap can only take so much.' At which point the
voice at the other end said: 'What's that noise?' I said:
'That noise is the sound of a lot of racing cars going round
and round a concrete road in the middle of nowhere, and

that noise is the reason I'm asking you, begging you, to get me on a flight home. Tonight.' The voice replied: 'It sounds more like a whining noise.' I replied: 'Whining noise? That'd be me.'

'You cannot be serious!' John McEnroe's celebrated line has had many an airing in conversations with sports desks down the years, every time they've hit you with an assignment you just knew would have you muttering 'Beam me up Scotty' from the moment you got there. High on my own personal list was anything to do with Formula One, a turgid enough experience when you're actually at a race, but on this occasion someone had decided to send me to Formula One testing. It had all started a couple of days earlier when the office called me at home. 'Testing?' I said. 'Formula One testing?' I'd hoped that I'd misheard this through a dodgy connection, and added: 'Could you just repeat that?' But the voice at the other end duly confirmed that a story on Formula One testing was indeed what they were after. A long pause ensued while I considered an appropriate response.

'Now then. Let me get this right. You want me to go along and watch people changing tyres, undoing things with a spanner, and peering at electronic instruments which are not the remotest bit interesting even to those saddos with an annual subscription to *Autosport*?' Precisely that, was the gist of his reply. I tried one last throw of the dice, assuring him that if the object of the exercise was to render the reader unconscious before reaching paragraph two, I couldn't, off-hand, think of a better idea. But it was to no avail. I tried to put a brave face on things as the plane took off from Heathrow.

I'd never been to Barcelona, but I'd been told it was a lovely city, full of lively bars and fine restaurants, and a two-night stay at a four-star hotel couldn't be all doom and gloom. Wrong. The first thing I discovered, after jumping into a taxi at the airport, was that we were not heading into Barcelona, but away from it. And about fourteen miles later, we pulled up outside some ghastly chain hotel – I think it was a Holiday Inn – in as charmless a neighbourhood as you could possibly imagine. It was a good half-mile from the Circuit de Cataluña, but already your ears were being pounded by what sounded like a colony of mosquitoes trapped inside a rock band's amplifier, confirmation that testing for the upcoming F1 season was already under way.

Arriving at the track, my worst fears were realized. The drivers whizzed round a couple of times, nipped back to the garage while a small army of people in jackets peered at a computer screen, and sat inside the cockpit while a team of people in overalls made a surgical inspection of the innards. Then they drove off again. There was one moment of high drama, when the lollipop man released his team's car before the petrol nozzle had disengaged, but otherwise everyone just went round and round. Then everyone took a break for lunch, which allowed a PR man to escort a group of Japanese visitors around the pit lane, where they took photographs of absolutely everything. Why do the Japanese take pictures of everything? I once saw a Japanese girl in London taking photographs, from a variety of angles, of a parking meter covered by an 'Out of Order' bag, and it was almost as surreal watching this lot clicking away at stacks of tyres.

Tyres are very important in Formula One, as I discovered later in the day when the PR man in the paddock announced to the assembled media (and it amazed me how many of them there were, and from how many different countries) that an important press conference was about to take place. This threatened to be a welcome diversion, and the fact that the room was full of fire extinguishers suggested that the interview was potentially so exciting that a reporter's notebook might well be set alight. This thought lingered only briefly as two drivers, in flame-retardant overalls advertising everything from engine oil to cigarettes, wittered on for about half an hour about down-force and aero-dynamics.

They also found it difficult to complete a sentence without a gushingly complimentary reference to their Bridgestone tyres, which possibly had something to do with the fact that they were seated either side of the Bridgestone rep. This was a Japanese gentleman, who, once the drivers had finished and departed, launched into an interesting speech about tyre compounds. Ten seconds of this would have been enough to make you believe that the ancient Japanese Samurai must have invented ritual disembowelment during a tyre-compound seminar, but, thanks largely to the fact that the Bridgestone man's pearls of wisdom were religiously translated from his native Japanese into three different languages, it actually went on for close to half an hour. Finally, he sat down, but just as the audible sigh of relief was poised to leave my mouth, the PR man jumped up and threw the floor open to questions. 'How many people have died during one of your tyre-compound conferences?' I enquired. Well, no I didn't actually, but it was tempting.

What surprised me, though, was how many questions it was actually possible to ask on the subject. A hand shot up, and a girl came over and handed him a microphone. 'How many different compounds have you tested this week?' The Bridgestone man leant over his own microphone. 'Six' came the reply. Another raised hand, and another pause while the questioner was equipped with a microphone. 'When will the new grooved tyre finally be ready for the Bridgestone teams?' 'Before the start of the new season,' said the Bridgestone man, who then sat back to wait for this to be repeated in several more languages. And on it went. Hard rubber, soft rubber, tyre wear, track temperatures, rear-end grip. Which hopefully explains why I came to find myself underneath a stairwell, sobbing and whimpering, and demanding to be airlifted back to Blighty. 'I don't think,' I said, 'I need another two days here. I've got all the material I need for the story already.' 'Great,' he said. 'We're getting one of the local photographers to send us something that will go nicely with your story. Any suggestions?' he asked. 'As a matter of fact, I have,' I said. 'The pit lane is full of large stacks of tyres. Any one of those will do nicely.'

Reporting on an actual Grand Prix is more exciting than listening to people drone on about tyres, but not by much. Formula One has come a long way since the inaugural world championship Grand Prix at Silverstone in 1950, won by Giuseppe Farina in an Alfa Romeo, but not necessarily for the better. There was a bit of romance about those old cars, driven by men who spent most of a lap wiping oil from their goggles, and trying to keep all the fillings in their teeth.

The modern drivers are no less fast and brave, but now-adays it's more about the designer than the bloke behind the wheel. Unless something vital drops off, or someone drops a spanner in the pit lane, the chap spraying champagne from balconies every other Sunday is the one whose car has come out of its winter wind-testing tunnel with the most aerodynamically efficient wing mirrors. Or wheel nuts. There's far more going on in the pit lane, with cars pulling in for something or other more often than your average family heading to the seaside on a Bank Holiday weekend, than there is out on the track.

Which makes you wonder why the people who run it are forever tinkering with ways of spicing up the action when the cars are on the move, what with their KERS and DRS zones, when there's far more scope for excitement while they're all sitting around in the equivalent of Newport Pagnell services. You could start by making them all pay for their petrol by credit card. Imagine the tension as the crowd looks up at the big screen at the Red Bull driver fuming and fretting behind a guy buying two bars of chocolate and a packet of crisps. And when he finally gets to the front of the queue, the machine doesn't recognize his pin number. Another improvement to what has frankly become a tired old format would be to make all the cars two-seaters, and have the driver's wife or girl-friend accompany him. We all know how cool these guys are under pressure, but when you've paid for your petrol, and come back to find that the wife is in the queue at Starbucks, or has nipped off to powder her nose, it would be a stern test of temperament if nothing else. It would give the poor hacks in the press room a different angle too, as by and large they're stuck with writing the same story every race. There are not many sports in which it's easier for the reporter to do it off the telly, rather than 'live', as it were, but with Formula One it's more of less impossible to know what's going on if you're not in front of a TV set. It doesn't matter if you're in Melbourne, Kuala Lumpur, or wherever. The cars roar off, you pull out your earplugs, and disappear back inside the soundproofed press room to watch it on the monitor. It is, in fact, the only way to watch it. Otherwise, you'd find yourself having the following conversation with whoever's been following the race on the office telly. 'Righto, 850 words it is. But before I start writing, could you just tell me who won?'

For Formula One fans, there is only one thing that has them drooling with more anticipation ahead of a new season than waiting to hear what compound of rubber is going to be used for the tyres. And that, of course, it the unveiling of the various new cars. The Ferrari F12 425WX is totally old hat by now, and ready to give way to the exciting new F13 425W, with its special brand of down-force-enhancing wing nuts, and (the talk of the paddock this one) revolutionary triangular sidepods. Imagine, therefore, my unrestrained outpouring of joy when the office asked me to attend the launch of McLaren's new car for the forthcoming season. I was, though, slightly taken aback by the choice of venue. I'd assumed it would have been in a garage. Perhaps – having just been reading about a new trend in subliminal advertising, which involved wafting product-associated smells through air-conditioning vents (freshly baked bread in supermarkets, that kind of thing) – with the seductive scent of carbon monoxide and old sump oil drifting down a ventilation shaft. However, the launch was in fact held at the Alexandra Palace in London, complete with ticker tape, dry ice, go-go dancers, and all-girl rock bands, at a cost you could only estimate to be roughly the size of a small nation's GDP. All this spanned a period of over three hours, with the various intervals allowing the punters the chance to wander past a very large tarpaulin and wonder what might be hidden beneath it? It was the nerve-jangling equivalent of waiting for those lights to go out on an F1 starting grid, but at last the great moment arrived. Someone pressed a button, the tarpaulin was whisked into the air, and the audience let out a collective gasp of astonishment. Followed by a spontan-eous outbreak of applause. This wouldn't have surprised me greatly had the tarpaulin's removal been followed by a troupe of naked go-go dancers leaping from a giant choc-olate cake, but the sight of a stationary racing car seemed to me to be something the audience might have expected.

The roars of delight were everywhere, including a group of middle-aged males in expensive suits, who I took to be high-ranking executives representing the makers of an American cigarette – stickers of which were plastered everywhere bar the exhaust pipe. I was told that the real objective behind the official launch of a new F1 racing car was not so much to benefit the fans, as to see which of the various teams could spend the most money on getting their car – and more especially their sponsor's logos – splashed all over the world's newspapers and TV screens. Which explained why McLaren's idea of leaving their rivals stuck in the pits included hiring The Spice Girls. And the girls duly gave a performance that confirmed what I'd recently been reading about concerning the growth in subliminal advertising – namely, a reminder to all F1 fans heading for a Grand Prix not to forget their earplugs. It was hard to believe that the evening could get worse, but get worse it did with a girl by the name of Devina bouncing out onto the stage to the backcloth of two large video screens advertising engine oil and batteries. Devina had clearly been coached in the art of grabbing the audience's attention with your first killer phrase, and she didn't disappoint.

Cooing into the microphone: 'We've got stars and . . .' (long pause to rack up the tension) '. . . we've got cars!' You longed to be back at F1 testing, listening to Japanese tyre people telling you about their compounds. 'This,' shrilled Devina, 'is the biggest event of its type ever held!' She then, though, rather spoiled this image of an entire planet tuning into the unveiling by adding: 'It's being broadcast all across the UK on Virgin Radio.' It seemed to me that 'all across the UK' and 'Virgin Radio' didn't sit entirely comfortably in the same sentence, but I nonetheless tried my best to conjure up a picture of millions of people huddled around a radio for the unveiling of a car. 'Cor, just listen to that chassis.' Frankly, though, it wasn't easy. Next up, after another song from a pop group and a few more plugs for the tobacco company, lots of people wearing ski suits and carrying torches started whizzing around the stage.

I was beginning to wonder what a Swiss mountain rescue team had to do with it when the MC explained that the suits were replicas of what the McLaren pit crew would be wearing for the new season, and I silently rebuked myself for not making the connection. Then it was back to Devina, to introduce the two drivers, David Coulthard and Mika Häkkinen, and she quickly moved to what she described as the 'big question'. Big? It was enormous. 'Tell me David. Is it Coul-tard? Or Coul-thard?' David, recognizing the invaluable experience this would give him should he ever be cornered by Jeremy Paxman, put up no resistance. He meekly pulled over like the driver of a Morris Minor spotting the new McLaren in his rear-view mirror. 'Coul-thard,' he croaked. Then it was Mika's turn for a grilling. 'Did you have anything to do with the design?' enquired Devina. To which Mika replied, in that deadpan way that Finns have, 'That's a bit technical.' Finally, it was left to The Spice Girls to round off an evening I would happily have ended a long time earlier by applying a McLaren mechanic's rivet gun to the temple had one been available. The song was mimed, presumably so the girls could save their voices to conduct interviews even more searching than Devina's. 'Tell me,' enquired the girl called Emma. 'Why aren't there any girl drivers?' Mika's eyes glazed over. So did Coul-thard's. And for the first and only time in my dealings with Formula One, I thought to myself: whatever vast amounts of money these boys are getting, it isn't enough.

In McLaren's favour, at least it was all over in one night, unlike the other high-profile unveiling I was assigned to, which not only lasted an entire week, but involved flying to the other side of the world and back. 'It's a quiet week,' said the voice from the office, 'and we wondered if you might fancy a trip to New Zealand.' 'What for?' I enquired. 'The All Blacks are getting a new rugby jersey,' he said, 'and we thought it might make a piece for next weekend.'

'Hang on a sec,' I said. 'Have I heard that correctly? All the way to New Zealand to write about a rugby shirt?' The voice came back: 'It's a quiet week, besides which, we're not paying. Adidas have stumped up 30 million quid for the deal and they want some publicity. Business–class flights, top-notch hotels, all paid for.'

Which is how I came to find myself in Queenstown, in front of a live audience in the city's Events Centre, waiting for someone to hold up a rugby jersey in front of a television camera. Anywhere else in the world, someone holding up a rugby jersey in front of a television camera could only have meant an advertisement for Persil washing powder, or Daz, but in New Zealand it was a serious news event, and it was going out live on the six o'clock news. Right across the hall was draped a banner inscribed: 'Rugby's Strip of the Century!', which, up until that moment, most people would have considered to be Erica Roe's topless half-time appearance in 1980 at Twickenham. However, this title had now been claimed by Adidas, and an entire nation held its breath as the TV New Zealand presenter broke off from some really dull stuff about the Americans imposing an import tariff on New Zealand lamb, and introduced their man from the Events Centre.

There then followed an obligatory film of All Black rugby players splattering opponents and diving over try lines, before the man from Adidas reached over to the string attached to the veil draped over the new jersey, and pulled it. Amazingly, in the same way as the audience at Alexandra Palace had failed to suspect that they might be about to see a racing car, so the packed congregation at the Queenstown Events Centre all but fell off their chairs when the veil fell off. 'Holy Rugger Jersey Batman!' Yep, that's what it was. A rugger jersey. What's more, a black one. Not orange. Not purple. Not blue with pink spots. But black. Aha. But this wasn't any old black jersey. The TV audience was presumably as gripped as the live one in the Hall as a number of radical new concepts were explained, such as a grip-enhancing rubberized chest panel. A bit like Velcro. One assumed that the jersey had met with the approval of the International Rugby Board, but people running in for tries without having to use their hands seemed somewhat at odds with the history of the game. Then there was the material itself, described as Climalite. The Adidas man droned his way through its various revolutionary properties, dropping in phrases like 'vital secret ingredient', which made it sound like an anti-dandruff advertisement. It also had, by all accounts, some kind of sweat transference process which kept you warm when it was cold, and cool when it was hot. If only Captain Scott had been wearing the new Adidas Climalite shirt when he sailed for Antarctica from New Zealand's South Island, he'd probably have come back again.

The captain of the All Blacks rugby team then came onto the stage to thank the man from Adidas for providing his side with just the kind of edge that could prove decisive in winning or losing a World Cup, and the Adidas man responded that it was an honour and a privilege. They could have gone on for hours, and probably would have done, had the MC not been told that it was time to hand back to the studio for the weather. While I was left to reflect, on the twenty-odd-hour flight home, where to rank, on the list of surreal assignments, a round trip of 23,000 miles to report that a black jersey with a silver fern had been replaced by a black jersey with a silver fern on it.

4

FOUR-LEGGED FRIENDS

Badminton Horse Trials, Horse of the Year Show, Punchestown, Melbourne Cup

I've always found it slightly puzzling as to what people see in horses. They're untrustworthy animals to say the least. My first memory of one was almost losing a hand when cajoled by an auntie into offering it an apple, and my first visit to a racetrack involved investing a hard-earned tenner on the second favourite in the 2.15 at Chepstow and watching its jockey go sailing over the first fence, the horse itself having declined the challenge. So when I joined the evening newspaper in Leicester as a youngish sports writer, the job I disliked most was being put in charge of the racing page. You were expected to write something interesting and informative to go above the runners and riders, and not just to rely on the agency copy, and I was quite pleased with how authoritative I must have sounded when I came up with the description for some nag or other that it was 'a decent type, but not good enough to win a Classic'.

The sports editor, who spent half his life with his head immersed in *Timeform* and the *Racing Post*, suddenly burst through the door clutching a page proof. 'You're spot-on about this horse,' he said; 'it'll certainly never win a Classic.' However, before the small swell of pride that was rising within me had a chance to develop into a full-blown puffed-up chest, he added: 'And I'll tell you why. It's because he's a twelve-year-old steeplechaser, and a gelding. That's why.' The upside to the story is that I was rarely entrusted with the racing page again, an arrangement I found entirely agreeable, and it wasn't for about another twenty years or so that I next found myself writing about horses. I still had no great affection for the things, but as I found myself driving through the leafy glades of rural Gloucestershire, heading for the Duke of Beaufort's private estate at Badminton, there was some small frisson of anticipation at the thought of watching them tackling the obstacles.

From what little I'd seen of the Horse Trials on the telly, it either resulted in an exhilarating glow of satisfaction for the rider, or a mouthful of ditch-water and third-degree bruising beneath the jodhpurs. And on the whole, I found the latter much the more entertaining. Disappointment swiftly followed, though, when it turned out I'd arrived on dressage day, when the hooves were not so much thundering and galloping, as prancing and tiptoeing. I'd never seen dressage live before, but it didn't take too long for me to realize that, for sheer gut-wrenching tension, it was right up there with watching Bernhard Langer consulting his yardage chart, or Steve Davis chalking the tip of his snooker cue.

Competitor No. 1 entered the arena looking like something out of a Jane Austen novel, although I didn't recall Mr Darcy's horse being spooked by a car alarm going off when he arrived to visit Miss Bennet. Once the offending vehicle had been located and disarmed, horse and rider trotted up to the parade ring, to which entry was denied until a man wearing a bowler hat and a tweed jacket had removed himself from a fold-up chair, unclipped a rope, and engaged in a mutual hat doffing ceremony with the rider. His bowler came off, and the rider responded by removing his topper. Whereupon the tweed jacket returned to his fold-up chair and the action, if such it can be called, began. Marks (out of ten) were awarded for various routines, beginning with something called an 'entry and salute', which earned the horse, Cartoon II, three sevens. Cartoon then went about his various dance routines, all with twee-sounding names such as 'medium trot' and 'half past left', and the whole thing ended with the rider removing his top hat, saluting the judges, and taking his leave.

After watching three or four of these routines, and not having the faintest idea what it was all about, I wandered off for a while – not just to try and get the pulse rate down a bit, but also to get a bit of live commentary from the Mitsubishi Motors Radio Badminton Tent. 'Lovely moment there in the extended canter' came floating through the speakers, not just to me, and a couple of people in Barbour jackets, but apparently to a live radio audience in New Zealand. There are certainly parts of New Zealand you'd be hard pressed to describe as racy, and where it's just about possible to imagine people huddled around radio sets listening to Two Way Family Favourites, or the Billy Cotton Band Show, but dressage? Somewhere in Wanganui, you thought, there must be a family groaning in disappointment when the New Zealand challenger only gets a 6.5 for his half parade routine.

Back at Badminton, meantime, you could also stay in touch with events in the dressage ring by stumping up a few extra quid for headphones, giving you access to two lady commentators sitting in a Four-by-four parked just outside the parade ring. I duly stumped up, and tried to make sense of their various expert judgements. 'He was,' said one of the ladies, referring to the performance she'd just seen 'technically correct, but just the teeniest bit boring.' Mmmm, I thought. Maybe the teeniest bit bored might have been nearer the mark. Not every horse, you'd imagine, responds to being mounted by a man with a top hat by turning into the equine equivalent of Gene Kelly.

Perhaps the animal needed a bout of cheering to get him going, or a Mexican wave, but this isn't allowed at Badminton, where spectators are obliged to watch in absolute silence so as not to put a horse off his routine. Which is slightly at odds with the origin of dressage, which required total equine obedience while delivering messages on eighteenth-century battlegrounds. Why not, it seemed to me, jazz the whole thing up a bit and make it more like Balaclava and Waterloo? And give first prize to the horse which made a decent fist of the extended trot or Spanish walk despite having musket shots exploding around his hind quarters. They've probably ruled that it's tough enough on the horses at Badminton having to perform to a permanent backcloth of yapping dogs. There are more dogs at Badminton than there are horses, and having at least two on a lead appears to be a condition of entry. And as they are all taken for walkies around the cross country course, you could argue that the obstacles for spectators are even trickier than they are for horses.

Badminton is as much a social event as a sporting one, and the estate is so vast at 1,500 acres that you wouldn't get around every one of the trade stands if you spent all four days there. One of the more incongruous ones on my visit was the HM Prisons stand, which provided a fascinating insight into life inside a cell, and offered to smudge both of your thumbprints onto a certificate for only 50p. Mostly, though, the more rural pursuits were catered for. Barbours, tweeds, horse-feeds, bridles, saddles, the whole range, including copious amounts of horsey literature. I wished I'd visited the Countryside Alliance tent before the dressage, rather than after it, as there were vast amounts of informative books and videos on the subject. *Dressage Judging Explained* seemed a snip at £24.99, though for only an extra fiver you could purchase *Dressage in Detail* by Dr Reiner Klimke, intriguingly subtitled *The Work of the 4 to 6 Year Old Horse in the Snaffle*. I looked in vain for *The Essential Guide to Dressage* by Major Snoring, subtitled *Don't Forget to Bring a Knitting Pattern and a Hammock*, and assumed it had already sold out.

The Horse of the Year Show promised more in the way of equine excitement, and on my way to Wembley I even found myself humming the BBC's old introduction music. 'Da da dum da da dum, dada dada dada dum . . .' It used to come on after *The Nine O'clock News*, with Dorian Williams and Raymond Brooks-Ward engaged in the human equivalent of sweating up in the paddock as a regimental Brit cantered towards the final fence. 'And it's Group Captain Bulldog Drummond-Haystack on Bengal Lancer IV. Can he go clear? Come on Bulldog! You can do it! Big stride now! Yes! He's . . . Oh no! It's gorn! It's gorn! Oh what a tragic end for Bulldog.' And poor old Dorian would then have to talk bravely over 'Deutschland Über Alles' as the dastardly Hun, Alvin Schockabsorber, riding Kaiser Bill's Batman III, collected the coveted rosette from Major General St John Something-Orother.

However, on my visit in 1999, the BBC had just ended forty years of broadcasting the event since its debut on the first ever Saturday-afternoon *Grandstand* in 1958. Forty-one years on, there wasn't a single outside broadcast van outside Wembley, and an event which once boasted a television audience of millions, finally ended up generating, over a five-day period, 20,000 tons of horse manure. No wonder the flower displays around the fences looked so good. Sadly, by the time I got there, the show which once had half the nation hooked watching the puissance – a giant wall which got bigger and bigger until there was only one rider left standing – was now reduced to cheap gimmickry in a sad attempt to get the patient back up onto its hooves. Smoke machines to create a moody atmosphere, and exhibitions that were pretty close to circus acts. Including a toe-curling performance from a bloke dressed up as a cowboy, who stood in the centre of the arena crooning 'Oh What a Beautiful Morning'.

It was all very sad, especially as the Horse of the Year Show was for a while compulsive viewing for people like myself – namely those who had no interest at all in watching faultless clear rounds, but would purr with pleasure at the sight of the animal making such a last-minute decision to put the brakes on that the only thing to clear the fence would be housed inside a pair of flying jodhpurs. Followed – as a crane was summoned to clear up the mess – by a priceless piece of commentary. 'Well, jolly bad luck there, but a very exciting prospect, and definitely one for the future.'

One difference between horse jumping and horseracing is that in jumping it's the riders who become famous, and in racing it's the riders *and* the horses. In jumping there was once a rider famous enough for a two-fingered gesture at Hickstead to pass into the vocabulary as a 'Harvey Smith', but if the horses are generally forgotten, it's perhaps not surprising given that they've all got names like Sanyo Music Centre, and Kellogg's Corn Flakes II. In racing, though, you can actually get sent by your sports editor to cover a horse (in the journalistic sense, that is) rather than a person, as was the case when I pitched up at Ascot to write a piece about an animal called Kauto Star.

I was told that this was more Hollywood star than horse, a sort of Clark Gable of the equine kingdom, and when the nag was led into the parade ring by its stable girl, there was undeniably the kind of excited gathering you get when a film star steps out of the back of his limo on Oscar night. All that was missing was a pair of sunglasses, a flash of pearly white teeth for the cameras, and the jumping world's pin-up of the day to wander across and provide a few autographed hoof-prints for his adoring public. So it was mildly disappointing when I caught sight of him for the first time. I examined the creature from every angle, but there was no getting away from it. It looked like – er, how can we put this – a horse. Four legs, two ears and a tail. Looking round, though, I was just about the only person present not totally smitten by National Hunt racing's glamour boy, who was destined, everyone agreed, to take his place in the pantheon of steeplechasing greats, and end up, like Red Rum, spending his retirement opening fetes and supermarkets. His great rival for the Cheltenham Gold Cup was an Irish horse, called Denman, and, every March, Cheltenham racecourse is thick with the accents of Galway and Kerry as they pour across to support their own.

The Irish equivalent is the April National Hunt festival in Punchestown, which is now nearly a hundred and fifty years old and brings together the two ingredients that make up an Irishman's DNA – horses, and gambling. Only Hong Kong and Australia wager more money per head of population on the gee-gees, and when I booked into my hotel in Naas, and asked for a morning paper, the receptionist said: 'It's the *Independent* you'll be wanting then. It's the best for tips.' Hundreds of people had already laid out the equivalent of a tenner, even before the three-day meeting had started, to attend an 'expert tipping seminar' in a pub next door to the Curragh racecourse. And you could even get tips in church from the Punchestown parish priest, who asked only, should he come up with a few winners, for a little more generosity the next time the collection tray came round. There was a time, before the Church realized it was fighting a losing battle, when priests weren't allowed to go to the races, but they solved the problem by building a large mound, known as Priests' Hill, and employing local youths to run to the track and back with their bets.

When the day's racing ends, the serious craic, as they call living it up in Ireland, begins, and nearby Naas is ideal for the job in having about six pubs for every ten houses. After the races, they used to carry on gambling with pig racing down the main street until the ISPCA decreed that the 9.15 Porkers' Handicap Hurdle was injurious to the health of their clients, so they now have things like obstacle races for bartenders instead. Any traffic passing through has to compete with the craic spilling out from the pavements to the road, and when I was there the traffic ground to a complete halt behind a bloke on stilts. Most of the motorists were content to turn off their engines and enjoy it, although the joys of being stuck behind the Patrician Primary Pipers may have been lost on anyone running late for the Dublin–Holyhead ferry.

Outside on the pavement, a girl by the name of Georgina was taking part in a karaoke contest, and making the sort of noise that would normally have prompted residents to empty chamber pots on her from the upstairs windows. 'Give her a big hand,' boomed the MC, adding a sympathetic: 'she's got a sore throat.' Then, to the accompaniment of stationary car drivers winding up their windows, Georgina launched into 'The Greatest Love of All.' She murdered it, and the next girl, Gail, performed a similar act of homicide on 'You're So Vain'. Next day at the races, the bookmakers made a handsome profit, albeit not as handsome as the local dry cleaners after torrential rain turned the car park into an ocean of mud. We took tea in the Irish Thoroughbred Marketing Tent, where the waiter was up to his ankles in muddy water, and respectfully felt obliged to point out to the lady hostess that the proximity of the electric tea urn to water leaking through a flap in the tent might result in something more serious than turning his hair a bit crinkly. And would it be possible to move it? Her solution was in the best traditions of Irish science. 'Can you not,' she said, 'stick something rubbery down there?'

The only race meeting I've been to which compares to Punchestown is the Melbourne Cup, for which the entire nation of Australia comes to a halt on the first Tuesday every November. It's not hard, in fact, to picture a scene in which some bloke in a corked hat drags himself out of the Bush, slightly the worse for wear after donating both legs to a saltwater crocodile's lunch. He crawls up the hospital steps and croaks: 'Give it to be straight, doc. Am I too late?' And the doctor replies: 'Nah, mate. But yer'd better look sharpish if you want to get a bet on. They're just coming under starter's orders.' When Nevil Shute wrote *On the Beach*, set in post-nuclear-holocaust Australia, he may have got the idea from a stroll down Bourke Street on Melbourne Cup day. No cars, no trams, no people – at least while the race is on.

It makes rich men out of bookmakers, hat-shop proprietors, morning-suit hirers, and the local equivalent of Fortnum and Mason's champagne picnic-hamper department. Vast sums of money will be wagered on the outcome of a two-mile handicap, and if you were to fill the favourite's saddlebags with the previous week's racing pull-outs, it would be putting up something like five hundred kilos overweight. Local news bulletins end with the bloke reading the news saying: 'And now over to Tracey with the weather . . . and what's your tip for the Cup, Tracey?'

Furthermore, when it comes to providing the punter with everything he or she needs to know to make an informed judgement, they get battered with information overload. When I picked up the paper, expecting nothing much more than the state of the going, I was required to digest the following. 'Track report: Good. Penetrometer: 3.64. Inside: 3.68. Outside: 3.60. Rail: True. Last meeting: Out 9 and 11 metres. Last time true: Sept. 5. Rainfall: 6.5mm for week. Irrigation: 23.5mm for week. 3mm Thursday. Preparation: rolled yesterday. Radar: morning showers.' Personally I think they were missing a trick by not giving their readers more information about the actual horses. Along the lines of: Ned Kelly. Health: minor case of the sniffles. Mane: sleek on Sunday. Diet: crushed oats and apples (Granny Smith). Shod by: Gucci. Travel: Seaboard crossing from New Zealand, weather cloudy, swell: moderate to choppy. Form on voyage: runner up in deck quoits.' If picking the winner isn't hard enough, it's nothing to what the women have to go through in trying to choose the right outfit, especially in a city where it can be 40°C and scorching one minute, and 5°C and piddling down the next. It's a hell of a day out, and with the champagne starting at breakfast time, one curious statistic about the Melbourne Cup is that there are more eye injuries from flying corks, and more aspirins and Alka-Seltzer sold the morning after, than after Christmas and Australia Day combined.

5

'SORRY, DIDN'T MEAN TO CAUSE OFFENCE'

Apologies to: Ian Poulter, Dermot Desmond, David Gower, Ted Dexter, Bikers, Motor Bikers, the Women's Tennis Association, and the United States of America

'Have you seen Ian Poulter?' It was the press officer speaking, as I was busy extricating my work bag from the boot of the car on the Sunday morning of the British Masters golf tournament at the Forest of Arden. 'Er, no,' I replied. 'Any reason why I should have done?' 'Well,' said the press officer, 'I sort of guessed you hadn't seen him just by looking at you.' 'Pardon?' I replied. 'It's just that, if you had seen him, you'd probably have two black eyes and a bloody nose.' I was certainly puzzled enough to want to know more, but I'd had an early start from home, and was keener to get to the press tent for a cup of coffee. When I got there, though, I encountered several journalists equally keen to know whether I'd run into Ian Poulter, and I was

finally forced to say to one of them: 'Okay. I could probably work it out if I gave it some serious thought. I can see
perfectly well, so it can't be that I've been blinded by his
trousers, so I give in.' 'You only missed him by about five
minutes on Friday,' he said. 'He burst into the press tent
and said, and I quote, "I'm going to kill him."' 'He said he
was going to kill me?' 'That's what he said.' 'Well, tell him
there's a queue,' I replied, 'and he'll have to wait his turn.'

I actually couldn't think for the life of me how I'd irked
Poulter, but the story finally emerged. I'd spent the first
day of the tournament, in my role as the provider of a
'colour' piece to go alongside the correspondent's main
article, following the threesome of Poulter, Lee Westwood
and Colin Montgomerie, and my notebook at the end
reflected that a large chunk of five interminable hours out
there had involved watching Monty play quite well, and
the other two not so well. To the point where Monty had
spent most of his round helping search for the other two's
golf balls. It seemed, therefore, not too unkind to suggest
that Monty might have wondered whether he was still
playing in Wednesday's pro-am, an event in which the
pros – many of them in return for lots of money – endure
hours of pain playing with people who haven't visited a
fairway since the old King was alive, and trying to offer
helpful advice to someone whose swing is not too dissimilar to Basil Fawlty beating his car with a branch when it
broke down on him. I once played in a Seniors' pro-am,
when Maurice Bembridge put his hand around one of our
amateurs who was having a particularly horrid day, and his
face lit up at the thought of Maurice about to give him
the tip that would provide an instant cure. 'Tell me,' said

Maurice, 'why do you swing a golf club as though you've got a champagne cork stuck up your arse.'

In Poulter's case, he was clearly keen for my own posture to involve having a biro inserted into where Maurice had identified the champagne cork. So when he emerged from the recorder's hut after a second round of 64 – or something equally brilliant – he whipped out the newspaper containing the offending article from his golf bag and waved it at the assembled hacks. 'Not bad for an effing amateur,' he said, whereupon he embarked upon his mission to have me exterminated. As he may well have done had I not already written that day's piece and driven off home. I wasn't to know it as I arrived back on the Sunday to be informed that Poulter was not best pleased with me, but I hadn't yet finished with causing offence to golfers during that particular tournament.

The winner that year was Greg Owen from Mansfield, a very good golfer who went on to become a successful member of the PGA Tour in America, but he's never been the kind of player liable to cause a queue at the turnstiles. Not to get in, at any rate. For every Colin Montgomerie there are a hundred Greg Owens, the kind of golfer who makes up what they call in America 'the hot dog group'. A spectator peers at his programme waiting for the next threeball to come through, his mate asks him who they are, and he replies: 'Fred Funk, Nolan Henke and Tom Pernice Jnr.' 'In that case,' comes the reply, 'seems like a good time to go grab a hot dog.' Greg, with a four-shot lead going into the final round, churned out a firework-free but winning performance, and admirably though he played, it was the kind of round in which I observed, a little unkindly upon reflection, that even Mrs Owen might have taken time out to purchase a hot dog. In my defence, Greg had actually gone on record before the tournament in acknowledging that he wasn't exactly box office. I quote. 'Boring? Yes, fair enough. You could call me boring. But Faldo made a living out of it, and I'm not doing too badly at the moment.' But it was the headline writer who did for me. 'Greg Grinds His Way to Victory' would have been fine. 'Pulse Rates Low as Owen Holds On' perfectly acceptable. But what did my sub-editor put on top of the copy? I couldn't believe it myself when I saw it. 'Mansfield Bore Finds He's Not Such a Draw'.

Ye Gods, the poor bloke had just won one of the most prestigious tournaments on the European Tour calendar, and he picks up the paper and reads that. No wonder the poor bloke was upset. I won't pretend that the copy was entirely complimentary, but quite often it's the headline that causes more offence, and not everyone is aware that the headlines are written in the office. Several years later, when they had become home owners in America and regular players on the US Tour, I was asked to interview both Poulter and Owen, within a month or so of each other, via trans-Atlantic phone calls. And I have to say that both of them were utterly charming, which led me to believe that they either didn't have very long memories, or had long since become successful enough to stop caring what was written about them in the newspapers. Opinion always has the potential to cause upset, which is why it is sound advice for the people you're writing about never to read the newspapers at all. And, in my experience, none of them ever do. I've lost count, in fact, of the number of sports people who have come up to me down the years and said: 'I never read the newspapers – but that piece you wrote last week was complete crap.'

It's entirely possible to upset people by simply getting your facts wrong, as I found out as a junior news reporter on the *South Wales Argus*, when a mistake with the calendar meant that I was responsible for several hundred people turning up to watch a tidal phenomenon known as the Severn Bore, when it had actually been and gone the previous week. It was my first experience of what is known in the business as the switchboard being jammed, although that wasn't too difficult in a district office with only one phone in it. However, if getting your facts wrong is never a great idea, it's opinions that cause most of the arguments. Try walking into an office on a Monday morning, walking up to the bloke in accounts who supports West Ham and whose team has just lost on a controversial penalty decision, and casually remark: 'I thought the ref had a good game on Saturday.' Then get ready to duck. Likewise writing about players. Rubbish the central defender and half the people who've read it will say: 'Couldn't agree more. Two left feet and half a brain.' And the other half will say: 'Which bloody match were you watching then? Best player on the park.'

I found this out when inheriting the job as rugby correspondent of the *Leicester Mercury*, despite the minor drawback of never having written about the sport before. My first report, for the now defunct Saturday afternoon sports paper, was simple enough. No opinion required. 'Tigers kicked off into a stiff breeze, and in the third minute took the lead when Dusty Hare landed a thirty-yard penalty.' That kind of thing. For Monday's paper, however, they expected eight hundred words or so of informed, thought-provoking opinion, which is why I mingled with players, supporters and officials in the clubhouse afterwards, keeping my ears peeled for any pearls of wisdom I could claim as my own original thoughts. I encountered a group which included the club secretary, who said to me: 'The pack was good today, and Smith especially. He was just outstanding.'

Later, finding myself in a group that included a couple of committee men, I decided it was time they realized that their new local reporter knew a thing or two about the game. 'I'll tell you what, though,' I ventured confidently, when there was a convenient pause in the conversation, 'the pack was good today. And Smith especially. What a player.' One of the committee men turned to me, with an expression that was quizzical to put it kindly. 'Smith?' he said. 'Rubbish game. He'll be lucky to keep his place for next week's match.' Which told me two things. One, that rugby is such a complex game that no one ever really knows what's happening. And two, that you can write just about anything you like. Some will agree with it, and some won't. Normally, the person not agreeing with it will hurl the paper across the breakfast table, mutter some dark oath, and carry on spreading marmalade on his toast. Sometimes, though, he'll hurl the paper across the breakfast table, mutter some dark oath, and dial his lawyer. One such a man, on the occasion of my covering a pro-am golf tournament in the West Indies, was Dermot Desmond.

Desmond was one of a group of wealthy Irish businessmen – among them John Magnier and J. P. McManus – who bought the exclusive Sandy Lane Resort in

Barbados in 1998, and turned it into such a luxurious hotel that Tiger Woods had his honeymoon there in 2004. One of its features was a golf course named 'The Green Monkey' – reputed to have been the most expensive golf course ever built, and a rival to the golf course hosting the pro-am I was attending, the Westmoreland. After the round, I was chatting in the bar to some of the locals, one of whom mentioned the new course just down the road, adding: 'Shame about the green monkeys, though.' The monkeys were all over the island, but according to this chap, the ones who used to inhabit the trees around the new golf course were all gone. Wiped out, he said, by the green-keeper using too much fertilizer.

I decided this was worth a mention in the piece I sent back, fairly well buried somewhere in the middle, and months went by before the subject cropped up again. The phone went, and it was Keith, the sports editor. 'It seems that your mention of the green monkeys got picked up and reproduced in some American magazine, and Dermot saw it. Anyway, he says the green monkeys are alive and well, and they're suing.' I laughed. 'The green monkeys are suing?' I said. 'Maybe we can settle out of court with a bunch of bananas.' A few more weeks went by, and Keith was on the phone again. 'I've had a long chat with Dermot,' he said, 'and there is a solution that doesn't require us going to court, or even having to apologize, or pay him any money.' 'Excellent,' I said, 'we've had a result there then.'

There was a bit of a silence, before Keith said: 'Well, Dermot's idea of an out-of-court settlement is not a bad deal for the newspaper, but you might not care for it too much.' 'Tell me more,' I said. Keith chuckled. The conversation, apparently, had ended like this. 'Keith,' said Dermot, 'there is a way to settle this, without lawyers, and to my entire satisfaction. All you have to do is to send me Martin Johnson's testicles, and I will then feed them to my green monkeys.' I paused to consider Dermot's offer. 'Sounds reasonable enough,' I said. 'How's about if I buy a couple of old prunes, shove them in a jiffy bag, post them off to Barbados, and include a note reading: "Dear Dermot, in full and final settlement, please find enclosed Martin Johnson's testicles. Yours in sport, etc., etc." If Dermot has a sense of humour, he might just drop the whole thing.' 'It's a thought,' said Keith, 'but I think I ought to tell you that when Dermot mooted the idea of turning you into a eunuch, I didn't get the impression that he found the idea amusing.' I never did find out what they finally agreed on, but whatever it was, people can still say to me – happily – 'I don't know how you've got the balls to write that.'

The only other time I've been sued was by David Gower, in 1989, after England lost the opening Test of the Ashes series at Headingley. The game had been seemingly headed for a routine draw, with Australia not having nearly enough runs to declare and give themselves time to bowl England out on the final day, but in the two hours before lunch the boundary boards took such a battering from a hapless home attack that Australia found themselves far enough ahead to invite England to try and survive for the final two sessions. A modest task, but one which proved to be comfortably beyond them.

The space originally reserved for the article had been a modest one, in anticipation of a fairly dull draw, but when

England lost, the instruction was altered to keep writing until I felt like stopping. I don't think I've ever been in a situation, before or since, where I couldn't type fast enough to get to the end of one paragraph before starting another, and not many of the words that came pouring out could be described as anywhere close to complimentary. In fact, I was so worked up that when I found myself reporting that Gower was due for an examination on an injured shoulder before the next Test match, I found myself wondering whether a scan between the ears might be worth considering while they were at it. I'm not sure why I'd picked on the captain quite so ruthlessly, as he'd been as stunned by his side's incompetence as the rest of us, and not unnaturally his agent felt it was worthy of recompense.

It upset Gower even more as we were both chums and near neighbours at the time, thanks to the fact that when he first started playing for Leicestershire, I was the evening paper's cricket correspondent. We socialized quite a bit, and were friendly enough for him to ask me a favour during an away match against Somerset at Taunton. 'Hey Scoop,' (Ray Illingworth had given me the nickname when he was captain) said Gower. 'I've been invited to the pub by Botham tonight, and I'm worried I'm going to end up with the hangover to end them all.' 'Just tell him you're not going, then,' I said. 'I don't think you quite understand,' said Gower. 'An invitation from Beefy is not an invitation at all; it's an instruction.' 'Okay,' I said, 'what can I do about it?' 'I've got a plan,' said Gower. 'I'm meeting him at eight, so you turn up at nine and say: "Come on Gower, drink up. You know I've got an interview piece to do with you for tomorrow's paper. We need to get back to the hotel and get it done now.'" 'No problem,' I said. 'I'll be there.'

So on the stroke of nine, I walked through the door of the Four Alls pub, and Gower, already looking slightly the worse for wear, swivelled on his bar stool and shot me a look of undying gratitude. We started to go through our previously rehearsed routine, but hadn't got far when Botham intervened. 'Who's this then, Gower?' Gower explained. 'Press, eh?' said Botham. 'Shall I tell you what I did to some reporter who got right up my nose in here one night?' 'Not entirely necessary,' I said. 'But if it's a story you're fond of telling . . .' 'I picked him up, opened the door, and bounced him over the road. Haven't got so much bounce from a delivery since I last bowled at the WACA in Perth.' 'Well I won't upset you,' I said. 'So, I'll just wait for Gower to finish his drink and . . .' Botham wasn't even listening. 'What are you having? Pint? Hey Bill! Pint for the press here!' And so, there we remained, until the clock chimed eleven, and the sanctuary of closing time had been reached. 'Bill!' chimed up Beefy. 'A couple of bottles of red please. The Australian stuff.' 'Er, isn't it closing time?' I said. Botham looked amused. He left his stool, walked over to the door, pulled the bolt across, and said: 'I'll be sure and let you know when it's closing time.'

I don't recall whether Gower got any runs the following day – if he did, it marked him down as a genius – or whether I managed to file a report – if I did, it should have won a prize. It may be that he never forgave me for not saving him that night, but after what I wrote about him in that Test match, there was a distinct frost in the atmosphere when I approached him on the outfield on practice day before the next Test at Lord's. 'I gather you're not happy with me skipper?' 'Correct.' 'And your people are looking to litigation.' 'Correct again.' 'Ah well,' I said, 'can't say I blame you. A trifle over the top upon reflection.' At which point Gower broke into a smile. 'We've decided to settle out of court, on condition you go along with our terms,' he said. 'Which are?' I said. 'Well, you have to take yourself off to Lay and Wheeler (a Leicester wine merchant), buy a magnum of vintage Krug – that's a magnum by the way, not a bottle, and it's got to be vintage – and bring it round to my place. Then I'll get a couple of glasses out, and we'll drink it quietly together.' What class. And no mention of providing – on an hors-d'oeuvre plate, speared with a couple of cocktail sticks – my testicles for an aperitif.

That was the summer Ted Dexter was installed as chairman of the England selectors, such a nice man that no one in the press box ever wanted to write anything bad about him. Unfortunately, the incorrigibly scatty Ted made it more or less impossible not to. He routinely mistook his players for someone else, or didn't recognize them at all, or got their names back to front. Ergo, Devon Malcolm became, for the rest of his career, Malcolm Devon. That first series ended not so much in defeat by Australia, as humiliation, and when the final press conference took place at the Oval Ted was asked whether he himself took any of the blame. We thought he might at least offer a mild *mea culpa* to the assembled hacks, but instead he came up with: 'I am not aware of any mistakes I may have made.' Cue a loud crash from the back of the room, caused by the cricket correspondent of the *Evening Standard* kicking over a chair in his rush to get out of the room. 'My God!' he gasped. 'What a quote! Out of my way, I've got to get this into my last edition!'

Ted really did make it difficult at times for the press not to portray him as a figure of fun, often using the word 'lampooned' to describe the kind of ridicule he was regularly subjected to, such as the mock apology which appeared in the satirical magazine *Private Eye* towards the end of that disastrous Ashes series.

In common with other newspapers, we recently published a number of articles under such head-lines as 'Lord Ted's Test Tonic', which may have given the impression that Mr Dexter's appointment was in some way likely to lead to an improvement in the performance of England's cricketers.

The passage 'Make no mistake – Dave and Ted will stuff the Aussies this summer. Border's boys can XXXX off back Down Under' may in particular have given rise to the unintentional inference that Mr Dexter and Mr Gower would somehow play a part in reviving England's fortunes. We now accept that Mr Dexter is nothing more than a loud-mouthed PR man who has done for English cricket what Michael Foot did for the Labour party, and we apologise to all English cricket-lovers for any distress that may have been caused by our earlier articles, which we now unreservedly withdraw.

More of the same followed later that year when he travelled to watch the team play in a one-day tournament in India called the Nehru Trophy. These limited-over international competitions were beginning to proliferate everywhere and always with a fancy peg to hang them on in a vain attempt to kid people that they were being played for prestige rather than money. This one was being held to commemorate the hundredth anniversary of the birth of Jawaharlal Nehru, although they could just as easily have made it the twentieth birthday of the Eden Gardens tea urn.

Nonetheless, it was at least destined to be remembered for providing the first error of Lord Ted's reign – one which even he would have admitted to – which was deciding to pop over to India himself. Having planned to watch England's group matches against Pakistan in Cuttack and India in Kanpur, the chairman never made it to the former when his flight was delayed because of a bomb scare, neither did he to the latter, which he spent propped up in bed in his hotel room watching on TV after being struck down by one of the local bugs. Having lost his voice, he issued a handwritten note in praise of the lads – like young Mr Grace telling the staff 'You've all done very well' – and when he was finally fit enough to get out of bed, it was straight to the airport to embark on the second leg of his 10,000-mile round trip without having seen a ball bowled.

India was something of a banana skin for Ted. The 1993 Test series there produced another memorable gaffe when the touring party was announced to the assembled media at Lord's. It had been rumoured for several days that Gower, who'd been fired and replaced as captain by Graham Gooch at the end of that 1989 Ashes summer, was not among the sixteen players selected, and sure enough, when Ted read out the names, Gower's was not one of them. The only left-handed batsman in the party was Lancashire's Neil Fairbrother, a brilliant one-day batsman, but a player that most people felt was not terribly effective in the longer form of the game. Which led to the correspondent of the *Evening Standard* (the same one who'd knocked his chair over) laying a carefully baited trap. 'Excuse me.' His face flushed with genuine anger at Gower's omission. 'But would the chairman care to explain how he's managed to preside over the selection of a touring party without a single left-handed batsman?' Ted digested this for a few moments, before a slow smile spread across his lips in a kind of 'gotcha!' moment. 'Well, let me see now,' said Ted. 'Yes. I'm fairly sure that the last time I looked Neil Fairbrother was in fact batting left-handed.' And with that, he leant back in his chair with the satisfied expression of a man who has just despatched a gentle leg-stump half-volley to the boundary. He had, however, as had many of his press colleagues in fairness, failed to recognize that it was actually a verbal hand grenade. The man from the *Standard* clambered back to his feet. 'Oh, I'm sorry. My mistake. Dear oh dear. I really should have made myself a little clearer. I meant,' he said softly, before delivering the rest of the sentence with a venomous spit. 'I meant a *Test class* left-hander.'

If Ted had looked behind him, metaphorically speaking, all three stumps would have been out of the ground. A Gower-less England were whitewashed 3–0 in that series, with Ted blaming one of the defeats, in Calcutta, on hazardous smog levels, and when England lost the second Test of the following summer at Lord's to go 2–0 down in the Ashes series, the chairman put it down to the alignment of the planets. 'Maybe,' said Ted, 'Venus was in juxtaposition with somewhere else.' He then claimed that the side had made significant progress since the defeat in India. 'There's been quite a difference between the winter and this series,' he said. 'In India, we were outspun . . .' At which point one of two journalists who, over the series so far, had been writing in their notebooks little else but 'bowled Warne' (sixteen wickets in two Tests) and 'bowled May' (six of the spinners' fifteen wickets at Lord's) tried manfully to suppress a titter, but failed. 'I must have missed the joke . . .' said Ted, and the comparison remained unfinished – unlike his optimism, as he then went on to predict that England would win the next four Tests and take the series 4–2. Sadly, with Australia about to take a 4–0 lead in the fifth Test at Edgbaston, the end came in appropriately bizarre fashion. Australia's openers must have been puzzled as to why their meeting in mid-pitch for an end-of-over chat should have been deemed worthy of a spontaneous cheer and burst of handclapping from the capacity crowd, but the announcer then let them in on what the spectators, or those of them plugged into their transistor radios, had just heard. 'For anyone wondering what that round of applause was,' he said, 'it was to mark the resignation of Ted Dexter.' There was, by contrast, a concerted groan from the press box, whose inhabitants all knew that whatever else it meant for English cricket, it would certainly be a lot duller.

It's one thing upsetting an individual when you write an article, but it's a rare achievement to get up the noses of an entire country – as happened after the 1999 Ryder Cup golf match at Brookline, when the American team, and their wives and girlfriends, ran across the seventeenth green to congratulate Justin Leonard on holing a putt while José María Olazábal still had a putt of his own to take for Europe. The following morning, the postbag was full of contributions from 'Disgusted of Denver' and 'Appalled of Atlanta', and all, apparently, because I'd made one or two uncomplimentary observations about the host nation. I'd found it, for example, mildly amusing to hear Colin Montgomerie being heckled about his portly figure by people tipping the scales at roughly the same weight as a baby elephant, or the spectators in general providing comfortably the most shining example on the planet of the old adage about noise and empty vessels. What seemed to put them out most of all, however, was my suspicion that the infringement of just about every known etiquette in golf had nothing to do with malice, or poor sportsmanship. It was the same kind of bone-headed ignorance which made most Americans believe that the Second World War was won, with only minor assistance from Great Britain, by John Wayne. I was phoned by a radio station in Chicago, and invited onto some chat show to explain myself about the John Wayne remark, which turned out to be enjoyably light-hearted, and ended with the interviewer telling me to get my facts straight. 'I gotta tell ya, Marty,' he said, 'you got it all wrong when you wrote that most Americans think John Wayne won the Second World War. Most Americans will tell you it was Tom Hanks.'

The Women's Tennis Association turned out to be slightly less capable of seeing the funny side judging by their reaction to a couple of articles I wrote during one Wimbledon fortnight, the first involving a ladies' singles match in which a well-built French player, Amélie Mauresmo, bludgeoned her way to victory over a more petite opponent. Not long before, it had been reported that she'd opened a bar in the south of France with her girlfriend, and I proffered the observation that she probably wouldn't have had too much trouble dealing with awkward customers at chucking-out time.

It was also around this time that, in the ongoing argument about whether women players deserved equal prize money, some of the men were calling for them to justify it by making them play five-set matches. I found this pretty horrifying, and wrote a piece suggesting that it should be resisted at all costs. The reason being that women's tennis was so awful that making people sit through five sets, rather than three, should only be seriously considered as a sentencing option for High Court judges, and a possible solution to the problem of overcrowded prisons. A couple of days later the sports editor phoned to inform me that the Women's TA had taken grave exception to this – so much so that I'd been banned from interviewing any of their members for twelve months. It seemed to me to be a curious penalty to impose, and I asked the boss whether he might consider writing a letter of protest, and demanding they make it twenty-four months instead of twelve.

But not only did he decide that it wasn't worth the cost of a stamp; he was still grappling with a complaint from the British cycling governing body about a report I'd recently done on their annual round-Britain race. I'd given up cycling myself at about my early thirties, having decided that taking to the open road on a bicycle was about as conducive to a long life expectancy as smoking sixty non-tipped fags every day. I'd actually started to become an expert on British hedgerows, mostly as a result of being propelled into them by motorized vehicles, and professional cycling seemed to me to be even more dangerous. In the race I attended, there were dozens of riders all bunched together reaching mind-boggling speeds travelling downhill, added to which police motorcyclists were whizzing ahead to flag traffic across to the side of the road until the convoy had past – breaking just about every commonsense rule of motoring in the process. Sure enough, a police escort rider was killed, travelling way too fast and on the wrong side of the road according to eye witnesses, but while it seemed to me to be perfectly reasonable to draw the conclusion that taking part in this race was the second best way of attempting suicide – just behind trying to interview Colin Montgomerie after a triple bogey at the eighteenth, it resulted in a long letter of complaint from the cycling people. Not as long, though, as the one the motorcycle people sent to the paper after I was sent to report on an even more dangerous annual road race, the Isle of Man TT.

The Isle of Man has few serious rivals when it comes to macabre tourist economies, in that nowhere else relies quite so heavily on filling its coffers by filling its coffins. The start line is sited alongside a cemetery, not inappropriately in that while most of the bikers arrive on the ferry, not all of them get to use the other half of their return ticket. In the year I went, the TT claimed eight dead, two in races, and half a dozen more in public outings around the course. My visit came during the Grand Prix fortnight, and the coroner's court was again in session investigating the cause of a thirty-three-year-old bank clerk ploughing into a wall during practice. The TT was founded around the start of the twentieth century, by an English motoring enthusiast by the name of Gordon Bennett – whose name must be constantly on the riders' lips as they find themselves wiping dead gnats off their goggles while hurtling towards a lamp-post. When a Formula One driver leaves the track, he invariably slews safely to a halt in a gravel trap, but when a biker parts company with the road on the TT course, the choice of final resting places embraces brick walls, hedgerows and greenhouses. I spoke to one local resident who had had no less than eight cases of riders paying involuntary visits to her back garden, mostly on what is known as 'Mad Sunday', when something like twenty thousand bikers take to the road without the inconvenience of speed limits.

The course itself measures nearly thirty-eight miles, and is narrow enough to induce a fair amount of caution if you're behind the wheel of a milk float never mind four times around on a machine that occasionally gets up to 180 mph. Every year there's a fresh clamour for bike racing to be banned, at least in its traditional format, and every year the island cocks a deaf 'un, perhaps because it's their one and only claim to fame – unless you count the Manx kipper. I tried to get some info from the racing office about accident statistics, and a mafia-style wall of omerta descended, apart from being told (and you can't make this up) that someone recently produced figures to prove that there are as many injuries sustained in cheese-rolling contests as from racing motorbikes around the capital, Douglas. Armed with this interesting information, it was nothing less than my journalistic duty to conduct my own market research in several of the island pubs, but of all the people I pinned to the bar in Paxman-style interrogation, no one would admit to hearing of anyone who'd been crushed to death by a giant gorgonzola.

Talking of big cheeses, the most famous rider in the Isle of Man's long history was Mike Hailwood, who ironically died in a 1981 car crash while nipping out to his local chip shop. I found a small shrine dedicated to Hailwood memorabilia at the Douglas museum, although the entire island is a Mecca for bike worshippers during the races. You can barely move for machines, ranging from state-of-the-art modern Japanese things, to the kind of antique relic Lawrence of Arabia used to ride around on while the camels were being re-shod. Most of the interest seemed to centre on the 500cc Classic race, in which four-time world champion Phil Read was the oldest competitor, at fifty-nine. Read once made himself as unpopular as a journalist reporting road-kill statistics when he declined to ride, although the most famous refusenik was Barry Sheene. He rode around the island once, fell off, and never came back. Read, who finished a creditable sixteenth out of eighty-eight starters, was riding because of the rule denying people the chance to bid for a plot in the cemetery – at least in an official race – beyond the age of sixty. And he only ever rode in the TT when he felt he had no choice, when it was an official world championship event and he needed the points. He told me he remembered Hailwood telling him: 'They should pull the plug on this effing death trap. You need to know where all the wet patches are, the walls, the bumps, kerbs; and some of the people who didn't know got caught out.' 'Caught out?' I said. Whereupon he confirmed that 'caught out' was the biker's euphemism for killed. He himself said that he could recall parting company with his bike four times around the island, but that all of them were 'little accidents'. I asked him what he meant by little. 'Oh, doing about 70 or 80 mph,' he replied.

The Classic 500 he had entered was held up for three hours owing to mist covering Snaefell Mountain. When you're biffing along at 160 mph, it helps if you can see where you're going, and when the visibility was adjudged to be okay, the bloke on the tannoy had encouraging news about the track conditions. There was, he said, a strong crosswind all the way up the mountain, wet leaves, twigs and other windblown debris on the road, oh, and he'd had reports of inconsiderate riding during practice. 'So,' he signed off, 'please be careful.' Read told me he'd been lucky to avoid any serious injuries in nearly forty years of racing. 'Let's see, I've broken a few ribs, a collar bone, shoulder blade, legs, arms, done a few discs, and that's it. Oh, and lost a bit of skin of course. Apart from that, nothing really.' The race passed off relatively safely, in that the rescue helicopter took off only the once to ferry an injured rider to hospital. And not every rider took risks – some of them phut-phutted around at the back of the field at roughly the same speed as a supermarket shopper on an invalid scooter. However, if you write that it might be dangerous, they write you gruff letters of complaint, even though when I was there I made quite sure to balance out the article by mentioning one important safety measure they absolutely insist upon. Which is that no rider is allowed to wear the number 13.

6

ON TOUR WITH ENGLAND:
MY GOD, IT'S MURDER

All the cricketing countries

India

We were off to play golf somewhere in Delhi, and after the taxi driver had narrowly missed cleaning up several bicycles, a couple of bullock carts and a sacred cow, he sailed so close to a traffic cop that in taking the evasive action required to stay alive the poor chap must have come perilously close to swallowing his whistle. It wasn't so much that the cabbie was a worse driver than anyone else out there trying to negotiate the potholes. Far from it. Compared to some, you'd have put him down as a courteous road user. Or that his cab – with both wing mirrors missing in action and the air conditioning provided via a rusted hole in the floor – was in a poorer condition than any of the other MOT failures on the road. No. It had more to do with his disconcerting habit of continually removing his eyes from what lay in front of him to swivel his head sideways and stare at his front-seat passenger. Finally, on about stare no. 12, he broke into a huge smile, and spoke. 'My God!' Chris Lander, the front-seat passenger and cricket correspondent of the *Daily Mirror*, was understandably startled. He checked his fly buttons, leaned across to look into the rear-view mirror in case he'd broken out in spots, and after satisfying himself that nothing appeared to be seriously amiss, carried on chatting to his back-seat colleagues. 'My God!' There it was again, and he turned to see the driver staring across at him with an even wider grin than before. Lander was about to ask for clarification when the driver spoke again. 'My God!' he said. Followed by, after a longish pause : '*You!* . . . *You* are my God!' Lander, understandably confused, replied with something along the lines of: 'Nice of you to say so, but I'm really not . . .' when the cabbie cut him off in mid-protestation. '*You!* . . . *You* are my God! You come to India, I eat. You no come to India, I no eat. *You* are my God!' All was now clear. It was an unusual way of thanking someone for hiring their cab, and one you don't often hear from the front seat when you're being driven down Tottenham Court Road, but India is, as they say, different. Lander's newly acquired deity didn't do much for his golf, and while his caddy was also in the habit of gasping: 'My God!' at regular intervals, it was more in sheer disbelief at the shot he'd just witnessed.

The fare came to about four pence for half an hour's travel, which made the cabbie something like middle class in a country with such extremes of wealth and poverty that houses with ceilings resembling the Sistine Chapel's are rarely too far away from shacks with ceilings made of corrugated iron. And it's when you hop into a taxi that you realize why Indian batsmen are so quick on their feet when it comes to playing the spinners, because if you're not, crossing the road is a more or less guaranteed death sentence. One day, on the media bus to the ground, we saw one young lad flying in and out of the traffic on a skateboard. He had no legs, and it would have been impressive enough watching him steer and change direction on two arms, never mind a couple of bandaged stumps. He had a begging bowl attached to his neck, and when we got stuck at the lights, he burst into a chorus of 'God Save the Queen'. Later in the same traffic jam, we spotted him serenading the occupants of a taxi with 'Lily Marlene', although how he knew they were German – if indeed they were – we couldn't tell. There is, it would seem, no easy way to earn a living in India, and when we got to the golf course we'd see scores of women, of all ages, manicuring the grass by the side of the greens with what appeared to be nail scissors. It was easier being a caddie, even though they'd have had a pretty short life expectancy if any of them had landed a job with Colin Montgomerie.

An Indian caddie selecting 'the bleedin' obvious' as his special subject on *Mastermind* would score pretty heavily, and if half the battle in golf is to try and forget a bad shot as quickly as possible, you certainly won't manage it with an Indian caddie on your bag. A typical hole would go something like this. Huge divot, followed by shank into stagnant pond. 'Terrible shot, sir.' Leave putt five feet short. 'Not hard enough, sir.' Charge putt five feet past. 'Too hard, sir.' We once set off for a game at the Tollygunge club in Calcutta, where Graham Gooch is on the honours board for a hole in one, and one of our number was having a particularly poor round. He topped his opening tee shot, and received the inevitable: 'Bad shot, sir.' 'Yes, I know that, thank you. Now hand me the three wood.' He hit it about two feet, and was promptly apprised of his caddie's opinion of it. 'Very bad shot, sir.' 'Now listen here. I've been playing this game long enough to know a bad shot when I see one, and I really don't need *you* to tell me. Gottit? Now, the six iron if you please.' Air shot. 'Oh, terrible, terrible sir.' 'Right. One more word from you and you're fired, you understand?' By now, the tension was unbearable, and when his next shot managed to propel the ball roughly five of the hundred and fifty yards required, an eerie silence descended. Until it was broken, after several seconds of admirable self-restraint, by a murmured 'tsch, tsch' from the caddie. Who was, indeed, summarily fired. Personally, the running commentary bit doesn't bother me at all, as long as my caddie remembers to keep throwing up bits of grass to check which way the wind is blowing. Not so much because I'm concerned about the effect it might have on my golf ball, but because I want to stay upwind of him. Whatever an Indian caddie spends his money on, it does not, in my experience, include bars of soap.

On most overseas tours, if the cricket is dull, the whole experience is dull. But that's never the case in India, a country which teaches you patience if nothing else. Try changing a travellers' cheque, for example, an exercise that will perhaps occupy five minutes of your day in Australia, and about five hours of it in India. Apart from: 'My God', the two words you hear most often in India are 'No problem'. The normal context being something along the lines of: 'I know all your luggage is in Ahmedabad, the match is in Jamshedpur, and we've accidentally flown you to Nagpur. But please. It will be no problem.' There is nothing a Western visitor can ask for in India that can conceivably qualify as a problem, and if you doubt me, try amusing yourself at your hotel by picking up the phone in your room, dialling room service, and asking them to send up two lightly boiled eggs, the Aberavon Male Voice Choir, and a partridge in a pear tree. The voice at the other end will say, without a hint of hesitation: 'Coming right up sir, no problem.' I once filled in one of those room service breakfast cards in a hotel in Jaipur, hung it on the door knob, and retired to bed. In the morning, fifteen minutes after the scheduled delivery, I rang. 'Any sign of my breakfast?' 'Coming sir, no problem.' Another ten minutes went by. 'Look, where's my breakfast?' 'On way now, sir. No problem.' However, the problem was that one of our number had downed more than his usual quota of Cobra ale the previous night, and on the stagger back to his room, had removed everyone's breakfast order from the door knobs. The hotel had, in fact, no knowledge of my order, or indeed anyone else's, but rather than say, as most hotels would, 'Sorry sir, there's no record of you ordering anything' what they say in India is: 'No problem.' Presumably in the hope that you'll eventually get tired of phoning, or die of old age.

Nothing much works in India, including the electricity. When someone pops the kettle on in downtown Cuttack, all the lights go out, as indeed they did during the Nehru Cup tournament in 1989, when a coachload of roughly a dozen English journalists pulled up outside the hotel in

Gwalior, with about an hour to go before first-edition deadlines, and everyone in need of a telephone. No one was greatly surprised to discover that the hotel had just the one international telephone line, or indeed that a recent power cut obliged us to sit in darkness waiting for our various London offices to try and get through. At last. The phone rang. 'Mr Otway!' came the cry from reception. 'For you.' The man from the *Today* newspaper rushed to the receiver, and we heard him say: 'Really darling? He's just started teething? That's great.' The howls of derision prompted him to hang up quickly and keep the line clear for more important matters. It rang again. 'Mr Otway!' This time the conversation at our end went something like: 'Is that you mother? Yes don't worry. I'm not eating the local food. My stomach is fine . . .' More howls of protest, and he hung up again.

That's how it is in India. On my first visit there we were filing by telex, and one day I descended into one of the underground dungeons which passed as a telex office, and was greeted by the lone operator. He had approximately three teeth, none of them white, and the walls were dripping with the betel leaf juice he expelled from his mouth at regular intervals. I paid him, impressed upon him the urgency required, and watched him dump my typewritten copy into a basket with a pile of other papers. I had a plane to catch, and had to go, and never once imagined that the piece would ever reach London. However, a few days later I came across a copy of the relevant newspaper, and was amazed to see the story in there word for word. Every cricket tour to India has its stories to tell, from lost kit to the dreaded Montezuma's, and sometimes you know that things are going to go wrong from the moment you land. On an England tour there in 1993, the team physio posted a letter home from the first port of call in Delhi. Three days later, he arrived back from the ground, opened his hotel-room door, and there it was lying on the carpet.

Which was at least preferable to opening your bedroom door and finding a rat on your carpet. And not any old rat, but a rat roughly the size of your average family cat. It was at the Park Hotel in Calcutta, which is far and away the worst hotel I've ever stayed in, and the irony was that a sign in the lobby read: 'No Pets'. I shot down to reception and said: 'I have a confession to make. I have smuggled a pet into my room. It's got a long tail, very sharp teeth, and likes to curl up for a nap on the end of my bed. So would you be so kind as to ask room service to send up a saucer of milk please?' The chap behind the desk gave a typically Indian smile, with half a set of white teeth, and the other half stained with betel juice. 'Oh, to beg your pardon, sir. No pets please. This is not allowing.' I gave him a long stare. 'I was actually joking,' I said. 'It's a rat. A very large rat. In my room. And I don't want him there. Understand. Now get upstairs, find it, and remove it. Now. Please.' About five minutes later the room was full of people, peering under the bed, in the wardrobe, around the bath-room door, under the mattress, and after a while they all headed for the door. The main man smiled and said: 'Rat gone sir. All is clear now. Wishing you a very good night.' I said something along the lines that I failed to share his opinion that the case was now officially closed, and that sleep was under any circumstances hard to come by in one of his hotel bedrooms, on account of a damp mattress, threadbare curtains and an electric light bulb (without a shade, of course) that had a disconcerting habit of hissing in the middle of the night despite being turned off. But with a rat on the loose, it was actually an impossibility. So I got moved. To an equally appalling room, but at least it was – as advertised – for single occupancy.

One of my favourite hotel stories, though, which just about gives you India in a nutshell, involved the late Christopher Martin-Jenkins. We were staying in a smallish hotel in somewhere like Nagpur, and the shirts he'd sent to the hotel laundry had come back not only four sizes smaller than they'd been previously, but also looking as though they'd provided a four-course meal for a colony of moths. The manager was summoned, invited to inspect what remained of CMJ's shirts, and asked to consider the possibility that his hotel's laundry service was possibly the worst in the entire world. 'Oh no sir,' said the manager. 'It is not the quality of the laundry service I am thinking is no good. It is the quality of your shirts.'

Australia

Of my first two impressions of Australia, one has changed, but the other hasn't. Happily, the beer no longer tastes as though it's been brewed from wet cardboard boxes (or at least not all of it) but the place is still nauseatingly patriotic. The commercial for Qantas sounds more like the national anthem than the real one, and the first thing I ever saw on a TV set in Australia was a lisping Shirley-Temple-like girl concluding a breakfast cereal advertisement with: 'I love Othtralia, and I love my cornflaykth.' The inference being that Rice Krispie consumers run the risk of being tried for treason. That was a time when the players and press travelled pretty much together, and when tours went on for so long that when you finally got home your wife opened the door, took one look at what appeared to be a salesman holding a suitcase, and said: 'Not today thank you.'

Nowadays, overseas tours are like weekend breaks by comparison. This one lasted 132 days, but on day one I still had no real inkling about how vast a place Australia was until I was returning to the hotel after an exploratory first walk around the city centre in Brisbane. As I waited to cross the road, a man I estimated to be in his early sixties came up and asked me if I knew where there was a Gents. I told him I'd only been in Australia about two hours, but that there was certain to be one at my hotel if he'd care to follow me. As we walked, he told me he'd moved to Brisbane about two years before, to live with one of his children after his wife had died, but was so homesick he was planning to go back in a few months' time. I asked him where home was, thinking he'd say something like London, or Bristol, but the answer was Perth. In the same country – but, as I later discovered, four hours away by aeroplane, with Singapore its nearest big city neighbour. In fact, flying from east coast Australia to Perth was three time zones away, and almost guaranteed you a mild case of jet lag.

I've been back around twenty times since, maybe more, and still can't really grasp how big Australia is. On one tour, when the former England fast bowler John Snow was the media travel agent, I asked him if he could organize a hire car from Brisbane, as I wanted to drive up to see the

Great Barrier Reef. 'Yes I can sort that,' said Snowy. 'And how about hotels?' 'No hotels,' I said, 'it's just a day trip.' To which he replied: 'Well if it's just a day trip, you'll get about a sixth of the way there before you have turn the car round and come back again.' The two places might be in the same State, but they're about eleven thousand miles and twenty-four hours apart by road.

The food is as good as you'll find anywhere on the planet, or at least it was until a new wave of chefs started becoming impossibly pretentious; and the bars are, as you might expect, pretty lively after dark.

For some reason, though, Australia after dark on a Friday night is a little too lively for most tastes, with the entire country – at least between the ages of about sixteen and forty – setting out to become as pissed as possible in the shortest possible time. And I have yet to spend a Friday night there without this objective being comfortably achieved. I remember once being in a bar in Hobart with a few colleagues one Friday night, and being fascinated by a row of drinkers on bar stools, and the fact that one of them was clearly only able to remain upright due to the proximity of his two neighbours either side. 'If one of those guys propping him up needs the Gents, it could be interesting,' I suggested, and no sooner had I spoken, than it happened. A sway to the left was safely halted by his neighbour's shoulder, but the sway to the right now had nothing to impede its progress. He hit the floor with a bang, whereupon so much blood spouted from his forehead it was like watching a fireman's hose. His chums were clearly concerned, as two of them dismounted from their stools, dragged him across the room to the jukebox, propped him up against the wall, and left him to carry on bleeding while they returned to their drinks.

Australia hasn't changed all that much in the years since my first visit in the mid-1980s, except perhaps in one area. A nation once second to none at cricket, and winning Olympic medals, is now only No. 1 in the world in the art of nannying its subjects. So much so that it will shortly become illegal for anyone to die, and if you do manage to pass away before the government's decreed life expectancy age (175 and rising) it will be because you haven't read the 'Watch Your Speed!' warnings or have failed to observe the list of safety instructions before cleaning your golf shoes. We'd just finished a game of golf in Brisbane, and there on top of the high-pressure boot-cleaning machine was a notice headed: 'Danger of Death!' And underneath it were listed four different ways of killing or maiming yourself by misusing the nozzle. One of them cautioned against employing it for removing particles of sand from your hair, as if it might prove attractive for dandruff sufferers as well as for cleaning your boots, and another counselled against using it in the pursuit of 'practical jokes'.

This seemed reasonable, given that Australia is a country not renowned for its chivalry towards sheilas, and sticking the nozzle up the lady captain's skirt would probably be considered fair game at all but the most exclusive golf club. Speeding has been all but eliminated, and careful motorists (which means all of them) are regularly rewarded by neon signs flashing messages like: 'Kept Your Speed Down? Well Done!' You would, therefore, be highly unlikely to suffer more than mild bruising should you be run over, but even that possibility has been eliminated in Australia, where stringent fines apply for crossing the road without getting permission from a little green man. A journey of, say, half a mile, can take either fifteen minutes or an hour, depending on what colour the traffic signal is when you want to cross a road. Australians wouldn't dream of trying to nip across on red, so while it's now been several years since anyone had 'getting run over' inscribed on their death certificate, you can still end up in the morgue from an attack of deep vein thrombosis waiting for the little man to change from red to green. Oh, and don't forget to apply the factor 30 sun block while you're waiting to cross, as dire warnings about skin cancer are posted on every street corner.

By the way, should you happen to fall ill in Australia (and government measures are already in hand to forbid it) make sure you complete your illness in the same State it broke out in. When I slipped a disc in my back on the 2006–07 Ashes tour, I found out that if a doctor issues you with a prescription in Adelaide, and you try to cash it in Perth, you can stand at the counter foaming at the mouth and sprouting a second head for all the chemist cares. They won't serve you. However, should you ever find yourself feeling suicidal in Australia, and utterly determined to defy the government's banning of premature death, there are still several ways to go about it. Swimming out beyond the anti-shark net is an option, as is snorkelling through a school of box jellyfish, but the most painless is to hail a taxi in Melbourne and ask for the airport. A: they won't know the way, and B: they won't speak English. So as long as you clamber into the back seat without emergency food and water rations and a box of flares, you can set off in the certain knowledge that when they eventually find you, the buzzards will have made you identifiable only by your dental records.

In almost all other respects, however, Australia is as nice a place to visit as you can find on the planet – albeit having become so hideously expensive that if you pop into an Accident and Emergency department anywhere between 10pm and midnight, you'll almost certainly see an English cricket journalist being treated with smelling salts as a result of the restaurant bill he's just been given.

However, the biggest pain about covering cricket, or anything, from Australia, is the time difference. You cannot, for instance, say something like: 'England have had a decent day, but they really need Strauss to kick on from his overnight 46 not out and make a century.' For the simple reason that by the time the report appeared in England, the next day's play would already have been over. In Australia, you can only look back, never forward. Especially in the middle of a cricket match. I only got it wrong once, I'd like to think, in seven Ashes tours there, but on the day I did get it wrong, I got it about as wrong as you can possibly get it. It was after the fourth day of the Adelaide Test in 1994, when England were getting their customary stuffing, and Australia were looking at a target they could have knocked off with a rolled-up copy of the *Adelaide Advertiser*. Defeat was inevitable, and it was time for a few harsh words when it was all over. It certainly was a little too early to demand that the entire squad be sent home in disgrace, and either be tarred and feathered or put in the stocks and pelted with rotten tomatoes, which was the rough gist of my overnight report. Next day, with Australia's bowlers needing half an hour – or so we thought – to mop up the England tail, Craig McDermott thudded a nasty delivery straight into Phillip DeFreitas's unmentionables, a happening which for some peculiar reason never fails to produce a collective outbreak of giggling while the victim lies writhing about, tears streaming down his cheeks, and clutching that which he holds most dear. DeFreitas, on the other hand, failed to see the funny side, and instead of remaining bravely in line with the ball, placed himself safely out of further harm's way by taking a fresh guard somewhere close to the square leg umpire. He also came to the decision that if he was going to perish, he might as well go down swiftly, and whenever McDermott dropped one short thereafter – which was most of the time – DeFreitas had an almighty heave. And what's more, he kept connecting. He ended up with 88, all of them scored with his eyes closed, and instead of needing just over a hundred, Australia needed more than twice that many. Added to which, they were now seriously short of time. They could have blocked out the last couple of sessions comfortably, but such was their dismissive opinion of England's cricket team at that time, they gave it a thrash, and lost. It was such a rare event to see England win a Test in Australia that elation should have been the primary emotion as the English hacks walked back to the hotel to compose their pieces, but it was as much as I could do to resist the urge to throw myself into the River Torrens. It was the thought that, in a couple of hours' time, the alarm clocks would be going off all over England, and the nation's breakfast tables would be full of people with the newspaper propped up against the marmalade jar. And I had this vision of them reading

102

the back-page headline 'What a Shower! Sack 'em All!' shortly before turning on the radio to hear the dulcet tones of the newsreader. 'And now, over to Adelaide for news of England's stunning victory in the fourth Test.'

Some of my fondest memories of a cricket tour to Australia involve Christmas Day. It can be a little bit strange watching department-store Santas sweating buckets in 40-degree heat, but if you've got to be away from home over Yuletide, Australia is probably the place to be. It certainly has the edge on India, where, on England's 1976–77 tour, Keith Fletcher and Mike Selvey celebrated – if that's the right word – with Xmas lunch in a Calcutta coffee shop. The only food on the menu was mutton curry, which prompted them to inquire: 'Er, any chance of something a bit more Christmassy?' 'Let me see sir, one moment please,' replied the waiter, disappearing back into the kitchen with their plates. And he re-emerged a couple of minutes later holding the same two plates of curry – only this time with a sprig of holly embedded in the rice.

New Zealand

An old Australian joke has the captain of the airliner touching down in Auckland, or Wellington, announcing to the passengers: 'Welcome to New Zealand. Please wind back your watches forty years.' There was a time when this might not have been far from the truth, when the fastest car away from the lights was a Morris Minor, the hula hoop was still being rotated around teenage hips decades after it had died a death in Europe, the Beverley Sisters were top of the bill at the local Palladium, and if you twiddled the knob on your radio you'd either get the Billy Cotton Band Show or an episode from *The Archers* that was so old Dan Archer would be ordering a pint at the Bull. That was the popular view of New Zzzzzzzzzzzzzealand, but it's become a much livelier place in recent years, even though the cricket is normally attended by crowds arriving in the back of the same taxi, and who have to be woken up by the stewards when it's time to go home at the end of play.

The weather can be a bit iffy as well. I've twice come close to contracting frostbite and hypothermia attending sporting events – and on both occasions the venue was Dunedin – the furthest city in the world from London, 11,870 miles away. I'd expected to shiver at the All Blacks v South Africa rugby match in mid-winter, and it was no great surprise when the bottom set of my teeth spent the entire game colliding violently with the top set, but to watch your outer extremities turning purple at a one-day cricket international in the middle of summer was a bit much. The stewards had to be on their toes to deal with various spectator disturbances – all of them in the press box as reporters grappled with each other to get closest to the one-bar electric fire. Then there's Wellington, a North Island city famous for its wind. It's sometimes quicker to get to the South Island by opening an umbrella than catching a plane, although if you plump for the latter, and find the stewardess in your lap, it'll have more to do with a sudden 80 mph gust than Air New Zealand's friendly in-flight service. Flights into the city can be so hairy that there's a notice in the airport arrivals hall which reads: 'You've only been in Wellington for a few minutes and already you feel happy to be alive.' And the wind can also have a big effect on the cricket. Jackie Hendricks, the former West Indian wicketkeeper, once stood close to the sightscreen with Charlie Griffith coming downwind, and up to the stumps for Wes Hall bowling into it.

Auckland is a nice enough place, but wouldn't be short of votes in a competition to find the ugliest venue in the world for a game of cricket, which is Eden Park. Made even less attractive by the fact that while each one of its 50,000 seats is occupied for a game of rugby, there are about 47,000 empty ones at a Test match. In fact, if you wanted to stage a cricket match somewhere with less atmosphere, a taxi wouldn't get you there, but a space-ship might. New Zealand, though, is also home to one of the world's prettiest cricketing venues, Pukekura Park in New Plymouth, where the spectators dip into their picnic lunches on grass terracing cut out of the steep hillsides, and if the cricket isn't particularly interesting, you can enjoy spectacular views across the ocean instead.

Lancaster Park in Christchurch is another attractive venue, and on England's 1988 tour it became the first ground on which (stump microphones being very much an experimental innovation then) an on-field conversation in a Test match was listened to, live, in the living rooms of those TV viewers watching at home. New Zealand still being a staid kind of country in those days, it didn't go down terribly well, in that the conversation mostly con-sisted of expletives from the England fast bowler Graham Dilley after having an appeal for a catch against the home team's star batsman, Martin Crowe, turned down. Dilley could have avoided the fine he collected from the England team management if he'd only taken a leaf out of the late

Christopher Martin-Jenkins' book and substituted the names of famous composers in place of swearwords. Not many people ever heard CMJ swear, which was not to say he didn't have the odd flash of temper – he did – but his unique method of substituting the name of a great composer for an oath was the product of his fear of inadvertently letting slip an expletive during live commentary. Which is why pouring red wine all over his lap, or the loss of his entire match report pressing the wrong button on his laptop (neither of them infrequent occurrences), would invariably be followed by an agonized yelp of 'Mendelssohn!' Or if things were really bad: 'Beethoven!' He had other quirky substitute words and phrases, among them: 'Billingsgate Harbour!', 'Fotheringay Thomas!', 'Fishcakes', 'Bishen Singh Bedi!' and 'Billy Goat Gruff!', but by and large he dedicated his moments of anguish to the great creators of classical music. It was so even on the golf course, where his mastery of the violent duck hook and yipped three-foot putt would occasionally result in him exhausting his entire collection of famous composers in the course of a single, gruesomely played hole.

My favourite CMJ composer story, and there are many to pick from, came on a cricket tour of New Zealand, when he was playing a round of golf against the then correspondent of the *Evening Standard*, John Thicknesse. I wasn't playing myself, just walking round as an interested observer having broken a thumb keeping wicket in the England v NZ Press cricket match, and the match had reached a critical point when CMJ lined up a shot to the green from the middle of the fairway. Thickers, as Thicknesse was known, needed some help from above having lost a ball off the tee, and he turned to me and whispered – pointing to some invisible presence up in the sky – 'I'm badly in need of a Schubert here. If I pray hard enough, you never know. I might get one.' Whereupon CMJ produced a hook of such awesome proportions (we later found the ball in an empty milk crate in a school playground) that it prompted – in his own league table of where the various composers ranked – the Manchester United of all his expletives. 'Ye gods,' exclaimed Thickers, once the air had cleared from CMJ's nuclear fallout. 'More than I dared hope for. A Beethoven!'

West Indies

The West Indies is, on the face of it, not a bad place to spend a couple of months on a cricket tour, but it's really not all it's cracked up to be. There are probably parts of Jamaica which are very nice, but you wouldn't count Kingston among them, and the same goes for Port of Spain in Trinidad. The local airline Liat has the irritating habit of flying you to one island and your luggage to another, and on the one occasion they flew both myself and my luggage to the same destination, they put me on a flight to St Martin instead of, as it said on my ticket, Dominica. Then there's Georgetown in Guyana, on mainland South America, in which almost nothing works, including the telephones. I did an entire Test match there in 1990, where the phones were those old-fashioned types, manu-ally turning the dial with my index finger. Like they did in old Humphrey Bogart movies. Dialling England involved about fourteen numbers, and the success rate for getting through was about one in twenty, all of which conspired to leave your right index finger looking, by the end of the day, like something you'd normally find between two pieces of bun, smothered in ketchup or mustard.

It also rains most of the time in Guyana, and in the days Test matches were held at the Bourda Oval, which is below sea level, the term fishing outside the off stump could actually be taken literally. You could take a rod and line down to deep square leg and be reasonably confident of landing a sea trout to take home for tea. I don't know if the golf club is still going, but if it is, it's well worth a visit. All the green-keeping staff have four legs – i.e. the grass is kept in check by goats, cows and sheep – and if you fancy a game of darts after your round, bring your own. They've only got the one dart, and the flight on it consists of just the odd strand, as though in the latter stages of alopecia. As a result, you have to hurl it like a javelin thrower, and even then it expires halfway through its journey, and falls out of the sky like a Second World War doodlebug. The dartboard doesn't get a lot of use, judging by what happened when we played, when the first time the dart hit the target, the board fell off, and a large bat flew out from behind it.

It was a warm day, and a cold beer would have been nice, but the stuff we got was at room temperature. Not far off boiling point in fact. The barman/steward/caterer/owner informed us that the beer cooler had been stolen and they hadn't yet decided whether the amount of custom they did made it worth replacing. 'How long ago was it pinched?' I asked. Our man thought for a while, and said: 'Round about sixteen years ago now.'

Aha, but what about Barbados and Antigua I hear you say. Well, they're both attractive enough places, but they're hideously expensive, and on one tour we were so far out of pocket on expenses we thought about inventing our own taxi firm, and having some blank bills printed up. We even got to the point of inventing a catchy slogan – *'We may drive slow, but our fares are low'* – before deciding it perhaps wouldn't fool our respective expenses departments. Barbados is so small that when England are playing cricket there, there's no avoiding the influx of Barmy Army followers, enormous beer bellies struggling to remain inside their Gulliver's Travel T-shirts, and creating gridlock in their hired mini mokes. You'd spend half your time stuck in a tailback, wondering why it is that Barbados has the curious distinction of commemorating their most famous cricketers by naming roundabouts after them. You stop and ask the way and someone say: 'Yes man. You take a left at the Sir Garfield Sobers Roundabout, turn right at Sir Frank Worrell Roundabout, and keep going. You can't miss it.'

Among the more pleasant memories of visits to Barbados were the beach parties held by the cricket journalist and broadcaster Tony Cozier (after several hours on the local rum the trip back to town in the mini moke involved several off-road short cuts through cane fields) and the ground. The Kensington Oval was full of atmosphere, although the press box was a bit on the small side when England were playing, given that no other country sends remotely as many journalists on a cricket tour. On one visit, the *Daily Express* correspondent was congratulating himself on getting there early enough to bag a decent seat, when he got a tap on the shoulder from a late-arriving local with a Rasta haircut. 'You in my seat, man,' said the local. 'Listen, pal. Where I come from, bums reserve seats,' said the *Express* man. 'And where I come from,' said the Rasta, reaching into an inside jacket pocket to retrieve a large knife, 'this is what reserves seats.' You don't need me to tell you which one of them was in that seat when play got under way. The *Daily Telegraph* reporter once had a knife pulled on him crossing the Savannah in Port of Spain, and downtown Kingston in Jamaica is not the sort of place in which to wander off after dark, but I've only once found the West Indies a particularly dangerous place, when I got stuck in a bar with Ian Botham.

It was in Jamaica in 1998 when a newly re-laid pitch disintegrated and caused the Test match to be abandoned after less than an hour, the early finish meaning that everyone was written up by about mid-afternoon. Hence the large gathering of hacks at the poolside hotel bar, including Botham. The thing about Beefy is that he's an exceptionally generous bloke, and every time he orders a drink, he orders one for you also. The only problem being that he orders a drink quite often. Very often in fact. And if there's no plant pot handy, in which to tip it every now and then when he's not looking, you're in serious trouble. You can try saying: 'Whoops, is that the time Ian? Well, it's been great fun, but I really must be . . . Sorry? Another one? Well, it's getting on a bit, and er, I think maybe it's about time . . . What's that? Er, yes thanks Beefy. Down the hatch. Absolutely.' It's a question of timing, and the trick is to slide off without him noticing. I was a bit slow that day, and as I looked across to the other side of the pool, and watched another victim, Vic Marks, emerging from the Gents with a smug smile on his face, I knew I was in trouble. Vic gave me a triumphant wave, and scuttled off towards his room. And I was now on my own. How to escape, that was the key. 'Er, is that the time Beefy? Well, it's been a jolly good day and I really must be going now. It's going to be a long day tomorrow, and, er, pardon me? Ah. I see. You've got a bottle of L'Aphroaig malt whisky in your room. And I'm welcome to join you. But not before they close the bar. Of course not. Er, what time is that roughly? Aha, 3am. Great. Terrific. Yes, a few more down here before we get stuck into the malt would be just the job.' Of what happened thereafter, the only thing I have even the remotest memory about was eventually being allowed to return to my room, a journey of roughly forty yards, which involved getting there in one-yard increments, largely by bouncing off both corridor walls, which took me the thick end of two hours.

Even if you managed to avoid Botham, the Caribbean could still be a dangerous place, and during one tour there had been a double murder involving two Brits on a yacht moored in the harbour of the Antiguan capital St John's. Back in England, the *Today* newspaper asked its cricket correspondent, Graham Otway, to investigate and send back a story, and not surprisingly, someone whose detective work involved nothing trickier than informing his readers that England were 122 for 3 at tea, found himself a touch out of his depth. So much so that one morning over breakfast, when I picked up the local paper to see how the investigation was going, there was a quote from the Antiguan chief of police remarking that the crime might get solved a bit quicker if he didn't have to spend all his time on the phone to some English cricket journalist asking idiotic questions. Otters certainly took his new crime correspondent's role with *Today* pretty seriously. One night, several of us were having a beer at one of the hotel bars, when *Today*'s photographer, Chris Turvey, walked by and said: 'I really shouldn't be walking about out here without a police escort. The phone just rang in my room, and it was Otters. He said: "Keep your door locked tonight, Turvs. There are some people on this island who think I know too much."' There was a long, astonished silence, finally broken by a thud as Peter Hayter of the *Mail on Sunday* fell to the floor clutching his ribs, followed by the voice of the *Guardian*'s Mike Selvey. Having taken some time to digest the concept of Otway knowing too much, he said: 'And there's a lot more people on this island who think he knows bugger all.'

Pakistan

It is worth visiting Pakistan on an England cricket tour for the journey to the ground alone. What with the smoke-belching auto rickshaws, bullock carts, bicycles carrying entire families, emaciated dogs, and donkeys humping everything from pots and pans to full-sized billiard tables, it's a little different to walking down St John's Wood Road to Lord's. There are a variety of aromas, none of which put you in mind of a French parfumerie, and if your nostrils can cut their way through the noxious traffic fumes, you can just get a hint of what can best be described as essence of cow pat. Which is what they set fire to for cooking on.

Then, in the absence of much excitement of an evening, there's the television. The adverts are the most entertaining, mostly because Pakistani TV has an endearing habit of cutting off its commercials before they're quite finished, and nipping straight to another one. Which throws up some terrific combinations, along the lines of: 'Painful piles? Put a stop to them now with . . . Cornetto ice cream!'

Then there's the red tape, which is almost as suffocating as India's. There are plenty of beards worn in Pakistan, mostly grown for religious reasons, but you can also grow one while filling in the forms at your hotel check-in. The Barmy Army, England's travelling band of winter supporters, is pretty much down to platoon strength compared to a trip to Australia or the West Indies, but there is still a hard-core who come over hoping to inspire the lads by draping banners with 'Bristol City FC' over balconies and singing tuneless songs. There would doubtless be more Barmies coming over if the place was full of bars and pubs, but this is a tour which at least gives the liver a fighting chance to recuperate. You can get alcohol in Pakistan, mostly in the five-star hotels, but you technically still need a permit, and if you want to buy the stuff in any kind of quantity, you need to know who you're getting it from. You can pick up the paper on almost any day of the week and read about entire parties of wedding guests being wiped out after drinking homemade hooch made in bathtubs, apparently from a base of substances belonging to the same family as the stuff you put in your car radiator to stop it freezing up in winter.

On one tour there, David Norrie of the *News of the World* was undertaking his customary role of organizing the end-of-tour press party, and he'd arranged for none other than the Pakistani batsman Javed Miandad to supply the bottles of proper foreign spirits for some non-extortionate price. It was hard to imagine Javed supplying anything but the real thing, but there had been previous instances of journalists buying black-market bottles of booze, taking them round to a party they'd been invited to, and becoming extremely popular when handing over a bottle of whisky with a 'Famous Grouse' label on it. Only, after glasses had been raised, and toasts been made, to find out that the stuff was more closely related to PG Tips. The trick was, apparently, to siphon the booze out of the bottom of the bottle, refill it (either with tea for whisky or water for gin) and carefully solder the hole back up. In that way, the seal would remain unbroken. Being a non-spirits drinker, Norrie invited me up to his room where approximately a dozen, maybe more, bottles were sitting on his room table, and my job was to take a sip from each and confirm the veracity of the contents. And about half an hour later, when I started colliding with the fixtures and fittings and slurring incoherently, Norrie was reasonably satisfied that Javed hadn't ripped him off. Norrie organized virtually everything on an overseas tour, including the traditional Press cricket match against a team of home journalists.

The first time I played in one of these was in Lahore, and it was an interesting sort of game to say the least. The home team chose to bat after winning the toss, and by the first drinks break they were 30 for 7. One ball after drinks they were 30 for 8, and at that stage not a single one of their players looked as though they'd ever so much as held a bat before. However, from 30 for 8 just after drinks, their innings lasted the full forty overs, and by the close, courtesy of their No. 10 striding out and batting like a combination of Javed and Zaheer Abbas, they were something like 240 for 8. I later recounted this story to a London-based Pakistani journalist, and asked him how it was that two extremely fat middle-aged men with no ability at all could open the batting, while some lithe nineteen-year-old who dealt entirely in fours and sixes came in at No. 10. He didn't seem at all surprised. 'Simple,' he said. 'Lower caste.' And that was it. No matter how good or bad you were, your place in the batting order was all down to your status in society.

Pakistan also witnessed the second biggest row – after Bodyline – in cricketing history. The on-field spat between the England captain Mike Gatting and Shakoor Rana resulted in an entire day of the Test match in Faisalabad being lost while the umpire demanded a written apology from Gatting, which he eventually got. Albeit, ordered by his bosses, on a piece of paper which looked as though it had been appropriated from one of the on-ground lavatories rather than Basildon Bond, and (deliberately) mis-spelt 'Fisalabad.' I got into a bit of trouble at the time after being told by one of the England players that they'd heard the umpire use two C words to Gatting during the course of their on-field contretemps. One was 'cheat' and the other was a word I'd never seen printed before in an English newspaper. I told the sports editor over the phone what Rana was alleged to have said, and he asked me to include it in the piece exactly as quoted. 'I can't do that,' I said. 'My mum will go ballistic.' My mother, at the time, ran a small hotel in Stratford-upon-Avon, and used to plonk the newspaper in front of the guests over breakfast and say proudly: 'My son wrote that.' The sports editor told me they'd probably censor the quote, but to send it anyway, and they'd decide whether or not to print it verbatim. Which they did. It didn't go down very well with Kelvin McKenzie, then editor of the *Sun* newspaper, who took both myself and the editor of the *Independent* newspaper to the Press Council on the grounds of offending public decency, or some such thing. Which I'd say was a bit rich coming from the editor of the *Sun* (although it had the distinct whiff of a publicity stunt to it) and was eventually thrown out.

I was, though, far more worried about my mother than Kelvin, and sure enough I discovered (via an irate phone call) that she'd done her usual trick of placing the article in front of some guests, and informing them proudly that her boy was responsible. That was a particularly long tour, starting with a series of one-day internationals, followed by the World Cup in Pakistan and India, and culminating in that rancorous Test series. It would have been a gruelling three months even without the usual health problems – on at least two days of the Faisalabad Test I read the quotes of the day to a stricken colleague through his bathroom door – and to say that everyone was looking forward to getting home just in time for Christmas was a serious understatement. The day before the flight, some of us were relaxing by the poolside at the Holiday Inn, Karachi, when a breathless Norrie burst through a door on the veranda, flopped onto his sunbed, and said: 'I don't bloody well believe it.' Needless to say, I inquired as to precisely what he was having difficulty in bloody well believing, and he replied that there'd been a cock-up on tomorrow's flight to Heathrow, with only eight of the seventeen seats now available, and that the airline had allocated those eight seats by alphabetical order. 'That's me buggered,' groaned Norrie. 'N is way down the list.'

By now, my mouth having been opening and closing for some time without any noise coming out of it, I was beginning to make strange whimpering noises, and Norrie said: 'Ah, you'll be fine. J. There's Lander, Lee, Selvey, Smith, Weaver, Woodcock. All after you.' At which point, he started going through the list. 'Let's see now, there's Allen. Bannister. Bateman. Botterell. Deeley. I think that's all. Oh hang on, though, what about Dellor? Ah, and I forgot Gibson.' And so on. Eventually, I appeared to have qualified right on the cut line, to put it in golfing parlance, but no sooner had I started to relax than Norrie piped up: 'Hey, that's a point. I hadn't thought of that.' I shot upright again. 'Hadn't thought of what?' 'Martin-Jenkins. Everywhere we've gone on this tour they've had him down as Jenkins. And if they've got him as Jenkins on the BA list, well . . .' I didn't hear the rest of it. There was a BA office one floor down in the hotel's shopping mall, and the chap behind the counter gave me a radiant smile as I burst through the door. 'BA flight 101!' I yelled. 'To London. Tomorrow. I'd better be on it d'you hear? Johnson. British Media. Show me the passenger list. Now. At once. This minute.' He tapped something out on his computer keyboard, looked at the screen, and smiled again. 'Johnson. Right here sir. Mr Martin. Oh yes. Tomorrow. Booking all confirmed. No problem.' Those last two words tipped me over the edge.

'Listen here, chum,' I said. 'I've been in this bloody country for three months now, and whenever there's been a major problem, it's always been two seconds after someone has said "no problem". So when you tell me there's not a problem, I know for a fact that there bloody well *is* one. So turn that bloody computer screen around and let me see for myself . . .' It was at that point that something made me glance to my left, and there, with noses pressed against the window, and tears rolling down their cheeks, were Norrie, and the media tour leader Peter Smith. Their wheeze couldn't have worked any better. I was so desperate to get home, I'd totally lost the ability to see through what was clearly a wind-up. But the relief was so palpable, I too began to see the funny side of it, as did the Pakistani behind the BA desk. Not that he had a clue as to what was going on. I gave him the thumbs up. 'No problem!' I said. And I thought he was going to break a rib he laughed so much. Next morning, sitting on the plane next to David 'Toff' Lloyd of the Press Association, and Graham Otway of *Today*, Toff raised his glass and said something like: 'England here we come!' Pause for a chuckle. 'No problem.' I was about to tick him off, on the grounds that these two words in Pakistan were invariably followed by disaster, when the bloke immediately in front of me decided he needed a kip, and his seat shot backwards to pluck the celebratory glass from my grasp and deposit its contents all over me.

South Africa

I never felt entirely safe in South Africa, largely as the result of getting mugged, along with a colleague, leaving a

Chinese restaurant. In what was supposed to be their least dangerous major city, Cape Town. It's hard to imagine what must go through people's minds when the point of a twelve-inch kitchen knife is tickling their Adam's apple (I didn't ask my assailant whether he'd mind if I measured it, but it looked like twelve inches to me) and I still find it difficult to believe the first thought that came into my head while the knifeman's accomplice was relieving me of my wallet was: 'Christ, there's two weeks' worth of restaurant receipts in there.' I wasn't bothered about the credit card, or the small amount of cash in there, just the receipts.

At best, it meant several days of written explanations and form filling, at worst, I wouldn't get reimbursed at all. So when I saw the two muggers sitting in the back of a taxi (presumably the driver was in for a cut as well) sifting through the wallet, instead of being grateful for being allowed to go on living (not a favour granted to many muggees in SA) I made the irrational decision to have a quiet word with the two guys.

'Excuse me,' I said, a safe distance back from the open window, 'but you've missed this 100-rand note.' Which they had. 'It's only the cash that's any good to you, so if I give you this, can I have the wallet back please?' Amazingly, the deal was done, but instead of quitting while ahead, the euphoria of being reunited with the receipts made my brain flip once again. 'Might I be so bold,' I said, 'now that you've come into a bit of money, as to suggest a very good Chinese restaurant. I can especially recommend the Singapore noodles.' At this point the guy with the knife reached inside his jacket to remind me that he still had the blade about his person, and his expression suggested that he might feel inclined to use it if any more smart-arsed comments came his way. I took the hint, and took off.

Even away from the major cities South Africa comes across as a not especially safe place. During the 2003 cricket World Cup I found myself in Pietermaritzburg to cover a group game, and while it wasn't what you'd call an attractive town – a bit like Milton Keynes without the charm was how it struck me – it didn't seem particularly threatening. I was staying in one of several individual chalets in the large grounds of a family home, and after checking in decided to walk to a nearby pub for a couple of beers and a bite to eat. I could actually see the pub from my chalet, so it hadn't occurred to me to take the hire car, but it was dark by the time I set off back, and after walking for about ten minutes in what I thought was the right direction, I found myself pretty much going around in a circle. I phoned the number the family had given me, and told them I was on the junction of such and such and so and so streets, and could they tell me which way to go. 'Don't move!' shrieked the voice at the other end. 'Stay right where you are. And don't for God's sake look lost! I'll be right there.' A couple of minutes later the owners turned up in a big Four-by-four, bundled me in the back, and sped back to the house. 'Don't ever wander around after dark looking like a stranger,' I was warned, 'unless you're tired of living.'

I thought they were over-reacting a bit, until I picked up the paper the following morning and glanced through it while having an alfresco coffee downtown. It wasn't even the lead item, but the day before an elderly woman had been loading her groceries into her car in a supermarket car park, when a man approached and offered to help. The packing finished, she got into the driver's seat, and didn't see him jump into the boot and pull it shut as she drove off. This strange incident was, luckily for her, spotted by a private security firm hired by the supermarket, and they followed the woman to her home, helping her into the house before springing open the boot. Out jumped the man, wielding a machete, but instead of being confronted by a little old lady – whom he presumably intended to slice into chump chops before burgling the house – he came face to face instead with three heavily armed security guards. Who did not, it became clear from the story, invite him to drop his machete and come quietly. They instead turned him into a colander with a fusillade of bullets from automatic weapons, after which, presumably, they went back to finish their shift at the supermarket. Not the kind of thing you often come across at your local Tesco.

There are, of course, fond memories of South Africa as well – difficult not to have them in such a beautiful country – and one of my fondest is the day I managed to put one over on the England cricket captain Michael Atherton. It was in 1995 in Johannesburg, my last Test as cricket correspondent of the *Independent*, and Atherton had just played one of the truly heroic rearguard actions, batting for ten and three-quarter hours to rescue an improbable draw against South Africa. That night I found myself in some bar or pub, along with a few other English press men, having a few celebratory drinks with the players, and for reasons that escape me now, I ended up in a drinking contest with Atherton involving a particularly lethal concoction known as cane and coke. I lost comfortably, and although I was unable to concede the match verbally, owing to an inability to speak at all, the fact that I tipped an entire table full over drinks over one of the bowlers, Peter Martin, was taken, and rightly so, as the equivalent of the towel being thrown in.

Next morning, I bumped into a surprisingly sprightly England captain, who asked me whether I felt as bad as I looked. 'And just how do I look?' I asked. 'Terrible,' he said. 'In that case,' I said, 'I feel much worse than I look.' Atherton fixed me with a superior kind of expression and said: 'It's high time you realized that drinking is a young man's game. You're forty-odd now, and clearly past it.' He was far too smug for my liking, and when, not long afterwards, I happened to bump into Ian Botham, the chance for retribution suddenly fell into my lap. Botham had just celebrated his fortieth birthday, less than a week before the start of the Test in fact, and after recounting my drubbing in the pub, I gave him a potted version of our conversation the next morning. With a few small embellishments.

'In fact, Beefy, he went so far as to say that anyone over forty is completely past it. Ready to fall over after two halves of shandy. And when I said to him, "How about Beefy? You surely don't include him?" You know what he said? "Especially him." That's what he said. "He might have been good in his prime, but after a night out with me nowadays the old dodderer might just about make it home again, but only in an ambulance." I wondered whether I might have overdone it, but Botham's 'Oh he did, did he?' kind of expression told me I had instead hit the spot. As the team and press flew on to Paarl for the next match, I flew back to England, and got a phone call from one of my colleagues during the next Test match in Durban. I can't remember the exact reason for the call, but during the course of the conversation he casually mentioned the flight from Paarl. 'You should have seen Atherton. Had to be helped onto the plane. Had a night out with Beefy apparently.'

Zimbabwe

Zimbabwe 1996. Forever to be remembered as the 'we murdered 'em' tour. It was, with New Zealand to follow after Christmas, supposed to be the lower-key part of a two-legged winter tour, and virtually every newspaper's main correspondent gave it a miss on the grounds that (a) England were bound to win every game and (b) there would be nothing much worth reporting. Which, as misjudgements go, turned out to be a pretty impressive double. The players and the press fell out pretty early on, when most of us reported, accurately as it happens, that the tourists weren't winning too many friends by declining to socialize with the opposition. A local magazine described the captain, Atherton, as 'aloof', 'grumpy' and (over the top, this one) a 'miserable sledger'. The team itself was harangued (fairly, I felt) as 'narrow minded' and 'bad mannered'. Atherton was not, therefore, in the best humour of his life when he also kept getting out for next to nothing in the opening matches. So quickly that some of the press guys — myself included — had still not made it back from the golf club in time to see him out.

The nature of the grounds was such that we'd turn up, with golf bags still on our backs, and walk past the players' enclosure en route to the press tent. Usually with a smouldering Atherton halfway back to the pavilion. One morning, spotting me and colleague Chris Lander from the *Daily Mirror* making our way towards the press tent with golf bags still slung over our backs, he actually made a detour on his long walk back from being dismissed to say, with what I took to be the merest hint of sarcasm, 'Glad you could make it. Nice of you to pop in.' Next morning off we went to golf again, and I said to Lander: 'I think we'd better try another entrance this time. If he's in the players' enclosure when we walk past with the golf bags again, he'll most likely blow a gasket.' So next day we came into the ground through one of the back entrances, golf clubs around shoulders, and about twenty minutes into the day's play.

'Oh my God,' said Lander, at the same time as I was thinking it. Two people dressed in cricket whites were leaning on the boundary fence, and though they had their backs to us, we recognized them pretty much straight away. Graham Thorpe . . . and Atherton. Thorpe, it later transpired, was a bit depressed over some domestic issue back home, and Atherton had taken him away from the dressing room for a therapeutic heart to heart. Which, considering that Atherton's batting average on the tour was heading in the same direction as a Zimbabwean bank-note, was a conspicuously kindly act. However, his mood of gentle compassion (or I assume it was) failed to survive the moment something made him turn round and espy myself and Lander, frozen to the spot, and failing badly in trying to look nonchalant. 'Bloody hell,' said Atherton, or words to that effect.

There was clearly something he wanted to add to that cheery greeting, but while the lips continued to move, no further sound came out. I cannot now remember whether either of us essayed a 'Morning Michael' or 'Hi Athers' but I suspect we merely kept our heads down and carried on towards the press tent. Later that day, with the daily reports of hopeless performances and even more hopeless PR having struck a chord with the public back at home, another walk round the ground (minus golf clubs this time) found us strolling past the England assistant coach John Emburey giving a radio interview to someone or other. We didn't stop to listen, but as we walked past I was just able to hear him say: 'What would they know about how we're playing? They're never off the golf course.'

This was true up to a point, but missing the first few minutes of a day's play really wasn't a huge handicap when it came to informing our readers as to how the team was playing. They might just have given the Barmy Army a game, but only after several hours in the beer tent, and why they might have thought that losing three of their opening four games in a country ranked ninth out of nine in international cricket's league table deserved a sympathetic press is a hard one to fathom.

Relations nosedived even further after a fractious first Test in Bulawayo, which ended in a draw with the scores level, and England furious at Zimbabwe's tactic of bowling wide of the stumps in the closing overs. David Lloyd is now a brilliantly dry-witted commentator for Sky television, but in those days, as England's coach, the boundless passion he has for the game rather got in the way of reasoned judgement. His performance on the boundary edge as Zimbabwe's tactic of just staying on the right side of the umpires allowed them to hold out for the draw was that of a man whose underpants have just been invaded by a colony of ants, and it wouldn't have been a total surprise to see several men in white coats bearing down on him brandishing syringes.

Neither did it improve his mood when the match referee issued a written warning for bringing the game into disrepute – not to Zimbabwe for bowling wide, but to England for unacceptably aggressive appealing. 'We murdered 'em,' was Bumble's verdict after the match – a point of view he expressed not once, but about twenty-four times before, during and after the post-match press conference. 'They've got to live with it,' he said, in reference to the wide bowling, which prompted me to ask him whether, in similar circumstances, England might have considered doing the same. Whereupon Atherton fixed me with what can best be described as a glower and said: 'If that's what you think, why don't you write it?' I thanked him for giving me permission, and was in the middle of writing precisely that back in my hotel room when there was a knock at the door. It was Atherton, holding a couple of bottles of Bolinger. Not the French champagne, with two Ls, but the Zimbabwean beer, with one L. It was a nice gesture though, especially given the pressure he was undoubtedly feeling, and we ended the tour on fairly good terms I thought.

The rest of his team wasn't quite so keen on burying the hatchet, though. It was a long-standing tradition, when England were away from home at Christmas, for the press to put on a panto for them on Christmas morning, and despite the undercurrent of bad feeling, this tour was no different. However, just as we were putting the finishing touches to the script, they decided to take a dressing-room vote on whether to attend, and, with the exception of Atherton and the wicketkeeper Jack Russell, they gave it the thumbs down. Which was a shame, as I think they'd have enjoyed a couple of the sketches we'd written. One involved England's fine for over-appealing – "Owzat?' 'Not Out' 'Oh yes it is!' – and another had Bumble sitting down at the Christmas lunch table, and a waiter coming over with the cheeseboard. 'Crackers sir?' 'No, not really. Although a bit eccentric from time to time, I'll grant you that.'

7

NOT YOUR EVERYDAY ASSIGNMENT

Miami Superbowl . . . PGA Golf Fair in Orlando . . . Drag Racing in Northamptonshire . . . Croquet in Cheltenham . . . Real Tennis at Queen's

Miami Superbowl

When you tell people that you write about cricket for twelve months of the year, the general reaction is something along the lines of: 'Don't tell me you get paid for it as well?', but after a while it can get a bit samey. It's a bit like eating out on tour. I remember once, having been in Australia for over three months, pitching up at a restaurant one evening, scanning a menu full of usual stuff like 'Rack of Lamb', 'served with butternut squash purée, and drizzled with the chef's own red wine reduction jus', and thinking 'Oh Lord, not again.' I asked the waiter if they'd do me an egg on toast, and when he returned from the kitchen with the news that they would, I said: 'In that case, I'll have egg on toast to start, and egg on toast for a main.' I had to guess on the choice of wine that would best complement it, but they went together okay if memory serves.

I wrote more or less exclusively on cricket for ten years, home and abroad, and the job was an enviable one by most definitions. Apart from the fact that you were away for so long, you'd get home, head for your bedroom and wonder where the mini bar was. Or the tray with the kettle, wooden stirrers, and those cartons of vile UHT milk. But what really got to me towards the end – got to everyone in fact – was 'preview day'. You'd have to pitch up at the ground the day before the start of a match, watch people training, get injury bulletins, listen to boring interviews, then sit down to write a piece predicting what was going to happen. There were, on very rare occasions, preview days that perked you up, such as the time the then England chairman of selectors P. B. H. May called the assorted hacks across to where he was standing on the outfield for an impromptu press conference. 'Gentlemen,' announced PBH, 'I have an important message for you regarding the way forward for English cricket, which can be simply summed up in one word. POW!' It was very warm that day, and I noted that the chairman had been walking around in the heat for some considerable time without a hat. Delirium clearly couldn't be ruled out, but it turned out that 'POW!' was an acronym standing for 'programme', 'overseas players' and 'wickets'. Anyway, it gave us something different to write about for a change, not least as 'wickets' should more properly have been described as 'pitches'. Which turned the acronym into 'POP!', as in gun. A much more likely scenario given that England's opponents that summer were the West Indies, then in their absolute pomp, and a hideous drubbing duly ensued.

More often, though, preview day was so indescribably turgid as to make writing a piece that was supposed to whet the readers' appetites pretty tricky. Especially if it was a one-day international. On one tour of Australia, there were about a dozen of these one-dayers crammed into the schedule, and for preview no. 11, or thereabouts, I'd pretty well had enough. I wrote some rambling piece about something completely different, and finished with the following sentence. 'PS. There is yet another one-day international taking place tomorrow, if anyone is inter-ested. It will, as ever, follow a stupifyingly turgid formula for about ninety-eight overs, at which point a loud cannon will be fired to wake up all the spectators for a breathless run chase over the final twelve deliveries.'

The preview day that finally did it for me, though, was for a Test match in New Zealand. I'd had a pleasant walk to the ground with Mike Selvey of the *Guardian*, but a cheery mood did not survive coming through the gates to see a depressingly familiar sight. The coach was, as ever, simulating slip catches, someone in a baseball mitt was fielding throws from the outfield, and other players were running in and out of a set of traffic cones. This never varied, like the captain's press conference which followed, in which he would spend twenty minutes or so telling us that 'No, he hadn't quite decided whether to play the extra seamer or not' and 'No, he couldn't say whether he'd prefer to bat first until he'd seen the pitch in the morning.' This one was scheduled for 12 noon, and experienced campaigners such as Selvey and myself arrived for it at 11.59 prompt. However, we immediately bumped into the media relations officer, who told us: 'Slight change of plan chaps. One or two things have cropped up, so the skipper won't be talking to you until 3.15.' 'Correction,' I said. 'The skipper won't be talking to *me* at all. I'm sorry for my reader, naturally, who won't now get the benefit of what I'm sure will be one long round of fascinating insights into the battle ahead, but if I'm to be watching the match from the press box tomorrow, rather than a padded cell, I'm outta here.' Or something similar.

It wasn't difficult then, when the offer of a more 'general' sports-reporting job came along, to make the switch, even though one of my first assignments in the new role was a trip to an event I'd always found unwatchable (at least in its entirety), the Super Bowl. I was vaguely aware that the Super Bowl was regarded as a pretty big deal in America, but I wasn't quite prepared for a media centre housing no fewer than 3,200 reporters, inside which the feeding frenzy was the equivalent of dropping a rib-eye steak into a river full of piranha. The two teams, Denver and Atlanta, had forty-five-man squads, and all ninety players were wheeled out for interview, the more important ones more than once. The levels of interrogation were not exactly Paxman-like ('Do you always put your right sock on before your left?' and 'Is it true you train on mom's blueberry pie?') and one of the real fascinations of Super Bowl week seemed to be not so much who might win, as which journalist could win the daftest question award. I myself had nothing I especially wanted to ask, so listened with interest to the ruthless grilling the American reporters subjected the players to.

'Where do you get your inspiration for your offensive plays? In the shower? In the bath? In the middle of the night?'

'The chairman says you'd jump on a hand grenade for those guys. Would you?'

'On the flight over, what was the team's choice of tunes on the boom box.'

And, 'If your team was a car, which car would it be?'

The most surreal question I heard, however, came from a TV reporter who'd correctly taken note that the players and coaches were rarely able to make it to the end of a sentence without some reference to God. 'We've been hearing,' she said, 'a lot from you guys about Jesus this week. Who does he play for, and is he on the offence or the defence?' One of the players, fresh from a five-hour session at the barbers', announced that he wanted to 'go down in history as having the best hair in Super Bowl history', and there was also a contest to see which player would arrive for his press conference wearing the most jewellery.

One of the Atlanta players, who apparently owned a Rottweiler named Tyson, turned up wearing his pooch's silver-studded dog collar around his neck. Tyson, mean-time, was probably back at home trying on his top hat and tails, given that I'd earlier been reading over breakfast one of those peculiarly American newspaper columns entitled: 'How to Include Your Dog at Your Wedding'. This offered sound advice for all those grooms opting for a canine best man, such as: 'Keep him securely leashed so he doesn't bolt with all the precious rings' and 'Make sure he's thoroughly walked in order to avoid those embar-rassing accidents.' I had this vision of grief-stricken fathers all over America, having been given the news by their daughters that they'd opted instead to be given away by their pet Pekinese.

There was also a mountain of media information news-print devoted to the half-time extravaganza performers, including an interview with the proud person selected to warble 'The Star-Spangled Banner' before the kick-off. On this occasion it had fallen to Cher, who had apparently had an attack of cold feet (her feet being just about the only part of her that hadn't been altered by a plastic surgeon) over singing the thing live. So just in case, a pre-recording had been made with an eighty-piece orchestra. Every time you turned on the TV there would be some story about the game, and one day I wandered out of the bathroom to hear some female reporter wind up her dispatch with the words: 'and finally some good news for Denver. There aren't any raisins in French toast.' Intrigued, I scoured the press centre trying to find out what she could have meant, but apart from finding out that Americans eat more on Super Bowl Sunday than on any other day of the year bar Thanksgiving, the business with the toast remained a mystery. Touts were selling tickets for extortionate prices, getting round the law decreeing they can't be sold above face value by pricing them as packages. 'That'll be $500 for the ticket, sir, and $10 million for the souvenir hat.'

When the first Superbowl was held in 1967, the stadium was 30,000 short of capacity, but by the time no. 6 came around, it held such a grip on the national psyche that President Nixon phoned the Miami Dolphins' coach in the middle of the night with a tactical tip. How to bug the opposition's bench, most likely. At the one I attended,

133

Super Bowl 23, there were forty-seven official Super Bowl radio stations pumping out the latest bulletins, in between weather reports, and endless advertisements for constipation sufferers. Americans are so obsessed by bowel movements that when they describe someone as a 'regular guy', I'm never quite sure whether they mean he's a decent chap, or how often he visits the bathroom. On one floor in the media hotel, one of the TV stations was recording a commercial of the Denver running back Terrell Davis throwing a football through a hole in a giant tin in aid of a promotion for Campbell's Chunky Soup. The Campbell's man said: 'We'd like to think Chunky Soup has played a leading part in Terrell being the NFL's leading rusher', while Terrell, a migraine sufferer, informed the viewers that a bowl of Campbell's Chunky Soup never failed to clear his head. In another room, a 'voice alike' contest was being held to determine which one of three finalists could sound most like a famous (not to mention dead) NFL archive film commentator, John Facenda, and thereby win two tickets to the game. All over Miami, Facenda's voice could be heard to the backcloth of old Super Bowls. 'The sun was setting on the Rose Bowl Stadium . . . Man's greatest enemy – the clock – continued its deadly tick . . .'

And so, at last, to the game. For some time it was as spectacular an event as there has ever been in the history of sport. The crowd was going demented; the stadium was a vast cauldron of noise, and the action positively explosive. Then someone blew a whistle to start the match, and it was downhill all the way. It didn't help that the Atlanta Falcons could have swapped places with their cheerleaders and given Denver a closer game, but the real mystery of any Super Bowl is why people want to watch it live rather than on television. At least when you're at home you can do something to amuse yourself when nothing is happening, such as wander out to the fridge for another beer, or take the dog for a walk. American football is as hard as nails, performed by athletes so breathtakingly fast and powerful they'd brush off any rugby player like so much dandruff, but thanks to its total dedication to commercialism, it flows at roughly the same pace as an Arctic glacier. The sixty minutes of playing time actually took three and a half hours, with play constantly interrupted for important messages about breakfast wheaties and laxative tablets, but it certainly suits the coaches, who thus have more time to pore over more charts and diagrams than Columbus had in his cabin when – as some historians would have it – he discovered the place.

If it turned out to be a bad night for Atlanta, it was two bad nights in a row for their defensive free safety, Eugene Robinson. The Falcons' game was riddled with bad calls, and Eugene made an especially poor one the day before the game when he made a play for a lady of the night. Unfortunately for Eugene, when he protested that he wasn't interested in paying extra for the handcuffs, the lady in question informed him that far from these being part of the service, she was an officer in the Miami Vice Squad, and would be grateful for his cooperation in assisting with inquiries. What was especially embarrassing for Eugene was that he had just received a 'morality award' for charity work and general do-gooding. Nicknamed 'The Prophet' for his religious convictions Eugene had also written a book entitled *Endurance – My Journey to God*.

By contrast, this latest journey was in search of a forty-dollar blow job, and given that Mrs Robinson had been asleep next to him when he nipped out in one of the team's hire cars, she was not best pleased. Neither were his team-mates, after his major contribution to the game was to hand Denver a touchdown with an intercepted throw. Asked whether he'd apologized to his team-mates, Eugene said: 'I apologized first to the Lord', adding, somewhat curiously, 'there is a difference between righteous and innocent, and I just wasn't righteous'. It wasn't a great night for Cher either, who, having worked harder than anyone on the planet to retard the ageing process, decided to save any extra wear and tear on her vocal chords by miming the anthem. She might have been able to do it live if she hadn't talked so much during her pre-game press conference, which she turned into a party political broadcast. 'Put the effing Republicans into a rocket ship and send them away,' she said, although what this had to do with a game of football was not entirely clear.

During the game, we were bombarded with statistics – rushing yardages, pass completions, turnovers, and the really important ones such as the blonde–brunette cheer-leader ratios. Denver had to work harder to win that one, shading it by thirteen blondes to twelve on the official cheerleader sheet. Another statistic is that there are tra-ditionally more instances of domestic violence on Super Bowl Sunday than on any other day of the year in America, which must have made the Prophet a bit anxious when Mrs Robinson said: 'Just wait till I get you home.' There was a decent chance the Prophet was among the 6 per cent of working Americans who call in sick the morning after the Super Bowl, and not until two days afterwards does the country get back to normal. Or as normal as it ever gets.

PGA Golf Fair in Orlando

There is scarcely a golfer on the planet who would not sell his mother-in-law in exchange for shaving a few strokes off their handicap, which is why the annual PGA Trade Fair in Orlando is an exhibition so large it makes the Open Championship's tented village look like a boy scouts' camping site, and requires a walk of twelve miles to get round the thick end of two thousand stands. Given the fact that most Americans can barely walk twelve yards without suffering a dizzy turn, or requiring oxygen, the size of the crowds that make what's more of a religious pilgrimage than a visit is remarkable. Further proof, if any were needed, that there is nothing quite as gullible as your average golfer is the trillions of dollars spent around the world every year on golfing equipment.

You don't even have to be a good salesman to make a fortune at the PGA Fair. A large percentage of the visitors to your stall will, within the previous month, have hit a shot of such awesome incompetence that the ball would have travelled two inches, and the divot, coming to rest only after hitting the bloke playing in front of you in the back of the head, two hundred yards. So no sooner have you held aloft the special hat with lead weights in the brim – guaranteed to keep your head down – than there is an undignified cavalry charge from people desperate to be parted from their money, even though a house brick underneath the bobble hat would have same effect, and cost substantially less money. Then there was the Assist Swing Trainer, which told you if you were swinging poorly by falling apart either on the way back, or, depending on the precise nature of the fault, on the way down. It also beeped if you broke your wrists too early and came with the guarantee of 'No more hooking or slicing!'

There is always the danger of tiring yourself out on the range before you've even started, but thanks to the fact that the Americans have invented almost everything that involves the avoidance of exercise, a gadget called 'Be The Ball' was available to save you the bother of having to put another ball on the tee by doing it for you. Then there was the Carbite putter, with a revolutionary new insert made from 'over 23,000 miniature brass balls', which now left me incapable of hooking, slicing, or missing a putt. So what next? Bringing those par fives within reach in two blows, if not one, of course, so next on the list was a driver with something called 'hot isostatic processing'. The guarantee with this one (everything at the Fair was guaranteed) was to 'add 15–20 yards to your first tee shot', which meant that your only remaining worry at a par five was hitting your driver so far it killed someone putting out on the green.

Should you have been thinking green in the ecological sense, however, there was a 100 per cent biodegradable 'Wheat Tee'. The rep caught me looking at it and said: 'I'm a guy who loves golf, but I also love trees and animals, I don't shoot swans, and I believe God's earth is the only one we have.' I said: 'Shoot birdies not swans, eh?', and he replied: 'Hey, great line. You should be in the golf business.' Golf being a game played largely between the ears, the next gadget to get my attention was a glove that came with two little dials. The idea being to unclutter your head by not having to do anything as stressful as counting. For the fashion-conscious lady there was the Evertan glove, which allowed the sunshine through and prevented the embarrassment of returning to the clubhouse with one brown hand and one white one. The Lady Classic also came with holes in the finger ends for the long-nailed competitor, and another hole that allowed you to show off your wedding ring. It occurred to me that it was also handy for whipping the thing off should your husband start playing badly in the mixed foursomes. But how could he play badly I thought? Not with all this stuff to use. And in the unlikely event of hitting it even slightly crooked, there was a ball called a 'Smart Core', which apparently knew which direction it was supposed to go upon being struck, and was able to alter course upon looking up and finding itself heading for the out of bounds. However, should the Smart Core have been a little late in correcting itself, the next stall was selling a gadget, worn round the neck, which claimed to 'prevent anomalous electrical activity in the brain caused by EMF sensitivity'. It also cured jet lag.

Now then. Have you ever stood over a tricky four-foot putt and been unable to concentrate for worrying whether someone might pinch your golf clubs while you weren't looking? You have? Me too. Happens all the time. Which is why my eyes lit up upon seeing 'Forcefield', a patented sensor device which makes the bag scream, yes that's right, scream, when someone tries to take it. I thought the addition of a voice shouting 'Stop thief!' might have been worthwhile, and hang the extra cost, but had to agree with the manufacturer's motto: 'Don't let theft interfere with *your* game. Another cause of missing putts, on top of wondering whether your bag will still be with you after finishing the hole, is lightning striking on your backswing, so I was gratified to happen across 'Strike Alert', your very own lightning detector.

Then there was the towel which both cooled you off and dried your kit at the same time, concentration aids such as Siberian Ginseng and Gingko Biloba, and aerosol spray that identified your sweet spot, a cross between a Mae West and a straitjacket that eliminated slices, and an umbrella strong enough to withstand assaults (and I saw the video to prove it) from both a bulldozer and a fireman's hose. However, there was one absolute must-have exhibit. It was by now extremely unlikely that you'd ever again hit a bad shot, but, just in case, they were selling something called the 'Whackduck'. This ingenious invention was just as the title suggested – a duck that you hang from your golf bag, to which, should you feel a hot flush of anger beginning to overpower you, you administer a therapeutic thrashing. What made it so amazing was that when you whacked it, the duck said things that were, I quote, 'guaranteed to make you laugh'. It had no less than eighteen random expressions ('great for kids – no foul language in this fowl's messages!') all of which, was the claim, were delivered with 'the wit and wisdom of a Scottish caddie'. I have, down the years, encountered many a Scottish caddie, and can honestly say that none of them has ever exclaimed : 'You're not good enough to get angry!', or 'Many a man prefers the road less travelled.'

And certainly not 'Cor-Mashie-Niblick-Feathery-ball-Haggis-Lordlovaduck.' Not even at closing time.

Drag Racing in Northamptonshire

As I was strapping myself inside a vehicle capable of travelling a quarter of a mile in less than seven seconds, the thought occurred that this was a good bit faster than it would take to recite the Lord's Prayer. Followed, not long after, by wondering how much there might be left of you should you hit a wall at 300 mph. After Donald Campbell lost control of Bluebird on Coniston Water back in 1967 they recovered his teddy bear mascot Mr Whoppit about five minutes after the crash, but it took another thirty-four years to locate Donald. I'd also been told, ahead of my first experience of drag racing, that a machine with eight times the horsepower of a Formula One car occasionally had the same urge as Bluebird to take off. One minute you're chatting with a mechanic, and a couple of seconds later to an air traffic controller.

The passenger seat of the drag racer I was about to take off in was being driven – or perhaps piloted would have been a better word – by a Canadian by the name of Gordon Bonin. Gordon was taking me for a spin at Santa Pod, which sounds like some exotic location in California, but is in fact a disused runway airport in Northamptonshire. The car wasn't very glamorous, either. It looked a bit like an elongated cigar tube, with pram wheels on the front, tractor tyres on the back, and an engine the size of a medium-sized garden shed. These machines, I was told, cost upwards of a quarter of a million pounds, which seemed a bit steep for an interior without so much as a cigarette lighter or a radio, although it was unlikely, I felt, that anyone would start twiddling knobs looking for *The Archers*, or *Test Match Special*, in the four and a half seconds that were available before reaching for the parachute button. In the course of my pre-ride research I discovered that accelerating exerted five Gs on the driver, while stopping was a comparative doddle at only four Gs. Fuel consumption was a bit on the heavy side, as well. The car I'd just parked up returned roughly thirty-five miles to the gallon. Gordon's machine did twenty-nine to the gallon. Yards, that is.

If someone asked you to guess at the origins of a sport based entirely around noise, money, and a subtlety quotient of zero, you'd be hard pressed to plump for anywhere other than the USA, and you'd be spot on. Furthermore, it seemed to me that the driver didn't have to be especially skilled to drive a dragster, merely have a set of intestines that – more often than not – had the ability to remain in roughly the same place at the end of a race as they were at the start. My personal theory was that you could probably teach a chimpanzee to drive a dragster, given that all you really had to do when the green light went on was apply your foot to the floorboards and shut your eyes. Shutting your eyes is, by all accounts, what all dragster drivers do – involuntarily – at the moment of take-off, and research has shown that it takes a full second for them to open again. By which time, a fifth of the race is already over.

The first three things I saw when arriving at the track were the toilets, a fire engine and an ambulance. You know you'll need one of them, and just hope you won't need the other two. Then it was time to clamber into some overalls, which, when someone explained to me were fully fire retardant, made the prospect of having a tyre blow at 300 mph much more reassuring. The only optimistic note was struck by Gordon, who informed me that the car we were going in was a good bit slower than the top-of-the-range machines. Instead of clocking 300 mph in five seconds, this thing could manage only a miserable 210 mph in six seconds. Gordon gave me this information on the start line, as though we were just off to Asda's in a Morris Minor, but when the lights turned green, and he pressed the pedal, I didn't even have time to congratulate myself on my decision not to have breakfast before it was all over. In 6.6 seconds. As it turned out we'd only managed 191.90 mph, which Gordon was pretty disgruntled about. I wasn't too happy either, busy trying to return my eyeballs to their sockets, wondering whether the eardrum damage might be permanent, and hoping that the engine noise had drowned out the sound of cowardly whimpering. While the dragster was sent off to the mobile car wash (an extra high-pressure one on account of collecting a few more squashed flies than after your average trip down the M1 in a Ford Mondeo) Gordon returned me to the pits in a Ford Transit, which covered the quarter-mile back in a blissful two and a half minutes. It was time enough to reflect on a once in a lifetime experience – once being the operative word.

Croquet in Cheltenham

The All England Club still has 'Croquet' attached to its official title, but the hoop and mallet equivalent of the

Wimbledon final is a slightly less energetic affair. Croquet's equivalent of Murray v Djokovic involves Murray battling away on the grass, while Djokovic wanders off to the players' canteen for a cup of tea and a biscuit, occasionally peering through the window to see how the match is going. I'd been sent to cover a day at the British Open in Cheltenham, and I'd gone over to the secretary's office where one of the world's top players, Chris Williams, had agreed to have a chat. 'When's your match on?' I asked, not wanting to get in the way of practice, or whatever preparation it is that croquet players have before a big game. 'Or have you played already?' 'No, no,' he said, dipping a digestive biscuit into his mug and pointing a finger through the window. 'I'm in the middle of my game right now. That's my opponent out there.' 'Oh I see,' I replied, in just the right tone to convey to him that I didn't see at all, so he explained.

Croquet, or at least the pure form of the game they play for the British title, is a bit like snooker, in that only one player is in action at a time. And Chris nipping away for some elevenses in the pavilion was merely the equivalent of Ronnie O'Sullivan sitting in his chair and sipping some water. As in snooker, once a player is 'in the balls' his opponent can be in for quite a wait. 'How long of a wait?' I asked. 'Varies,' replied Chris. 'But the way he's going I've almost got time to nip down town and do some shopping.' He took another glance out of the window. 'Uh, oh. It looks like he's going for a TPO.' This didn't sound like good news, and Chris confirmed that it wasn't. 'It's an abbreviation for "triple peel on opponent". There are four balls in a game, two for each of us, and he's aiming to leave me with only one ball. It's definitely not looking good.' I nodded, although in all honesty, as I peered through the window watching Chris's opponent administer his TPO, I was more in TKO mode. As in boxing's technical knock-out, when you're led back to the corner waiting for your brain to remember who you are.

I could see some bloke in tennis-type gear biffing some coloured balls around on a lawn dotted with hoops. Occasionally he would pause to scratch his head, or for a thoughtful stroke of the chin. Other than that, I had no idea what was happening. You could, I thought, imagine a Martian spaceship landing on Wimbledon's Centre Court, and its occupants eventually working out what was going on. But it seemed to me you could sit for hours, weeks even, watching a game of croquet, and not have much idea at all. Unless you get an expert to explain it to you – and even then you're not much the wiser. At this point, the secretary's door opened and we were joined by Stephen Mulliner, runner-up in the previous World Championship. 'What's he trying?' he asked. 'A sextupal?' 'No,' replied Chris, 'he's trying to TPO me.' And there followed a lot of talk about 'peeling', and the difference between a 'roquet' and a 'croquet'. While they were talking I thumbed through the beginners guide I'd armed myself with, but after reading 'At the beginning of a turn you may roquet all three other balls and take croquet from them just once, but the moment you run a hoop in order you may roquet all three balls at once' my brain throbbed even harder.

Stephen may have suspected that the finer points of the game might be travelling slightly over my head, so he supplied me with some more understandable human interest information. Chris's opponent was a chap by the name of David Maugham, and was known among the croquet fraternity as 'the Beast'. Which dated back to the time he had a Union Jack shaved into his head by way of protest at being left out of the British team. According to Stephen, the Beast was reasonably cheerful most of the time, but when things weren't going so well out on the lawn, to be approached only with extreme caution. Stephen seemed to approve of the Beast, in that he came from Altrincham, and was the antithesis of the public-school-educated county types that croquet players take exception to being stereotyped as. The Beast, I noted, certainly didn't look like a cucumber-sandwich-and-a-glass-of-Pimm's man, and I imagined him completing his TPO with a snarl of 'take that chump' before heading off to the pub for a pie and pint. 'We still,' sighed Stephen, 'get associated with blazers, boaters, cucumber sandwiches and all that crap. The last vestiges of that were still around when I took up croquet in 1976, but it's been gone a long time now. The press like to perpetuate the image, but you boys never like to spoil a good story with the facts, do you?' I wasn't sure, but it sounded like he'd just TPO'd me.

Real Tennis at Queen's

Real tennis has not had a history of being plagued by crowd disturbances, at least not since 1536 when Anne Boleyn was heard to shout as she was being dragged away to the Tower: 'Hang on a minute. Unhand me. I've just had several groats on that chap serving from the Royal Box end.' Or something similar. Real tennis was a major gambling sport in those days, and although Henry VIII's decision to send the Beefeaters round to escort her from the Whitehall Palace to the Tower of London is widely put down to her inability to sire an heir, some might speculate that it had more to do with blowing all the housekeeping money on real tennis wagers.

It is an historical fact that Henry was a keen devotee of the world's oldest racket game, hard though it is to believe when today's players promote it as a game of pace, stamina and athleticism. Most of Henry's portraits suggest he would have been better suited to darts, or sumo wrestling, although you have to concede that he would have been extremely difficult to pass at the net. And by way of a reminder of the potential penalty for beating him, Henry's call of 'heads' at the toss-up for choice of ends would probably have seen off most opponents. The game is nothing like as big today, the full-house crowd of 125 when I visited Queen's Club for the British Open Championship having less to do with its popularity than with the nature of the venue.

Constructing a court is certainly not as straightforward as it is for the more popular game it spawned, for which a relatively flat surface, a net and a can of paint would just about get the job done. Real tennis, though, was originally played in palaces and monasteries, which made for a series of strange angles and obstacles. The Queen's Club courts looked like some kind of amalgam of barn conversion, church nave and semi-detached living room, with a low sloping roof on both sides, and the ball is never out of play unless it gets stuck in a ceiling joist, or an overhead light. There's a net, over which the ball has to travel, and there are three ways of producing a winner. You can hit the ball into a net behind your opponent (at one end only), or into a smaller net down the sidelines (at the other end only) or into a smallish rectangle called a grille. One other difference to lawn tennis is that the point is not necessarily over if the ball bounces twice, but it's far too complicated to go through all that. The 'real' in tennis is apparently a distortion of the Spanish for royal, as the game is called in Australia, with the Americans referring to it as court tennis, and the only other seriously competitive country, France, calling it Jeu de Paume, dating back to the days in which the racket was actually the palm of the hand. However, some racket players also believe that 'real' equates to 'proper', in that its devotees regard its more popular offspring as something of a game for cissies. 'Lawners', as the 'Realers' describe them, with more than a hint of condescension, are provided with chairs to sit down on, while a real tennis match doesn't stop until it's over. Which can be three hours or more.

When I was there, the British Open was won by Rob Fahey from Tasmania, who is so seriously good at the game that his 2012 world title was his eleventh in a row. It was a game, unlike the other one, in which the officials' decisions were rarely queried, and it's hard to imagine a real tennis player ever shouting (as Anne Boleyn possibly did when she was being frogmarched from the premises) 'You cannot be serious!'

8

DON'T HOLD THE BACK PAGE

Must have been a thin day on the sporting calendar.
Henley, bowls, ice hockey and darts

If you've ever wondered what it would be like to own a Time Machine, albeit with the needle permanently stuck in reverse, you could do worse than spend a day or two at the Henley Regatta. There, the monocle and the shooting stick is alive and well, and if you listen hard you can just pick up – above the general hubbub – conversations about the Boers kicking up in Pretoria, or Mr Gladstone addressing the House on the thorny issue of raising road tax on ponies and traps. Only the price of a Pimm's jolts you back into the realization that you haven't travelled back in time at all, and that you're still in the twenty-first century. The first thing that struck me was how many schoolboys were there – about a dozen taking part in the Prince Elizabeth Schools' Challenge Cup, and roughly several hundred more quaffing bubbly in the champagne tent. Not proper schoolboys, but old boys dressed up as schoolboys, and resplendent in their old school blazers and caps. They reminded you of Jimmy Clitheroe, or what Prince Charles would have looked like if he'd suddenly pitched up in his old Gordonstoun uniform.

On the stewards' enclosure gate the security guards were on the lookout for prohibited items, which given the number of middle-aged, hairy-legged schoolboys queuing to get in, possibly included catapults and stink bombs. I heard people talking about Bucks and Berks, which I took initially to be a reference to bucks, as in fizz, and berks, as in a gathering of people looking like a cross between a retired admiral and a sixth-form prefect. It turned out, though, to be an abbreviation for Buckinghamshire and Berkshire, the two counties separated by the river. Very few events can compare to Henley in terms of the disparity in energy output between those taking part and those (occasionally) trotting down to the riverbank to watch. Sitting in the Royal Box at Wimbledon comes close, but the agony levels between rowing and stretching out a hand for a Campari and soda refill are about as wide as it is possible to get. Public address announcements come thick and fast. 'At the barrier, Oberhausen lead the City of Oxford by half a length, with both sides striking at 37.' But you have to actually watch the race to get some idea of the pain being experienced out there. It's Roman-galley-type exhaustion, albeit without the whip.

The really major suffering is always experienced by the losers, who from positions ranging from the flat-out to the foetal are obliged to respond to the victors' 'Three cheers for Rowlocks-on-Thames!' with a croaked 'Hip, hip, hoo-rah!' of their own. This isn't always easy. After Pangbourne had been beaten by Canford, the losing stroke, looking as though he'd just had one, remained completely horizontal through the traditional exchange of hoorahs. One of his team-mates tried but failed to participate, the urge to retch forcing him to lean overboard midway though. 'Hip, hip, hooorrugggggggh!' Another beaten rower, from Imperial College London, tried to sit up for the row back to shore, but struck his head on his oar and collapsed back into the boat. Being physically ill is commonplace at the end of a rowing race, and at Henley the urge to retch is not diminished by the finishing post being adjacent to the Henley Brewery. The aroma of hop is quite a pleasant one if the extent of your afternoon exertion is to pull out a fold-up chair and gently apply some factor 30, but not so much when visited all at the same time by headache, dehydration and delirium. Everywhere you look at Henley, groups of young men are chundering over the side of a boat in front of groups of young ladies having to dab away any beads of perspiration which may have resulted from too many twirls of the parasol.

Henley might be regarded as a quintessentially English social event, but the intensity of the competition is fierce. A small group of spectators tucking into their smoked salmon mousse were startled by a nearby American crew whipping themselves up into a frenzy with a bonding routine that appeared to have its origins in a Sioux war dance. Eight of them, huddled in a circle, each held out a clenched fist, and listened, heads bowed, to their leader. 'Okay guys, we're going to win this race! We're trained! We're ready! We're the best! Let's go out and whip this fucking river!' The clenched fists banged into each other, followed by a collective whoop of 'Yeeeessss!' as they all leapt about thirty feet into the air. The whoop was blood-curdling, and so unnerved one of the lady picnickers she had to have her back thumped to retrieve the olive from her Martini. The Yanks turned out to be a crew from Boston, who had just saved enough energy from their war dance to beat Kingston Grammar School by half a length. 'Hip, hip, hoorah!' shouted the Americans. 'Hip, hip, hrrrer,' gasped Kingston. Sometimes, a race was won by such a vast margin that the winners had to put their 'hip, hip, hoorays' in an email. There should have been a total representation of seventeen countries, but this was reduced to sixteen when India didn't make the qualifying mark. Finishing three minutes behind the next slowest team, this was the equivalent of a runner being lapped in the 800 metres. There was the same disparity in times among the spectators as well. You could be ten yards from the beer tent and get there in either five seconds or half an hour, and it all depended on what type of badge you had and how many detours ('Sorry, sir, you're not allowed through this gate') you had to make. Class distinction isn't quite as rigorous as it used to be when Henley was first held in 1836 – when one of its rules stated 'no manual labourers' – but it's still there.

There was also an occasion when the 1936 Australian Olympic team was excluded on the grounds that the crew contained a number of policemen, an occupation Henley regarded as much too far down the social scale. This is not to say that there are no allowances made for the *hoi polloi*, it's just that they're kept well away from the snobby lot. I knew, for example, that I'd inadvertently strayed into riff-raff territory when I came across a caravan containing 'Gypsy Lee – World Famous Romany'. She didn't seem to be getting much custom, which came as no great surprise given that her major attempt at a drawing card was: 'One of my great uncles is the TV and radio personality Gordon Boswell.' I wished I received a pound for every 'Gordon who?' as people walked past her caravan. The racing stopped twice, for lunch (12.20–2pm) and for tea (3.50–5pm), but the Bacchanalian feasting wasn't subject to any specific opening and closing time, which led to heavy demands on the Portaloos, and the slightly distressing sight of manual labourers on the premises. Although it at least offered you the chance to prick some pomposity had someone stopped you to ask the way to the ('No Culottes, Divided Skirts, High Hemlines, or Trousers') Stewards' Enclosure. 'Certainly. Turn left at the C&R Cesspool and Septic Tank Emptying lorry. You can't miss it.'

Bowls

One obvious thing about bowls is that it's not a game to be rushed. Not even an enemy fleet off the coastline can hurry a chap when he's in the middle of a tight end, and if Drake's match in 1588 had detained him a little bit longer we'd all be eating paella and watching bullfights. It must have been a close game to keep Sir Francis otherwise engaged during the initial exchange of cannonballs, but even more surprising was the fact that, at the time, he was only forty-eight. For years, bowls was seen as a game only to be taken up after acquiring a Zimmer frame, a hearing aid and a set of false teeth. Furthermore, the fact that televised events are usually confined to afternoons suggests that the broadcaster believes that its audience is largely the type that starts making the bedtime cocoa by the time the six o'clock news comes on. However, at all levels, it's become more of a young man's game. The majority of newcomers to bowls clubs do so before legally qualifying for anything stronger than a ginger beer after showering down and heading for the members' bar, and the 2013 world indoor champion was only twenty-seven when he won it.

Its fuddy-duddy image is still hard to shake off though, possibly because of the fuddy-duddy nature of the apparel. Thumbing through a beginner's guide to the game on my first visit to a world championship, its what-to-wear advice would have put off most people under the age of 120. 'Socks,' it said, 'should be of an absorbent material, and the wearing of white underwear is recommended.' Pardon? 'Because,' it went on to explain, 'the synthetic material of some trousers is light – and in some circumstances, transparent.' There aren't too many scenarios in a game of bowls which would prompt the audience to let out a collective gasp, but one such might be when a competitor, upon bending down in his delivery stride, was seen to be wearing purple underpants. Bowls is continually looking at ways to make itself more sexy, and trying to find a way of competing with the likes of snooker and darts – far more sedentary indoor sports – in terms of attracting media interest and sponsors. Preferably, sponsors who are not necessarily associated with a pipe and slippers. There are few things more incongruous than watching two pasty-faced snooker players waiting to come out to play at the Crucible while some plonker wearing a shiny suit and clutching a microphone has deluded himself into believing that he's introducing a heavyweight boxing contest, but bowls could certainly do with a little bit more ceremony before a big match. At the championship I went to, the sport's biggest names simply wandered out, unannounced, from the fire exit. There isn't enough money for the players to give up their day jobs, and one of the bigger perks the male players receive involves being presented with knitted socks and jumpers. Which they doubtless have to register with the Inland Revenue as a taxable benefit in kind.

I got the impression it could do with a few more characters, although bowls is not the kind of sport where you can barge your opponent out of the way, or start sledging him when he pulls off a lucky shot. When I was watching, the conversation was mostly confined to that between a bowler and his bowl. Until then, I'd thought that golf was the prime example of a player talking to an inanimate object, but while Sergio Garcia will regularly instruct his ball to 'get down!' or 'be right!', an Australian bowler called Ian Schuback regularly pursued his bowl down the entire length of the rink, imploring it to speed up, slow down, or turn a bit to the side. As if, like a pet cocker spaniel, it would instantly obey. Bowls is also big on sportsmanship, with the ref never required to do much more than apply some chalk to a toucher, or take the occasional measurement. If a few more players trashed the drinks trolley, or hoofed their bowl into the crowd in a fit of temper, the TV audience figures would go through the roof overnight. I had thought also that it was a reasonably inexpensive sport until I wandered into the spectator shop, which was selling, apart from bowls obviously, tubs of wax, gripping powder, cloths, bowl holders, and no less than nineteen types of measuring device. There were also racks of white trousers, although given the warning in the beginners' guidebook about their potential transparency while in the bent-over position, it was mildly surprising to find nothing in the way of matching white underpants.

Ice Hockey

There's something to be said for a sport that can still provide an exhilarating spectacle even when the only way you can tell that a goal has been scored is when the players all gather round to hug each other. Even if you're at rinkside, an ice hockey puck is barely visible, and on TV you can't see it all. Or at least I can't. Which leads me to believe that the reason it remains as popular a sport as it is, is because the numbers on the players' backs should all come with a double O prefix. If not licensed to kill, then at least to break several ribs by splatting your opponent, Tom and Jerry style, into the Perspex boards. Which immediately causes such offence to the opposition that all their players jump up from the bench, and skate out onto the ice intent on breaking a few skulls. Which in turn prompts the other team's benchmen/henchmen to skate out onto the ice intent on escalating the conflict. And when both sides are all punched out, someone, or occasionally even one player from each side, is given a short cooling-off period in the penalty booth for being a very naughty boy.

Sadly, in my view, the punch-ups that make ice hockey the spectacle it is have got fewer in more recent times. Legal lawsuits in both the civil and criminal courts have resulted in much less of the old-style mayhem, in which games such as that between Vancouver and Colorado in 2004 were pretty commonplace. Todd Bertuzzi of Vancouver punched Steve Moore of Colorado in the back the head, knocking him unconscious. Bertuzzi then fell on top of Moore, crushing him face first into the ice, followed by the pair of them being buried beneath the combined weight of both sides as players rushed to get involved in a brawl. Moore ended up with three broken ribs, concussion, vertebral ligament damage, nerve damage, and facial cuts and bruises, while his assailant was charged with assault. Had it been a nightclub, he'd probably have done time. But as it was ice hockey, he got a conditional discharge. However, if the violence is not quite what it used to be, there's still plenty of it about.

Sitting in the press enclosure at the British championship play-offs during the first period of the first semi-final between Cardiff and Sheffield, I wondered why there was no correspondent from either *The Lancet* or the *British Medical Journal*. There were eight two-minute penalties, two roughings, two trippings, one slashing, one hooking, one elbowing and one cross-checking. The only thing that was missing was a goal. 'Cor blimey,' I said (or something similar) to a proper ice hockey journalist on my left. 'That was a bit physical.' He gave me a strange sort of look and said: 'Quietest play-off I've been to in years. Game's gone soft if you ask me.' However, it seemed to me that not even the spectators were safe from having their evening end in a trip to A&E. The puck only weighs six ounces, but it regularly flies over the safety Perspex, and if six ounces of vulcanized rubber travelling at 70 mph thuds into your Adam's apple, it'll be a while before you're able to resume eating your popcorn. There was barely a spare seat to be had at the Nynex Arena in Manchester, and that included the sin bin. Ostensibly a place of solitary confinement, a player is rarely without company for long, and one of the earlier occupants was Sheffield's Franc Kovacs. Not long before, Kovacs had given an interview in which he revealed that he had discovered religion. And when asked how his new Christian beliefs could be reconciled with an apparent history of ungentlemanly conduct, his reply was along the lines that he only whacked an opponent on those occasions when God came visiting and told him when to fight. And sure enough, with only thirteen minutes on the clock, God was on the line. 'Fight, Franc, fight,' said God, and verily, there was much fighting in the goalmouth. However, there was another god wearing a black and white striped shirt, and he too spoke to Franc. 'Repent thy sins,' said this earthly god, and lo, there was great sadness on the Sheffield bench as Franc was cast into the wilderness for 120 seconds. Although skating to the sin bin doesn't really come across as a journey of shame when the loudspeaker immediately pipes up with a blast of 'Hit the Road, Jack'.

The game, in fact, is only ever without music, and loud music at that, when play is actually in progress. Unless you include the pre-match rendition of 'God Save the Queen', which was just about the only time that every player on the ice was upright. Although given the nationality of most of the players, quite why they played 'God Save the Queen' instead of the Canadian National Anthem was a bit of a puzzle. Cardiff's two post-match spokesmen were both Canadian, and, as representatives of the losers, neither had much of a good word for the referee. One of them accused him of getting so excited at making a rare appearance on Sky TV that he wasn't about to let the evening go by without drawing attention to himself, while the other complained that he was out of his depth when it came to foul play. It was not that the ref was too lenient, they argued, but too authoritarian. 'In the end,' said the Cardiff Canadian sadly, 'we were too scared to go out and hit their guys.'

Every ice hockey team has what's known as an 'enforcer'. To an extent, everyone enforces, but there's always one who's extra good at it. Franc was Sheffield's equivalent of a nightclub bouncer, but when they played London, he was like Little Lord Fauntleroy next to the opposition's Dave Morissette. He too was Canadian, and had clearly adopted the motto of the Mounted Police in always getting his man. With the result that it was a rare event for him to ever finish a game. Afterwards, Dave was kind enough to spare some time to share his philosophy with me. 'It's in my blood,' he said, apparently unaware of the fact that most of the blood involved came from his nearest opponent. 'Hockey allows you to fight, and I have fun in what I do. The gloves come off, and you just go for it. I've broken my hand about six times, and my nose about four. Players like me are important. You go across to the other bench and say "Hey, you want trouble, you got it"; then you drop the gloves and put on a good show for the people.' And putting on a good show is really what ice hockey is all about. 'Listen,' said Dave. 'I can be a complete asshole out on the ice, but most of the guys I fight end up having a beer with me afterwards.' You don't say. And clearly, it doesn't matter whether they're drinking their beer from a glass, or sipping it through a straw.

Darts

Bathed in sweat, grey from exhaustion, and eyes so sunken in their sockets you'd have needed a crowbar to return them to their original position, he spoke movingly of his terrible ordeal. So movingly, in fact, that I could scarce record his words in my notebook without tear-drops splashing onto the page and smearing the writing. 'I prayed to God,' he said. The interviewer asked him exactly what form his prayer had taken. 'Please God, help me,' he said. 'Let me have the strength to get through this.' At which point, God having answered his prayers, the author concluded by embarking on a series of hugging sessions with tearful friends and relatives. It was, by any standards, a press conference raw with emotion, the kind of thing you might have expected from a released hostage, or an earthquake victim who'd been buried for a fortnight before finally being pulled from the rubble, rather than someone who'd just won a game of darts in a noise-filled tavern just off the M25.

Okay, it wasn't just any old game, it was a second-round duel in the world championship in which Raymond van Barneveld of Holland had just scraped through against Les Wallace of Scotland. It was a heavyweight contest in every sense of the word, given that both contestants could have employed their shirts to accommodate a family of four on a camping holiday, although Barneveld wasn't all that much bigger than his interviewer, a former darter himself by the name of Bobby George. Even so, Bob would have tipped the scales at roughly five stone heavier than Barney, if only for the fact that he had what appeared to be the contents of an entire jeweller's shop both hanging from his neck and attached to his fingers. The most exciting thing about darts, given that spectators are so far from the board that without the big screen you'd have no idea whether someone had scored 180 or 3, is the build-up.

In terms of making an entrance, boxing isn't in the frame. Led out by two young ladies wearing dresses containing less material than the shirt pocket housing Barney's darts, the man from Holland – a postman in a former life – was roared onto the stage by tables full of orange-shirted Dutchmen. Wallace, wearing a kilt, came out to a bagpipe rendition of 'Flower of Scotland', and – nicknames being more or less compulsory in darts – had the soubriquet 'McDanger' emblazoned across the back of his shirt. The following match was between Andy Fordham and Mervyn King, or to give it its official billing, the Viking and the Swerve. I assumed that the Viking must have some distant bloodline to Leif Eriksson – or at the very least, Sven-Goran Eriksson – but apparently not. Andy, in fact, was a genial publican from Woolwich, who drank lager from a bottle (and quite a lot of it judging by the size of him) as opposed to mead from a horn. He did, though, it has to be said, have more than a passing resemblance to Hagar the Horrible.

Andy's fans, of which there were many, were all wearing Viking headgear, while Merv's fans, of which there were considerably fewer, had somehow managed to make the journey from home to the Lakeside Tavern at Frimley Green without stopping off at a fancy dress shop. Both sets of supporters, though, were singing, or yelling to be more accurate, from the same hymn sheet when the MC went through his pre-match warm-up routine. 'Yo ho!' he shouted. 'Yo ho!' the crowd shouted back. 'Yo ho!' the MC shouted again. 'Yo ho!' the crowd responded once more. Given that the game's origins are said to date back to medieval battlegrounds, might this, I wondered, have been some kind of ritualistic reference to Agincourt. 'And gentlemen in England now-a-bed shall think themselves accursed they were not here. Yo ho!' yelled Henry. 'Yo ho!' replied his archers. There is a certain amount of historical evidence that Henry's archers warmed up for the battle with a game of darts – by cutting down the shafts and hurling them at barrel butts. With their eyes thoroughly 'in', as they say, the Froggies had no chance. Three arrows in a Frenchman's forehead, and a rousing chorus of 'one hundred and eighteeeeeeeeee!' Followed, perhaps, by a 'yo ho!' or two.

From Agincourt, darts quickly spread to the snug bar of the Fox and Firkin, and finally onto our television sets. Lord knows how they managed it in the early days, with no widescreen TVs around, but someone they managed to squeeze the likes of Leighton Rees and Cliff Lazarenko onto the same camera shot. The players of that era held their darts in fingers that resembled giant hot dogs, and part of the fascination for the television audience at home was the distinct possibility that one of the contestants might disappear through the floorboards. It was, furthermore, a clear requirement of entry to the tournament that not only did you guzzle half a dozen pints of ale between throws, but that your non-throwing hand had to contain at least one burning cigarette, stuck between podgy fingers the colour of Norwich City's home strip. Not unlike a bunch of over-ripe bananas, in fact.

There was a time, when darts was on the telly, when most of the audience had to reach for the mute button to stop the dog howling and the cat arching its back behind the sofa. However, if Sid Waddell's commentary didn't always meet with the RSPCA's approval, to many others it was better than the darts itself. One of the players made his entrance to a 1960s pop song, which prompted Sid, who's sadly no longer with us, to inform his audience: 'There was a gentleman who topped the charts called Thunderclap Newman. Well, this man came onto the stage to thunderclaps, but he's no new man!'

You can't teach this kind of thing; it's a gift. Sid had a field-day with players' nicknames. There was a Scot called 'Brave Dart', and Dennis 'the Heat' Ovens was particularly good pun material for Sid. Waddell's descriptive powers were certainly required for Alex 'Ace of Herts' Roy versus Alan 'the Iceman' Warriner, owing to the fact that someone overdid the dry ice machine, and you couldn't see either gladiator make his entrance on account of a fog so thick it would have kept Jack the Ripper indoors. It was a boring match, which would have benefited from keeping the ice machine going, with neither player capable of sending an audience delirious in the same way as a van Barneveld. Quite why this should be was frankly a mystery. A very large man, who perspired a lot, and was from Holland. But still they cried, as he hit another three-dart maximum,

'Een honderd en tachtig!' They also shouted, 'Doe maa eeen klomp!', although quite why his fans thought they might inspire their man by shouting what translates into 'Give me a clog!' still puzzles me to this day.

9

ENGLISH SPORTING HEROES: NO. 1: MARTIN JOHNSON. (NO, NOT THAT ONE)

My bid to win the World Snooker Championship . . .
Carnoustie 1999 . . . Hoisting spinnakers at Cowes
. . . Taming Augusta National . . . Fish pond finish
at the Old Course

'You any good at snooker?' It was the deputy sports editor on the line. 'Good?' I said. 'I'll have you know I once had a break of nine. Two reds and a black. And I've only once ripped the cloth. And that was after I'd had a few.' 'Well get practising anyway. I've just entered you in this year's Embassy World Championships.' You can't do it any more, but there was a time, for some strange reason, when all you had to do to claim a place in the world's most prestigious snooker tournament was to cough up the fee to become a member of the World Professional Billiards and Snooker Association (£250 I think it was at the time) and turn up wearing a waistcoat and a bow-tie.

I fancied I might have a decent chance of winning the thing given that snooker remains the only sport in which a complete unknown by the name of Johnson has won the world championship. If Joe could pull it off, I thought, why not me? The commentators were forever blathering on about the Crucible's gut-wrenching tension, but what did they know? I'd never seen Dennis Taylor or Willie Thorne in the Aylestone and District Conservative Club on a Sunday lunchtime, with the steward shouting last orders, nineteen balls still to pot, and only one fifty-pence piece left for the light. Pressure? They'd no idea what the word meant. Nonetheless, I decided that it wouldn't do any harm to get some coaching in, and who better to give me just that extra edge I might need at seventeen frames apiece in the final than the six-time world champ, Steve Davis.

Which is how I came to find myself at one of Davis's practice tables in his father's farmhouse near Romford, while he measured me up for whatever minor nips and tucks he might feel – once I'd breezed through the dozen or so preliminary rounds – I'd need to handle my first experience of playing in front of the TV cameras in Sheffield. 'First of all,' I said, 'I really need a nickname. I'm pretty fast – I reckon I can be out of my chair, give four away, and be sitting down again in about five seconds flat – so I thought Hurricane Mart or Rocket Johnson might fit the bill, but I gather they're already taken. Any ideas?' Davis replied: 'Well, let's see you hit a shot or two, and we'll see if something occurs to me', and sure enough, he'd got it before I'd even drawn back my cue. All it took was one look at a bridge hand which resembled a mole with chronic arthritis to prompt a cry of Eureka. 'Got it!' he shouted triumphantly. 'The Claw!'

And so, now armed with a moniker guaranteed to strike terror into the likes of O'Sullivan and Hendry, I set about attempting to pot a few reds, but after half a dozen whites had disappeared Davis called for a time-out in order to sit down and analyse my prospects. Which were, he opined, somewhat negatively I thought, not great. His argument appeared to be based around finding it hard to coach someone destined to spend 99.9 per cent of his career sitting in a chair, which would have deterred a lesser man, but I wasn't going to be put off that easily. 'In that case,' I said, 'if I'm going to be sitting down all the time, how about teaching me how to sip a glass of water?' No one in the game's history has ever sipped water with quite such style as Davis, and very soon I was fully conversant with the little-finger-off-the-glass technique, and the quizzically raised eyebrow as you reflect on the duff shot which caused you to return to your seat in the first place. Taking thirty-six sips a frame without actually consuming enough to drown a gnat is a skill in itself, and Davis also taught me how to alternate between both hands, so as not to keep reaching across and covering up your sponsors' logos. 'I take it you will be sponsored?' he said, but I had to tell him that none of the blue-chip companies, BMW, Rolex and the like, were as yet aware of my entry.

Davis then introduced more unwelcome hints of negativity regarding my prospects when he suggested we start working on a list of excuses at my press conference should I happen to lose. I hadn't, until then, seriously considered the prospect of an upset, but Davis was insistent that for the really top players, such as myself, there was always the danger of complacency. 'Who are you playing first?' he asked. 'I don't know,' I said. 'Never mind,' said Steve. 'Don't forget he'll never have heard of you. Sitting in his chair thinking: "Who is this Claw?" he'll be as nervous as hell. Mind you, this will only last for as long as it takes you to play your first shot, so if you win the toss, ask him to break first.' Steve was mildly concerned that one look at my bridging hand might give the game away, but when his father Bill suggested I might try having it heavily bandaged, Steve shook his head. 'It may affect the only strong part of your game,' he said. 'Sipping the water.'

And so to the big day. Not at the Crucible; that wouldn't be until I'd despatched, with as minimal fuss as possible, my next ten opponents, but at the Hazel Grove Snooker Club in Stockport. Davis, wise old bird that he was, had warned me that nothing can fully prepare you for that first appearance in the Embassy World Championship. Your throat gets so tight you can barely swallow, you get dizzy spots in front of your eyes, and you're in severe danger of choking. However, once I realized I'd tied the bow-tie a bit too tight, all was well, and when I got into my stride I soon began to reproduce the blistering form that once took me to a mere 138 tantalizing points away from snooker's Holy Grail, the maximum clearance. 'Work on your nod,' was Steve's last big instruction, in astute anticipation of a scenario more in keeping with a Sotheby's auction room than a snooker hall. And sage advice it was. Five glances from the referee, five imperceptible nods, and five frames stylishly conceded.

It was hard to believe that the road to the Crucible – the A523 between Stockport and Macclesfield in my case

– had ended in a first-round 5–0 whitewash. The papers, I thought, would have a field-day. 'Stockport Stunned as Claw Makes Early Exit!' As Davis had feared, though, a player of my pedigree had simply found it impossible to pump himself up for the small occasion. I sat down afterwards to share a beer with my opponent, Gary Challis, from Grimsby, who confessed to me that Davis's prediction that he'd be nervous about playing someone he'd never heard of turned out to be spot on. He had, therefore, sneaked a quick look at me warming up before the game on one of the practice tables, and after briefly wondering whether it might be a wind-up, began to relax a little. He was even more laid back during the fifteen-minute interval, which he spent, leading 4–0, pumping money into a fruit machine. The whole match lasted just over an hour, including a toilet break for Gary (nerves, I guess), and despite my slightly disappointing tally of five balls potted, only three of them were whites. It can be a cruel old game, and the turning point, I felt, came when – trailing by a mere four frames and 48 points – I crouched over the table and fouled the pink with my waistcoat.

Carnoustie 1999

Maurice Flitcroft had given up inventing bizarre *nom de plumes* and trying to sneak into Open Championships by the time Carnoustie came around in 1999, but this was the one occasion when the celebrated impostor could have played in the tournament pretty much undetected. Hacking it around in the rough with everyone else. The wind blew, and the grass was allowed to grow so long you had as much chance of locating a long-lost pygmy tribe in it as an errant Titleist. Ian Woosnam, all five foot four of him, was playing, and you wondered whether his partners would arrive back at the clubhouse without him, having searched for him for the regulation five minutes before declaring him lost under Rule 27. Nowadays, with all the Health and Safety regulations, the diminutive Welshman wouldn't have been allowed out there without a SatNav and a box of flares.

Walking around following the golf, we hacks struggled to come to terms with the eerie silence all around the links. Every now and then, it would be broken by a distant roar, and you'd think to yourself: 'Eh up, someone must have made a par.' After Day One, the R&A committee must have been wondering whether to introduce a fining system, along the lines of the All England Club at Wimbledon, for crimes such as audible obscenities and equipment abuse, and by the end of Day Two, grown men were close to tears. And one nearly grown man, Sergio Garcia, blubbed uncontrollably in the arms of his mother after signing for a round of 89. In the end, the combination of the weather, the course, and the pressure conspired to relieve a French golfer of his marbles. Requiring a double-bogey six at the seventy-second hole to become the Open champion, the way Jean van de Velde elected to play the hole was the most ill-conceived piece of strategy to come out of France since the Maginot Line, and it all ended up with him rolling up his trouser legs and going for a paddle in the Barry Burn. All that was missing to complete the seaside-postcard effect was a knotted handkerchief on his head.

To this day, no one quite knows whether it belongs in the category of sporting tragedy or sporting farce, but in the interests of providing a follow-up story, the sports editor phoned me on the last day of the championship and asked whether there was any chance of me playing the course myself on the Monday, to, in his words, 'See if you can beat Sergio's 89.' And so, with the kind permission of the secretary, I teed it up on the Monday morning accompanied by a one-armed Scottish caddie and a photographer. The caddie, Alex, had lost his arm in a butcher's mincing machine at the age of fourteen, and had won the British one-armed golf championship no less than seven times. At his peak, he played to a handicap of eight, which, as anyone who's ever played Carnoustie will testify, is no mean achievement even for someone who is able to get two hands on the club.

By the time he reached the pinnacle of his career and caddied for me, Alex was sixty-seven, and had been doing the job for half a century. In which time, if dishing out compliments was the best way to guarantee a generous gratuity, he wouldn't have made a heap of money in tips. At the first downwind par four, I managed to find the fairway with the driver, and only had a seven iron for my second. 'Not bad, eh Alex?' I ventured. To which Alex replied: 'Woods took six iron, sand wedge. And his tee was fifty yards further back.' Later on, a decent enough drive took an unkind kick and finished about a yard off the fairway in knee-high rough. 'A bit unlucky that one Alex,' I said. 'Nae unlucky laddie,' he replied. 'I told you to keep it down the left side did I not?' I couldn't deny that he had, but it was now time to seek advice on what to do with a ball that was lying at the bottom of impenetrable jungle. 'What do you think Alex? Could I get a wedge back to the fairway do you think?' Alex replied: 'D' ye think ye can write yer article with two broken wrists? If ye can, have a go, but if not, take a penalty drop.'

Scottish caddies traditionally have a nice line in deflationary wit, and on the potentially card-wrecking par five sixth, known as Hogan's Alley, I ventured a tentative: 'Driver Alex?' He replied: 'Aye. Then another driver, and maybe a driver for the third as well.' After a good shot followed by a duff he grunted: 'Ye're a hard man tae club, all right. Ye're either hittin' a four iron 220 yards or 10 feet.' And the one compliment wasn't really one at all. 'Great shot!' he chortled as I hit a horrendous slice off the tee at the fourth. 'Ye've hit it so far right we'll find it sitting up on the fifteenth fairway.' And so it went on. Finally we got to the eighteenth tee, having arrived there in 81 strokes, and needing to do it in the same number as van de Velde's 7 to beat Garcia's 89. Unlike van de Velde, I managed to avoid the Barry Burn, but in the interests of research I went down there anyway to see whether the shot he had thought about playing was in any way feasible. However, during the couple of minutes I spend thrashing around unsuccessfully trying to remove a golf ball from a slippery bed of rock covered by four inches of water, I came under what can only be described as a mortar attack. 'Splish', another ball arrived. 'Splosh', and another. I wondered whether the crazy Frenchman had decided to come back for another go, but instead of a cry of 'Mon Dieu!' floating across on the Carnoustie wind, this one sounded more like an 'Ah so!' And indeed it was. From a Japanese fourball following behind us. 'I suggest you take a penalty drop,' I shouted up. 'No good down here.' But all I got in reply was a lot of smiling and bowing.

Remarkably, I somehow managed to complete the hole in a regulation par four, my 85 beating Garcia's 89 with something to spare. The media tent was now deserted, sadly, otherwise I'd have happily spent the rest of the day giving interviews. 'Well played,' said Alex afterwards. 'I've caddied for worse.' High praise coming from him. I asked him who was the worst player he'd caddied for, and the story he told me certainly had an apocryphal ring to it. 'It was an American,' he said. 'I spent the entire round fishing his ball out of the Burn. He was staying at a hotel in St Andrews, and after we'd finished he asked me for directions. "Up tae Brechin, across tae Troon, doon tae Edinburgh, across the Forth Bridge, and on tae St Andrews," I said. "Are you sure that's the quickest way?" he asked. "Well it's no actually the quickest," I said. "But I guarantee ye'll nae have tae cross the Barry Burn."'

Cowes

One of the more romantic notions of Britain is of a rugged island nation of salty seadogs, whose sailing exploits were once responsible for turning half the globe red, and whose children are weaned on fireside tales of Drake, Nelson and Chichester. In reality, though, the sum total of most of its people's ocean-going experience is a pedalo ride around the bay, or a P&O ferry crossing. Yo, ho, ho, and a bottle of cheapo rum from a Boulogne hypermarket. On my first visit to Cowes week, though, it was hard not to get some kind of feeling for our maritime ancestry, not least for the fact that it had been going – in some form or other – since the scurvy and weevil-biscuit era of 1812. Some of the sailing is serious enough, but mostly it's more of a social gathering, like Henley and Ascot. Not so much first over the line, as first into the Pimm's tent.

Emotionally, I was more at home on boats propelled by engines, with waiters occasionally dropping by to plop a fresh olive into your dry Martini, and a gentle game of deck quoits representing the maximum possible exertion. Splicing mainbraces was my forte, not hoisting spinnakers. However, the office had decided that the main point of my being there was to convey the feel of a proper race to the reader, which is how I came to find myself forming part of the crew on one of the main sponsors' boats. We were due to go out on the Monday, but the Force Six wind was adjudged too strong for the amateurs, and our race was postponed until the following day. Sailing can be a dangerous business when the wind is up, and the first two yachtsmen I shook hands with were missing the full complement of fingers. Or at least the tips, which are regularly left inside a winch, or float away to provide a canapé for a passing shark. Apart from the skipper, James, our crew was entirely made up of invited guests, with varying degrees of experience ranging from Mike, who was apparently a dab hand on something called 505s, to myself, whose mastery of the pedalo even stretched to steering one while licking an ice cream. The first trick to learn was how to make it to the starting buoy amid a huge armada of sailing boats, pleasure craft and the occasional mainland ferry.

The skipper was not impressed when the gun went off ten minutes before we got to the start line, but once under way we soon got the hang of things, not least by the captain's inspired decision not to confuse us with too many nautical expressions. Ergo, when James let rip with comments such as 'That was effing diabolical' and 'Pull your sodding fingers out', they were readily understood by all concerned. There were times, I don't mind admitting, when the occasional blast of bad language was not just confined to our leader, as was the case during my first attempt to raise a spinnaker. It began with James shouting 'Get that bloody rope!', which sounded easy enough, but not when you've a choice of about twenty-three ropes. Red ones, blue ones, yellow ones, green ones with speckles, you name it. Not to mention attempting, at the same time, to avoid having your skull crushed by the boom, and your fingers turned into crinkle-cut chips by the metal rope clampers. I muttered a response under my breath, and the two words which preceded 'captain' were not 'aye aye'. However, raising the thing was a cocktail-and-hammock experience compared to getting it down again, and more than once I found myself parcelled up, like an en croute salmon, inside a wet expanse of billowing sail.

I made a quick mental note of the ten things I most wanted never to see again, and the spinnaker came in comfortably at no 1. I admired the skipper's competitive instincts, but when he decided upon one final spinnaker hoist in an attempt to get us across the line in something like thirty-seventh place of the forty starters, instead of thirty-eighth, I knew exactly how Fletcher Christian must have felt. But no sooner had I conjured visions of lowering

James over the side in a dinghy, with just enough water and ship's biscuits to give him a fighting chance of washing up ashore somewhere, than he announced that we'd crossed the finish line. And after four hours out there on the Solent, it was an announcement that was music to my ears. Or it would have been if my ears hadn't been full of water.

Augusta

'You haven't played it, have you?' 'Yes I have actually.' 'Bloody hell, what's it like? Is it as beautiful as it looks on telly?' 'Prettier, I'd say.' 'Impossible to play though.' 'Not really. Biffed it round in 86 as it happens.' It was a conversation I've had more than once, and it involved playing a round of golf at Augusta. Azaleas, pine trees, Amen Corner and all that. A place so exclusive that when Bill Gates unwisely let it be known he'd quite like to join, they deliberately kept him waiting two more years for being too pushy. The ironic thing about Augusta is that to get to a course with serious claims to being the most picturesque in the world you have to drive down a street with even more serious claims to being the ugliest. One long stretch of Dunkin' Donuts, Waffle Houses, Hooters, Gas Stations, Tire and Lube advertisements, grim, grotty motels that cost $50 a night for fifty-one weeks of the year and $500 in Masters' week, and finally, just outside the main gate to the golf club, the Christian Bookstore, with a giant neon sign offering 'free lemonade' at Sunday's service. The spectators, whom the TV commentators are obliged to call 'patrons' if they want to keep the contract for next year, are then obliged to form an orderly line until the gates open, listening to people with loudspeakers giving them a list of prohibited items – running to about a dozen – before finishing with the inevitable 'Have a nice day.' You don't see any of this on the telly, though, just a vast expanse of flora, and grass which hasn't seen a dandelion or a daisy since the turf was first laid back in the 1930s. It's almost a crime to take a divot out of it, which I was about to do after coming out of the hat in the media-centre draw.

Every year, the media is allocated forty spots in ten groups of four, to play the course – with the tees further forward but the same flagstick positions as for the previous day's final round – on the Monday morning. And one year, I got lucky. Most golfers know every hole at Augusta intimately, as the Masters is the only one of the four majors to be played at the same venue every year. And those who've only seen it on TV can't really appreciate what an awesome place it is. Especially seeing it for the first time. It was a bit strange walking across the lawn from the clubhouse to the first tee, and finding, for the first time in about a fortnight, no gathering of newspaper hacks and TV crews waiting to interview the players. I'd happily have stopped to give CBS or the Golf Channel some pearls. 'I'm hitting it real solid right now' . . . 'Sure, coming off forty-eighth place in the captain's day Fur and Feather, why wouldn't I be confident?' . . .

No player in the tournament, apart from Tiger Woods, can make the walk from clubhouse to practice putting green without being ambushed by several radio stations and groups of newspaper hacks, and though Woods makes himself deliberately unavailable behind a squadron of sinister-looking security men, they get round it by asking all the other players about him. One year, Jim Furyk was collared by a truly oleaginous presenter for the American Golf Channel (if that isn't a tautology, nothing is) who began the interview thus. 'Tell me Jim. Just what is it, that, when you're paired to play with Tiger, and you get to walk onto that first tee, and there he is, in the flesh, and you shake hands, and wait for the starter, Jim, what is it exactly, that, well, puts a mortal golfer in so much awe of him?' American golfers are well used to giving antiseptic replies to this kind of tosh, and Jim duly babbled out the standard stuff about Woods being 'kinda special', and a 'helluva player', etcetera. Like every other golfer on the planet, I'd love to play in the Masters, but only for the sheer joy of being interviewed by a pillock from the Golf Channel on the subject of Woods. 'Pardon me? I didn't quite catch that; would you mind asking the question again?' would have been a reasonable opening gambit, followed eventually by 'Oh, are you talking about Eldrick? Can't drive very straight, spits a lot, swears quite a bit, likes cocktail waitresses, that the chap?' And so on. And eventually, after my fiftieth Masters, I could start giving Gary Player-type interviews.

Every year, Gary turns up to give an audience, and every year, the theme never varies. In fact, the biggest danger to anyone in the field not winning the Masters is to bump into Gary on the practice range and miss his tee-off time, because when Gary is in full flow there isn't a donkey on the planet who'd go near him for fear of being parted from its hind legs. His regular hobby horse is obesity. 'Look at me. Can you believe I'm 190 years old? Did you know that

24 per cent of Americans are overweight? Twenty-four per cent!' Did you know that 100 million Americans will have diabetes in fifty years' time? One hundred mill . . .', and on and on he goes, until darkness falls, or, whichever is the earlier, everyone listening has died.

There's something about playing a golf course you know so intimately from television, and it wasn't hard to close my eyes and imagine that it was me the CBS commentator was talking about, as opposed to, say, Greg Norman. Ergo, while standing on the twelfth tee having just come off (as they say in America) double bogey at the eleventh, a slight shift in the breeze, and more than a slight leap of imagination, helped me pick up a muffled voice in the distance. 'Marty Jaanson . . . trying to stop the bleeding.' Followed by the summarizer. 'That's what happens when you try and get cute with Amen Corner. That twelfth hole might look innocent, but there isn't a golfer in the field who won't say: "Just take your par and get out of there".' But on the Monday morning after the Masters, the TV towers and the radio booths were all deserted, and the only voice I could hear was that of my caddie. Jimmy was his name, and he told me he'd once carried Doug Ford's bag in the 1976 Masters. Until 1983, the players were not allowed to use their regular caddies, and I asked Jimmy how he and Doug had got on. 'Just terrible,' he said. 'He played awful. Not as bad as you, but just awful.' I must have brought back many unpleasant memories of Doug that day, but was fortunate in that there were no specta-tors, as I could have inflicted quite a few injuries out there.

At least Jimmy was refreshingly honest, unlike Russ, who was caddying for an American journalist in our group, by the name of George. Russ had graduated with honours from the 'have a nice day' school of American sincerity, and his gushing observations when George hit a shot, mostly sideways, bore less relation to the quality of the stroke he'd just witnessed than the size of the tip he was hoping to get. QED for George's golf was the fact that he was seven strokes worse than me at the finish despite a method of playing at least two balls off every tee, and discarding the one he didn't much care for. His opening drive shot sharp left through the pines, and finished on the ninth fairway, but the ball was immediately abandoned in favour of another one, with which he holed out in five. 'Nice five George,' cooed Russ, opting, like his employer, to pretend that the first shot never happened. 'Thanks,' said George.

The rest of the round involved Russ trying to convince George that Augusta was a touch too easy for a man of his talents, and whenever George fouled up it was never his fault. So, when he dunked his ball into Rae's Creek at the thirteenth, it was the result of a capricious change in the wind. It's not, however, an especially difficult course, not off the members' tees at any rate, and it's only the speed of the sloping greens that really get you. I had a three-foot downhill putt at the sixteenth, and Jimmy's instruction was 'Just breathe on it.' So I did, and it caught two-thirds of the hole, spun out sideways, before coming to a brief halt on the left-hand edge. Then it moved imperceptibly, followed by slightly, then a bit more, then a bit more again, and when it finally came to a halt I had a nine-footer coming back. I finally signed for an 86, and thanks to years of listening to proper golfers give their post mortems, knew all the right things to say to the press afterwards. 'I left a few out there, and I couldn't quite get anything going on the back side, but I feel my game's almost where I want it to be at right now, and I just gotta coupla things to work on on the practice ground, and I'm looking to post a decent number tomorrow.' 'Thanks Marty.' 'Thanks guys. Appreciate it.'

St Andrews

There was a time when Tiger Woods viewed the Ryder Cup as an irritating intrusion on his busy schedule, and yet whenever the Deutsche Bank Open came around (a tournament that would otherwise have attracted the kind of audience you'd expect at a County Championship cricket match between Northamptonshire and Derbyshire) he could barely wait to clamber aboard his private jet to Germany. Why? I used to wonder. But once you'd ruled out the possibility of a fondness for sauerkraut, or a preference for having his drink served by cocktail waitresses wearing Bavarian corset dresses, you were left with the inevitable conclusion that it was down to the number of noughts on the cheque. Not for winning, mind you. Just for turning up. And that's how it was with the Alfred Dunhill Cup, which ran from 1985 until 2000 as an international team competition, until the sponsors got fed up with having to entice a country's best players with the promise of a nice fat bung. So they decided to spend just as much money, but this time turn it into a four-day celebrity pro-am, change the name to Dunhill Links, and invite all their pals. Which is why, every October, you can wander around the grey old town of St Andrews and stand a better than even chance of bumping into Hugh Grant, Michael Douglas or Gary Lineker. If indeed you can recognize any of them, invisible as they invariably are dressed up in the kind of gear you'd normally see on the deck of a North Sea trawler. Woolly bobble hats, several layers of turtleneck sweater, and the full set of waterproofs.

The weather for the Dunhill is invariably foul, which is probably no more than you deserve when you decide to organize a golf tournament for Scotland in October, although the weather is not the primary reason that the number of spectators turning up to watch it appear to have made the journey in the back seat of the same taxi. The Scots generally prefer to watch good golfers, as opposed to some barmaid from the Rovers Return hacking away at a gorse bush, and the combination of the weather and the admission fee tends to persuade most of the locals that a bout of pneumonia in return for Bobby Charlton's autograph is probably something they could pass up without a lifetime of regret. It's not much fun for the players, either, especially for some shivering American with a Florida suntan, bent double into an icy Force 9, with a marshal cheerfully assuring him that the weather in Scotland isn't always like this. 'Och no. Ye should try playin' aroond here in January. This is just a gentle wee breeze.' On one of my visits, wandering across the links trying, first, to grip a biro with fingers that had turned a deep shade of purple, and second, to inscribe something into a notebook with all the pages stuck together, Boris Becker suddenly emerged from a sea fret, such a picture of misery that it occurred to me that at least there wasn't much danger of him nipping down to the beach and pinching all the sun beds.

The aforementioned Hugh Grant was out there too, playing with Sam Torrance, and if they were having a good time, they were doing an impressive job of keeping it hidden. Sam had his head buried inside his windcheater, trying to light one of his roll-ups with a lighter when what he really needed was a blowtorch, and as a hunched Hugh muttered and cursed his way through the horizontal rain, he briefly looked as though he was playing one of the witches in the heath scene in *Macbeth*. As Grant lined up a putt, a husband said to his wife: 'He's not as good looking in real life is he?' His spouse appeared to want to say something in reply, disagree perhaps, but her teeth were too busy chattering for any words to come out. Everywhere you went there were celebrities of varying degrees of fame, and one of the bigger galleries – I must have counted as many as half a dozen people – were following Ernie Els and one of his amateur playing companions, Michael Douglas. There was a sizeable delay on one of the tees, during which time Douglas began discussing vacation possibilities. Malibu got a mention, although it was no great surprise that an East Fife timeshare cottage, or a weekend break at Mrs Auchterlonie's B&B, failed to feature on his list of possibilities.

Another feature of the Dunhill is the fact that they occasionally extend invitations to newspapers for one of their journalists to take part, and hopefully write a kind piece about the tournament, which is how I came to find myself arriving at the first of the three venues – Kingsbarns, Carnoustie and St Andrews – to register myself at reception. I was clearly in no danger of being mistaken for anyone famous, and when the girl looked up from her paperwork to see me standing there with the clubs slung over my shoulder, she pointed in some vague direction beyond the tent and said: 'Caddies over there.' My professional partner was a very large Geordie from Ashington, birthplace of Bobby Charlton who was also playing, named Kenneth Ferrie. Kenny was a gruff and genial companion in equal measure, who kept me regularly entertained by his dialogue with marshals when they made a noise on his backswing, but you'd hardly have called him – nor our fellow pro, Rolf Muntz – famous, and it came as something of a surprise when we finally attracted a gallery while waiting to tee-off on one of the par threes. Gallery is perhaps stretching it a bit. Two old ladies to be precise, who were alternately peering at the programme, and then at the group of us standing on the tee. The first old lady finally nudged the other one. 'Well,' she said 'that caddie has "Ferrie" on his bib, and according to this programme he's playing with Martin Johnson.' 'So it says,' came the reply. 'But maybe he couldn't play for some reason, and they had to replace him with someone else.' We were still waiting for the group ahead to clear the green, so I decided to clear up the mystery for them. 'Are you looking for Martin Johnson?' I asked. 'Well yes,' came the reply. 'Then allow me,' I said, taking the programme from the old lady, and producing a biro from my back pocket. 'Shall I sign it to anyone in particular? I've shrunk a bit from my rugby-playing days, and people say I don't look quite as mean in my civvies as I did in a rugger jersey. So I'm not really surprised you didn't recognize me.' They looked, understandably, puzzled, so it was time to reveal that this was not the Martin Johnson they'd been hoping to see. They saw the funny side of it, and we had an amiable chat until it was time to go and commit some atrocity with my golf ball. Curiously, they insisted before I went that I signed their programme anyway.

It was an enjoyable round, apart from the weather, made even more so by Muntz's amateur partner David, a young American, who managed at least one full-blown shank on every hole. Had we had any spectators following us, they'd have assigned a St John Ambulance crew to our match just in case one of David's throat-high sockets flew towards human flesh as opposed to a deep thicket of heather, or the bottom of a burn. After the opening two rounds, at Kingsbarns and then Carnoustie, we ended up on the Saturday at St Andrews and it quickly became clear to me that Kenny, whose mood, depending on the circumstances, was what you might call variable, was not a great fan of the world's most famous golf links, the Old Course. On the first green, he had a ten-foot birdie putt, which was making good progress towards the hole when it hit a bump and skewed off course. 'Bother!' said Kenny, or something similar. The Old Course gets a huge amount of traffic around it, mostly from Japanese and American tourists, and is not remotely in as pristine a condition as professional golfers are accustomed to, so requires a phlegmatic temperament to cope with the occasional putt taking an unkind detour. There are a number of words you could employ to describe Kenny's temperament, but phlegmatic would not be among them, and when his next putt, on the second green, suffered much the same fate as his first, I was neither surprised that Kenny had an opinion on the matter, nor that it turned out to be of a non-complimentary nature.

'Bother,' he said again, or another word to that effect. After which he said it again. Several times. It was then that I remembered the real reason I was out there playing golf – to write a piece for my employer. And as I walked towards the third tee, keeping a safe distance between myself and my by now seriously pissed-off partner, I spotted the chance for a ready-made intro to the story required for tomorrow morning's paper. I closed the gap, chose my moment carefully, and related to Kenny the much-celebrated and highly complementary quote about the course from the American amateur Bobby Jones, on the occasion of his induction as an Honorary Freeman of St Andrews. Whereupon I wondered, in the light of Jones's gushing admiration for the place, whether Kenny might care to proffer his own opinion. Accordingly, I was able to scribble down a reply that more than took care of the opening paragraph for the story I was to compose after we'd finished. Which was: 'If I could take everything out of my life bar my experiences of the Old Course at St Andrews, I would still have had a rich and rewarding life' (Robert Tyre Jones, 1958). 'The place is a total shit-hole' (Kenneth Ferrie, 2003).

I kind of had more of an empathy with Kenny's point of view than Bobby's, especially as it is a hopeless place to either watch or report on golf, but the history of the Old Course at least made playing it an experience not to be missed. I hit the finest shot of my life there, on the par five fourteenth, when I was facing a second shot towards the famous Hell Bunker. 'Ye'll want tae stay oot o' there,' said my caddie. 'Take a six iron.' I pondered his advice, then replied: 'What if I was to hit the fairway wood?' 'Well, if you nailed it, and ye hit it straight' (the way he said it suggested he considered neither very likely) '. . . ye'd be doon in that bunker for sure.' 'In which case,' I said, 'hand me the wood.' And I spanked it right out of the sweet spot, gun-barrel straight, and into the bunker. 'You see,' I said to my caddie as he shook his head sadly. 'That's made my day. I'll probably never play here again, and now I can say I've visited Hell Bunker.' There was disappointment, however, at missing out on the Old Course's most famous bunker of all. After driving off at the seventeenth, I found that my ball had ended up in an ornamental fishpond inside the grounds of the Old Course Hotel, and no sooner had I formulated a plan to roll up my trouser legs – Jean van de Velde style – and attempt to remove the ball (along with a few Koi carp if necessary) than I was told that my ball was out of bounds. Ergo, I was denied the chance of carrying on and hitting it into the Road bunker. It's all about history, really, and being able to say to yourself as you make the descent into the bowels of the world's most famous golf hazard, 'I wonder if I can get out of here in less strokes* than Tommy Nakajima?' I did wonder about briefly pausing on the Swilcan Bridge on the eighteenth fairway, and waving to the crowd as Jack Nicklaus did on his final appearance at the Open, but thought better of it. For a number of reasons, but mostly because there was no one watching to wave to.

* Four, when tied for the lead in the third round of the 1958 Open Championship.

10

THEY THINK IT'S ALL OVER

Tough at the top? Try life at the bottom

Snooker Qualifying, Blackpool

More often than not, when people find out that you report on sport for a living, they will let out an envious sigh, and tell you how lucky you are. And shortly afterwards they'll say: 'So tell me. What are you covering this weekend?' At which point, with no small measure of satisfaction, and very often truthfully, you reply: 'I'm covering Bristol Rovers v Stockport County. It'll be pissing with rain according to the forecast, you wouldn't house your pet dog in the press box, the Wifi is so hopeless you might as well try and send your story by carrier pigeon, and at the end of it you turn up to a press conference to listen to one manager telling you it was definitely a penalty and another manager saying it was never a penalty in a million years, and finally you get back to your car for a five-hour drive and get home at midnight.' It's the same for sports men and women, too.

For every Tiger Woods there's a Hiram Higginbotham III hacking away on the satellite tour for the kind of first prize Woods tips his caddie, and for every Ronnie O'Sullivan there's some young snooker hopeful spending all day long on his own on a practice table trying to become one of not very many players who can make a decent living out of the game. And seldom have I been assigned to report on anything less glamorous than the fourteenth qualifying round of the World Snooker Championship at Blackpool. In January.

Conspicuous by their absence were a television camera, a sponsor's advertisement, an autograph hunter, and a crowd. The venue, the Norbreck Castle Hotel on Blackpool's North Shore, lay three miles along the seafront from the town centre, sandwiched between a petrol station and an endless line of guest houses trying (in vain, judging by the number of 'Vacancy' signs) to seduce passers-by with the promise of en suite facilities, TVs in all rooms, and, for the more luxurious establishments, 'carpets throughout'. It was a large, uniquely unattractive building, just off the seafront, and rendered even uglier by an electrical storm. Rain battered the pavements, waves lashed the beach walls, and the hotel, lit up by lightning flashes, looked like Castle Dracula. It was essential to keep your head down walking down the promenade, not just because of the weather, but to tiptoe in and out of what appeared to be the world's biggest dog lavatory. It was a long way from the bright lights of Sheffield, and the Crucible, in terms of atmosphere at any rate. By round fourteen of the quali-fiers, the competitors were just two matches away from the televised stage of the World Championship, and young thrusters were pitched against old veterans in the bid to get there. Many big names had already been despatched by the new bum-fluff and acne brigade, although one survivor from the wreckage was a former world champion, Joe Johnson, who won in 1986 as a 50 to 1 outsider. Johnson's steady slide down the world rankings had now forced him to try and scrap his way back again at a venue known by the players as Heartbreak Hotel, partly because of its association with shattered hopes, and partly because of its depressing ambience.

One year, another former world champion – Cliff Thorburn – was forced to come to try and qualify at Blackpool, but after peering out at the rain-battered dog walkers through his hotel-room window, he put his cue back in the boot of the car, told the organizers to award his opponent a bye, and drove out of town. The playing area was partitioned into sixteen separate areas, with the players making their entrances through makeshift curtains. You could have made a more dramatic entrance going into an NHS hospital cubicle ('Just take off your clothes and the doctor will be with you shortly . . .') and while there was just about enough space in each for around twenty spectators, I saw no more than half a dozen in any of them. The occasional auntie, a nephew, and other assorted relatives, mostly. If you gazed skywards, which is what snooker players tend to do a lot when their opponent is at the table, the ceiling was pockmarked with holes, and appeared to have seen its last lick of paint when Joe Davis was in his pomp. You watched these players twiddling their bow-ties, sipping their iced water, waiting their turn to pot a few balls and then repair to the practice table, with increasing admiration, realizing that the likes of Davis, Hendry and O'Sullivan must have spent many years flirting with brain death before filling their garages with fast cars.

One thing none of them was required to do when they reached the top was keep their own score, as Johnson was obliged to do when the electronic monitor broke down midway through the first frame of his match against Nick Pearce. The game resumed only when someone in the audience assured the referee that Pearce was leading 34–16, or something close to that. 'Are you sure?' said the ref. 'Fairly sure,' came the reply. 'I think he was up to 31, and he's just potted the green.' And the scores were eventually pegged on the same kind of board used in British Legion clubs on a Sunday lunchtime. 'Do we have to play on like this?' asked Pearce, shortly before a repair man arrived to get the monitor working again. Within seconds, it had turned into a snowstorm, began making strange hissing noises, and had to be turned off again. The referee was so flustered by now that Johnson had to remind him to return the pink he'd just potted from the pocket to the table, and so it went on. You half expected someone to call for the rest and find that either there wasn't one in the rack, or else, just as he was lining up a pot, the end would fall off. The match itself was low on quality, and it wasn't hard to understand why. One man used to the big time, and the other trying to break into it, desperately trying to fire themselves up in the kind of atmosphere you'd normally find inside a dentist's waiting room. When they shook hands at the end, both of them broke into a broad smile, which initially struck me as odd given that Johnson had lost. Then it occurred to me that compared to the pleasure of getting out of Blackpool, the pain of losing wasn't even a contest.

Golf Qualifying, Spain

Sotogrande is a lovely old golf course on the Costa del Sol, and if you don't enjoy a round here there's something wrong with you. Apart, that is, from the occasions it's used to host the European Tour Qualifying School, which, by general consent, represents the nastiest inquisition in Spain since Torquemada: a six-round exercise in human suffering involving, in the year I was there, 168 starters playing for 35 slots on the European Tour for the following season. For the rest, it was a choice between playing for peanuts on the satellite tour, or joining the queue at the Job Centre. There are two kinds of pressure in golf – standing over a putt to win the Masters, and lining one up to win your playing card. Of the two, the latter is comfortably the more nerve-wracking. This is probably why a threesome routinely took longer to complete their round than caterpillars require to turn into butterflies, and in the time it took a Swede by the name of Pehr Magnebrant to work out whether to take on a shot over water or lay up, the builders working on a new villa by the side of the eleventh hole had installed a pair of patio windows.

The pressure also got to an Italian, Alessandro Tadini, who played off scratch in terms of immaculate dress sense, but who possessed a temperament as snappy as his apparel. One duffed chip resulted in a wedge buried so deeply into the turf that his caddie required both hands to retrieve it.

She also happened to be his girlfriend, doubtless working for love rather than pay, although whether the engagement ring would make it past one of Sotogrande's deeper water hazards after six rounds of golf with Alessandro seemed to be open to question. When she wasn't pulling the trolley, informing him how many yards it was to the green, or retrieving buried golf clubs, her main reason for being there was to listen dutifully while her man complained vociferously about things like bunkers getting in the way of his golf ball, and putts turning left when they should have turned right. The fact that she said nothing at all in reply suggested to me that she had, on one early occasion, attempted a 'Yes dear, very bad luck' and been verbally Rottweilered for her pains. This being November, it became pretty chilly once the sun started to dip towards the horizon, and she ended the round huddled beneath a scarf and anorak on the clubhouse terrace while Alessandro practised his putting.

It was a reminder that this event was about as far removed from golf being fun as it is possible to get. Ian Woosnam once put himself through this, and although he earned his card, he ended up eating cold baked beans out of a camper van as he trailed around Europe barely eking out a living, and after three years on the breadline he was close to packing it all in before something finally clicked and he won the Swiss Open. Just a missed putt, or a visit to a water hazard, away from ending up as a plumber in his home town of Oswestry, as opposed to a major champion and a tax exile in Jersey.

Others in the field at Sotogrande had apparently made it to the big time, only to fall back again, and a couple of those who'd been up the ladder and down the snake were Ireland's Philip Walton, who six years earlier had been mobbed on the eighteenth green at Oak Hill after securing the point which won the Ryder Cup for Europe. Then there was England's Paul Broadhurst, who ten years before had been on Europe's Ryder Cup team at Kiawah Island, for the so-called War on the Shore, winning both his matches – in the fourballs in partnership with Woosnam, and in the final afternoon singles against Mark O'Meara. And another golfer who'd somehow gone from destined to become famous to suddenly having lost the plot was Hampshire's Steven Richardson, who'd been at Kiawah with Broadhurst, winning two and losing two of his four matches. An extremely personable bloke, and a one-time winner of half a million pounds in a season, Richardson had apparently put it all in a savings account in case he needed it for a rainy day, and it had been chucking it down ever since. Apart from playing in one of the most raucous Ryder Cups of all time, Richardson had the same year finished fifth behind John Daly in the US PGA at Winged Foot. Here, though, I watched him hole a long putt at the second hole of his opening round for a birdie to the accompaniment of a couple of barking dogs, the distant squawk of a nesting green parrot, and the irritating buzz of a workman's drill plumbing yet another bidet into one of the luxury fairway villas. Richardson knew more than most about Qualifying School, having won his playing card in each of the previous three years, only to find himself back again in the winter for yet another attempt. Richardson's caddie was the teaching professional at the Portsmouth Golf Club, who had been working with him for the previous eighteen months in an effort to recapture whatever it was that made him appear destined for a long and lucrative career. However, as Ian Baker-Finch had reminded us in the previous year's Open Championship, when he missed the widest fairway in golf by such a margin that his ball almost got served up as a boiled egg in the Russack's Hotel, there is rarely such a thing as a swing for life, and Richardson's had somehow gone AWOL. And his week at Sotogrande was destined to end in tears when, requiring just a par four on the last of his 104 holes to be absolutely certain of a place in the top thirty-five, he took five. He then had to wait three hours for the rest of the field to finish, and when the final threesome was done, so too was Richardson. By one miserable stroke.

Walton also failed, as did Broadhurst, who said afterwards: 'I'll enjoy Christmas, and then get on with the rest of my life. Whatever that might involve.' 'Are you thinking of trying something else then?' he was asked. 'Might have to,' replied Broadhurst, still suffering from the emotional damage of blowing any chance he had with a final round of 77. There was also some physical damage to report, and the only card Alberto Binaghi of Italy ended up qualifying for after his own failure was a blood donor's. He was minding his own business waiting to play on an adjacent hole when a wild tee shot from one of Broadhurst's playing partners, a Frenchman, struck him straight between the shoulder blades. He went down as if hit by a sniper, and when the perpetrator arrived to apologize, Binaghi had not only recovered enough to speak, but turned out to be fluent in French. I couldn't get the gist of what Alberto was saying, but from the purple shade of his cheeks, and the tone of his voice, it appeared to be something a good deal less conciliatory than 'Don't worry about it old chap. These things happen.' Broadhurst's other playing partner was an Italian, whose caddie rather summed it all up by saying: 'It 'as been, 'ow you say, one of those days.'

Broadhurst himself began to lose heart on his sixth hole, when he failed to come out first time from a fairway bunker. A bogey was the result, and after his caddie tried to lift him with a cheery 'Never mind, we can make a birdie at the par five', Broadhurst's expression suggested it was not a view he necessarily shared. 'He's just not a confident player,' the caddie muttered to me walking down the next hole. 'Doing his yardages is the easy bit. I spend most of my time trying to talk positive to him.' However, after the ninth hole, when his man made two visits to the water en route to a triple-bogey seven, his caddie recognized the futility of continuing his cheerleader role, and the last hour of the round was played out in more or less total silence. He did make one last attempt at light-hearted banter as the pair of them sat on a wall waiting for the group in front. 'Blimey,' he said, as something large and black scuttled past. 'Have you seen the size of those Spanish beetles?' To which Broadhurst replied, without even lifting his head or opening his eyes, 'Mmmmmmmmm.' But by the final hole, with all hope of qualification gone, it was as if a huge burden had been lifted from all three of them. The Frenchman began smiling, the Italian chatted enthusiastically about Inter Milan, and when Broadhurst duffed his final approach shot into a bunker he shouted: 'Perfect!' And they all fell about laughing. They might have failed the exam, but at last it was all over.

11

OFF THE BEATEN TRACK

*Murder mystery on Norfolk Island . . . To the Orient
(not Leyton) with Beckham . . . Tomaszewski, the
Klaun Prince of Poland*

I was covering an England cricket tour in New Zealand
when the sports editor phoned and asked me if I wouldn't
mind stopping off on the way home when it was all over.
It's a long old journey, and breaking it up seemed not a
bad idea. 'There's a place called Norfork Island,' he said.
'It's somewhere in the Pacific. Population 1,800, nearly
all of them related to the HMS *Bounty* mutineers, and
they're sending a team to the Commonwealth Games in
Manchester. Might be interesting.' There were countries
taking part in the Manchester Games, such as Canada and
Australia, that took three days to cross by train, but this
country was so small that you could run round its entire
coastline and still not have gone far enough to complete a
marathon. In short, Norfolk Island was such a pinprick in
the ocean that if Captain Cook's lookout had nodded off

for ten minutes during the explorer's second South Pacific expedition in 1774, there might still be nothing there but parrots and penguins. But by the time I got there, they had not been able to hold back the remorseless tide of man-made progress, and traffic congestion had become so bad that they'd just been forced to put in a round-about. Mind you, cattle still had right of way over the horseless carriage, and my inquiry as to whether they had plans to add to the island's single streetlamp met with a resounding negative.

A semi-autonomous external territory of Australia, Norfolk Island measures five miles by three, and one of the slimmer books on the island was the telephone directory. Which, with nearly everyone related in some form or other to the *Bounty* mutineers, is full of entries for Christian, or Quintal. The mutineers were brought here when Pitcairn Island became too crowded, and like most prisons at the time, conditions were a tad harsher than you'd find in an episode of *Porridge*. One escaped convict hid in the trunk of one of the island's tall pines for seven years, until he was eventually found and hanged. His name, Barney Duffey, lives on, and the table mats at the Barney Duffey Charcoal Grill gave you a potted history of his miserable existence. The Grill, like most of the island restaurants, opened at 6pm, and calls last orders at 7.30pm. My first appointment was with the island's Commonwealth Games team manager Tom Lloyd, who also edited and printed the local weekly newspaper, the *Norfolk Islander*, in a small shed at the bottom of his garden. Tom showed me a few back copies to give me some idea of the racy nature of life on the island, with front-page headlines varying from 'Points from the Chief Minister's Radio Talk' to 'The New Marquee is Here'.

Normally, the island was so bereft of crime that the safest place to leave your car keys was in the ignition, but shortly before I got there the place had been shocked by its first murder since 1893. A twenty-nine-year-old local woman had been stabbed, a crime which eventually ended with an Australian chef, who'd been working on the island at the time, being convicted and sentenced to twenty-four years by a court in Sydney five years later. The investigation was led by detectives flown over from Australia, given that the island was a bit like Dixon of Dock Green land, where the local police rarely got involved in anything more serious than some motorist going the wrong way round the new roundabout, or noise complaints about a restaurant staying open beyond 8pm. The reason it took so long to apprehend the villain may have had something to do with communications not significantly more sophisticated than the ship's telegraph which nabbed Dr Crippen, and down at the island's telephone exchange, calls were still being put through a switchboard operator pulling coloured plugs in and out of one of those old solitaire boards. I wondered whether news of the island's only previous Commonwealth Games medal – a bronze in the women's individual bowls in Canada in 1994 – might have arrived via a note in a bottle bobbing onto one of the beaches.

Tourism was the island's main source of revenue, although there were two ways of telling an islander from a visitor. The first was the unique language derived from the *Bounty* mutineers' intermarriage with the women of Tahiti, and the second the locals' remarkable courtesy to strangers.

So much so that if the ancestors of these people got upset enough to cast Captain Bligh adrift in a boat, you leaned towards the feeling that the tyrannical old sea dog probably deserved it. The first competitors I met were Jamie Donaldson, who'd entered for the marathon, and his father Graeme, who was in the triathlon. Jamie, a twenty-three-year-old trainee chef, had never been off the island before, but revealed that he'd heard that Manchester had quite a good football team, and was a very pretty town. Which left me able to inform him that he'd got it exactly half right. Jamie's coach, Brentt Jones, was competing himself as a hammer thrower, and was descended from the mutineer Matthew Quintal. Brentt thought that Jamie had more chance of doing well than he did, but he hoped to have 'a good time, at least'. He wondered what clothing to pack for Manchester, and hoped he wouldn't have to spend too much. In which case, when he confirmed that he already owned a Macintosh and an umbrella, I was able to reassure him that no extra spending would be required.

Milton Bradley was the island's clay pigeon representative, and unlike most of the team, he had been to the UK before, working briefly in Poole in the early 1970s. 'I love the pubs over there,' he said, 'and I can still remember the names of some of them. Is the George Inn still going? It's on the quay in Weymouth. I used to drink Double Diamond in there.' The *chef de mission*, Dan Yager, another descendant of Quintal, revealed that the grant to get to Manchester was nothing like enough for the twenty-five-strong team, and that they'd be raising the extra through coffee mornings and garden parties. 'For most of the team,' said Dan, 'it will be the holiday of a lifetime as well as a sporting event.' I'd not visited many places as picturesque as Norfolk Island, and I wondered quite how a trip to the Arndale Shopping Centre in a thick drizzle would fit into the description of a holiday of a lifetime. In fact, I found myself thinking that, if their forefathers had known it would all have ended up in a trip to Manchester, it would have been Fletcher Christian in the rowing boat rather than Captain Bligh.[†]

When you're eating out in a country in which you don't fully understand the menu, you never really know what you're going to end up with, although my pidgin Spanish did once result in a bit of a triumph when me and my photographer, Frank, were on a football assignment in the Basque capital of Vitoria. The Spanish like to eat late, as we'd discovered the previous evening when we popped our heads round the door of a fish restaurant to ask what time they finished serving. Three o'clock was the answer, whereupon my look of surprise must have suggested to the patron that this might not be late enough for us. 'Please, no to worry,' he said, clocking my expression. 'Three o'clock ees when chef, he go home. After this, my wife cook. No problem.' I didn't think it odd, therefore, when we sat down to eat at around 8pm the following night – to fit in with the flight home – to find the restaurant otherwise deserted. The menu had no English translation, and because I knew six more words of Spanish than Frank – '*por favor*', '*dos cervezas*', and '*muchas gracias*' – I was

---

[†]*(Footnote: Thirty-nine countries won medals at the Games, but Norfolk Island wasn't among them.)*

in charge of ordering. The head waiter would appear at regular intervals, and each time, still trying to decipher what was what, I waved him away. Finally I gave him an exasperated: 'Please – *dos minutos*', at which point he broke out into a broad grin, snatched away the menu, and strode off towards the kitchen. 'What's all that about?' asked Frank. 'Beats me,' I said. 'I just told him to give us another couple of minutes, and off he went.' Soon after, he came back with a basket of bread, two bowls of soup, and a bottle of red wine, which Frank, not unreasonably, wanted to know whether I'd ordered. 'Two minutes,' is what I said, I told him, 'but the soup looks okay, and it might just be best to go with the flow.' So we did. Two plates of something else appeared, then two more plates, two more, and so on until the cheese and biscuits arrived. 'Bloody hell,' said Frank as we shook hands with the beaming *maître d'* and left to hail a taxi. 'Best meal I've had in months. You're a genius.' I never did find out what had happened, although one of my brothers, who speaks Spanish pretty well, did hazard a guess that the waiter might have thought I was ordering a set menu for two. Whereby 'dos minutos' might have become: 'Dos. Menus Dos.'

Still, at least I tried, as did David Beckham when he went to Real Madrid, giving his final press conference before leaving them for America, in Spanish. Or at least an attempt at it. I drew the line, though, at trying to order dinner in Chinese, as I imagine Beckham himself would have done when in Beijing for his first appearance as a Real player on the club's pre-season tour to the Far East. We had a local guide to interpret for us on our first night out in the Chinese capital, which was just as well given what we might have ended up eating. On our first night there, sitting at a pavement table having an al fresco beer, a street hawker wandered by with an interesting choice of snacks. To the first inquiry of 'What the bloody hell is that?' our guide informed us that it was sheep's intestine. Raw sheep's intestine. The next offering turned out to be boiled ox penis, and the next, fried scorpion on a stick. And so on. I later discovered, to no great surprise, that Real had brought their own chef with them.

Next day, when Real paraded Beckham at a press conference in the Great Banqueting Hall at the Beijing Hotel, the crowds outside were bigger than the daily hordes flocking to see Mao Tse-Tung lying under his glass bubble in Tiananmen Square. Those who managed to get a gawk at both possibly concluded that, of the two, Mao had the greater range of expression, although Beckham's blank stare might have had something to do with not having the faintest idea of what was going on or who was saying what. A dead ringer for Bert Kwouk, who used to play Inspector Clouseau's Chinese servant Cato, chuntered on about something or other for what seemed like several days, and it was a good effort for Becks to at least appear to be interested in what he might be saying. Some of his team-mates up there on the stage were able to pass the time with some giggly whispering, but with Beckham still on the 'Buenos dias, señor' section of his Spanish phrase book, this particular avenue of passing the time was denied to him. The only part of proceedings which broke through the language barrier was when the captain of Madrid exchanged shirts with the captain of the Chinese XI they were playing in the opening match, after which all the players got up and left. 'I thought,' said one of the English journalists to our appointed media guide, 'that this was supposed to be a press conference.' He nodded. 'Yes. Press conference.' 'But we never got to ask any questions,' the hack protested. 'Yes,' replied the guide. 'Correct. No questions allowed.' The Great Helmsman, as Mao was known, would definitely have approved of a press conference with no questions.

Never mind, at least the schedule included the Real players visiting the Forbidden City after the non-press conference, but with thousands waiting for the Madrid team bus to decant their heroes, word came through that the trip had been cancelled. Maybe it was fortunate that Becks was confined to barracks, given that everywhere a Westerner walked in Beijing, they were approached by a local asking if they could practise their English. Just imagine how many years of diligent study could have been destroyed by a few minutes' exposure to English as wot she is spoke. A twentyish-year-old student who approached me was already impressively advanced with his English, in that within two minutes of my asking: 'All this Forbidden City stuff has made me thirsty; where can I get a beer?' he'd escorted me unerringly to a local bar. 'Try the food,' he said when we sat down, which, to my later regret, I did.

Twenty-four hours later we were in Tokyo for the next leg of the tour, and for the first twenty-four hours of arriving in Japan I was either in the bathroom or in a local clinic being rehydrated with a saline drip. By the time I was well enough to be allowed back to the hotel, armed with enough potions and pills to open my own branch of Boots, I was handed the bill in a plain white envelope, and fully expected, upon opening it, my next medication to involve a liberal dose of smelling salts. This was based around the earlier discovery that the hotel's charge for a cup of coffee – that sump oil variety that sits around on a hot plate all day – was something close to a tenner. So it came as a pleasant surprise – especially given that at one stage I had no less than three nurses allocated to my recovery – to find that the total came to forty quid. Or if you prefer, four cups of hotel coffee.

I hadn't missed anything, as it happened, as Beckham had apparently checked into his room and remained there. Sensible chap, I thought, given that the hotel in Bejing had been surrounded by thousands of hysterical worshippers, hoping perhaps that their hero might just for a second draw back his bedroom curtains and give them a glimpse of pony-tail. I wondered whether Johnny Haynes got this kind of treatment when Fulham went on a pre-season tour of Rochdale, or wherever. No one was actually there for the football, merely for a marketing exercise designed to flood the Orient with billions of replica shirts.

When the players finally broke free of their hotel rooms for a practice session at the Tokyo Dome, no less than 50,000 people turned up. For the match the following evening, against FC Tokyo, Beckham showed the full range of his versatility, playing for the first half with his hair down, and taking advantage of the fifteen-minute interval to return after half-time wearing a pony-tail. Once upon a time a footballer was given half an orange and a cup of tea at half-time. Nowadays, he gets to spend it having a cut, wash and blow-dry. Every time Becks got the ball, the crowd cheered, so when he actually scored a goal, something close to bedlam broke out. It was a trademark one at that, curling a free kick from the corner of the penalty area around what neither in Japan, nor back in China, could be described as a great wall. He even managed to get himself booked for tripping an opponent, but the suspicion that Beckham had more or less taken over from the Emperor in the deity stakes was confirmed when the final whistle blew on a rain-swept night, and a Japanese official ran on to escort him off underneath an umbrella. The pop-star treatment in Japan was, in many ways, even more pronounced than it had been in China, and you wondered when Beckhamania in this part of the world would all end. A bit like persuading the last Japanese soldier that the Second World War was actually over, maybe, thirty years on, someone would take to the streets with a loud hailer and declare: 'You can come out now. He's totally bald, and managing Rushden and Diamonds.'

Even by Brian Clough's standards, it was a remarkable performance. At half-time, with England needed to beat Poland at Wembley in 1973 to qualify for the World Cup finals, and unable to find a way past the human octopus in the visiting goal, millions of frustrated viewers were informed: 'Sit back. Relax. The goals will come. The goalkeeper's a clown.' Then, at full time, after the draw that finished Sir Alf Ramsey's managerial career: 'Don't blame Alf! Blame me. Blame yourselves. Alf's not to blame! We're to blame! You're to blame!' A mate of mine recalls that his mother was doing some ironing at the time, and looked up to say: 'What's he on about: I'm to blame? What's it got to do with me?' It was as deranged a performance as Clough ever managed in front of the television cameras, and Lord knows he provided some stiff competition down the years. England were out after a 1–1 draw, the only goal put past the Polish goalie coming from the penalty spot, and with the programme's closing credits rolling, Clough was still calling Jan Tomaszewski a 'clown'. Although if anyone should have been wearing a red nose that night it was the then Derby County manager.

More than a quarter of a century later, I travelled to the clown's house in Poland to ask him about that night. He was then into his fifties, living modestly – the route to his house was strewn with graffiti-filled walls – in the industrial town of Lodz, around seventy miles south of Warsaw. I'd often wondered about Tomaszewski's performance that night at Wembley, and hadn't seen it since, so I was delighted when he offered to put the video on. He got up from his chair, opened a drawer and scratched his head. 'Ah yes,' he said. 'I remember, now. One of my friends has borrowed it. Sorry.' One of his friends, he said, was always borrowing it. Clough's assessment of his performance that night had caused almost as big a stir in Poland as in England, and the nickname had stuck. The 'klaun', as he was known (affectionately) in his own country, only met Clough once, about eight years later, when they were both in a Manchester TV studio to judge a save-of-the-season competition. 'He apologized to me,' said Tomaszewski, 'which is the sign of a big man. I told him I understood why he said what he did, because some of my saves were theoretically impossible. It's funny. England had beaten Austria 7–0 in the game before, and everyone thought it was just a matter of how many they would score. But football isn't always like that. In basketball, if you have the better team, you will win even if you are all drunk. But in football, anything is possible. It's like having a fire in your house. You find yourself doing things you wouldn't normally do. There was a fire in our house that night and we ran in and saved all the furniture.' Not to mention the kitchen sink.

In the ITV post mortem, Brian Moore, the presenter, speculated that the England goalkeeper Peter Shilton's concession of a soft goal might have been down to losing concentration as he'd had so little to do. Clough retorted: 'Brian, he'd have caught it in his teeth if it had been that clown at the other end.' Moore: 'Brian, you keep calling him a clown, but that fellow has made some fantastic saves and . . .' Clough: 'No he hasn't. No he *hasn't!*' foamed Clough. 'I never wanted to be a goalkeeper,' said Tomaszewski. 'I wanted to be up front scoring goals. But I was a big lad at school, and big lads nearly always are told to go into goal.' Like most of the leading Polish players, he had to go abroad to earn anything more than modest wages, and ended his career playing in Spain and Belgium. He only had one brief and unsuccessful dabble in management at his old club LKW Lodz. He will, though, always have that recording of Wembley 1973 – as long as he remembers which one of his chums he's lent it to.

12

WORLD SERIES OF POKER

From Happy Families . . . to taking on the high rollers
for a million quid

The online gambling firm Betfair were assembling a team for the first ever World Series of Poker event to be held in Europe, and they wanted me on it. Presumably for the publicity rather than to beef up their chances of winning, as what I knew about poker could have been accommodated on a fairly small postage stamp. Also, this was Texas Hold 'Em poker rather than the five card draw variety, or three card brag I occasionally played with a group of chums on a Friday night, when my presence at the table was desired not so much for my scintillating conversation as for the fact that the others could be reasonably confident of a large dona-tion towards their weekend drinks bill down at the pub. Apparently, I was incapable of not smiling when I had a good hand, and because I didn't know how to bluff, every time I did have a good hand the rest of them chucked their cards in. I warned the sports editor not to allocate too much space to the story, as I was pretty confident I wouldn't be at the table long enough to gather a lot of material. Betfair had stumped up £10,000 in stake money in a tournament with an estimated prize pool of seven million pounds, and their PR man was keen to hear about my gambling experience. I was able to reassure him that when it came to keeping cool under pressure then I was his man. 'You can't get stakes much higher than playing against your two brothers for who does the washing-up after dinner,' I told him. 'No such thing as dishwashers in those days. And no one ever accused me of dithering when it came to putting an extra house on Old Kent Road, or buying up Marylebone Street Station.' However, despite what I considered to be impeccable references, he didn't seem over-impressed. 'Listen, there are over three hundred and fifty players taking part, many of them full-time pros with millions of dollars in career earnings. Is that the extent of it? A game of Monopoly with the washing-up at stake?' 'Well no, not quite,' I said. 'I've had my moments at Ludo as well. And let me tell you this. These people may all be hardbitten pros, but how many of them will ever have peered through their dark glasses trying to work out an opponent who once went an entire evening – thanks to some judicious play involving Master Bun the Baker's Son – unbeaten at Happy Families.'

Finally, I was forced to confess that I had never, not even once, played Texas Hold 'Em Poker, whereupon he decided to secure some expert tuition for me in the shape of one of the UK's top pros, Ben Grundy. 'I know a bit about stud poker from watching Edward G. Robinson and Steve McQueen in *The Cincinnati Kid*,' I told Ben when he phoned me at home. 'Er, yes, well, better than nothing I guess,' he replied, 'but I really think we should get you into an online game, and I can give you some coaching.' So with Betfair having signed me up to some poker site or other, and given me some stake money to get me into a game, I found myself pitting my wits – or to be more accurate Ben's wits – against fifty-three other online players in a game with a £10 entry fee.

My brief was to tell Ben what cards I'd been dealt, what the others were betting, and whether or not to check, fold or raise. Occasionally, me having picked up a pair of kings, Ben would say: 'From the way the betting's gone I reckon he might have got something like pocket jacks, so re-raise him.' And more often than not, Ben had correctly worked out what cards my opponent was holding. I didn't really understand most of it, but in a game lasting about half an hour, I ended up finishing third and winning a few extra quid for my account. Ben signed off with a cheery 'Good luck', delivered in a way which suggested I'd need plenty of it, and left me with a few internet links for some extra tuition. However, I didn't find it easy trying to get to grips with tips like: 'If you have a suited connector, you are hoping there are enough callers and dead money in the pot to justify drawing to the straight or flush.' Whatever that meant. So I thought it would be more useful getting to work on the kind of thing my brain was better able to cope with, such as whether or not to wear shades. 'Up to you,' said Ben. 'I sometimes wear them myself, if I think an opponent can get a reading from looking into my eyes.' I recalled the old three card brag evenings, and my unfortunate propensity for my mouth to fall open in astonished delight whenever a good hand was dealt to me, and asked Ben whether a bag over my head, with just a few small slits to see and breathe through, would be acceptable attire, but he thought on the whole perhaps not. He also told me that while any fool could win a short game of poker, over the longer haul they'll lose every time – the widely held belief being that poker was roughly 30 per cent luck, and 70 per cent skill. Which is why, for a tournament scheduled to last for seven days, I didn't pack too many spare shirts.

I've stayed in some fancy hotels before, but when I arrived in central London to take up my Betfair-sponsored accommodation, I found myself checking into a room costing £1,000 a night, in which everything was con-trolled electronically. Including the bed. It was roughly nine feet wide, and I amused myself for about half an hour by fiddling with the remote and having it glide around the room like Fred Astaire. Then I had a shower in one bathroom, and, just because I could, had a bath in the other. There were four television sets, including one you could watch from the bath, and two enormous baskets of fruit, which, to my minor disappointment, I was unable to move around with a remote control. I went down for dinner, and after initially ordering a half-bottle of red with my meal on the grounds that I needed to be at my sharp-est for the opening day's play, I called the waiter back to change it to a full bottle on the grounds that a clear head wasn't going to make the slightest difference, so I might as well enjoy what threatened to be a single night's stay. I closed my eyes to the sensation of the ceiling spinning round, which I initially put down to the wine. However, I then realized that I'd left the remote on the pillow, and when I put my head down, it had sent the bed off on yet another foxtrot around the room.

Next morning, realizing that high-stakes poker was all about making the big move at the right time, I took a long hard stare at the bathroom mirror. To shave? Or not to shave? I decided to leave the razor in the washbag, but realizing that it's not much use looking mean and stubbly if the eyes are giving the game away, went 'all-in', as they say in poker, and slipped on the designer sunglasses to complement the whiskers. It was a simple enough piece of reasoning. When your only previous experience of moving chips around is when they're preventing you from getting the vinegar onto your battered cod its best to look the part, even if you've no real idea what you're doing. There were so many tables to fill in the early rounds that three separate venues were required, my own being at the Empire Casino in Leicester Square. I turned up, signed in, and the Betfair man told me I'd been assigned to table 12. I asked him whether you were supposed to stay quiet during a hand, and he replied: 'There's no hard and fast etiquette. Some talk, and some don't.' And after three hands, none of which I'd taken part in, the chap on my left decided to talk. 'Listen, buddy,' he said, 'because I'm only going to say this once. I've seen all three of your hands so far, and if you want to show me your cards every time, you won't be here for very much longer.'

The voice, I learned later, belonged to an American professional player by the name of Phil Gordon, and an author of several instructional books and DVDs on Texas Hold 'Em. But not even Phil had thought it necessary to include in lesson one the advice: 'Try not to let everyone at the table see what cards you've got in your hand.' The chap on my right, a Swede by the name of Erik, was a little more sympathetic, and gave me a quick lesson. Apparently my method of examining my hand was the equivalent of leaving your credit card lying around complete with pin number, and Erik taught me how to turn up the tiniest corner of the card and crane your neck downwards for a brief squint. Advice duly taken, I flicked up the corners on the next two cards and saw Ace–Queen, which even I knew to be a decent hand, and pretty soon half my chips were out there in the middle. Eventually, with just two of us left, we both turned our cards face up, and my opponent had Queen–Four. Which was, as it turned out, precisely what I had as well. When you're in squinting mode, the corner of a Four looks pretty similar to the corner of an Ace, I discovered. We shared what was called a 'split' pot, and I actually made a few bob. Phil gave me the kind of look which suggested he wasn't quite sure whether he was up against a bold adventurer or a congenital idiot.

Ben's last piece of advice to me after the telephone lesson was 'Don't play a hand at all until you've had a good look at what the other players are doing', so after the next deal, despite having a pair of Eights, I folded. 'Hey, whadya wanna fold for?' said a player opposite. 'You could have just checked.' I thought of giving him a cold stare. And possibly the hint of a knowing smile. Just to let him know that if he'd never seen someone throw in a hand when it would have cost him nothing to stay in it, he had now. And he'd better be worried. The puzzled opponent turned out to be another American pro, Kirk Morrison, and what with throwing in a hand when I didn't have to, showing the player next to me my cards, and several times having to ask the dealer how many chips I needed when the betting got around to me, Kirk put two and two together. 'Hey, I read a piece in a newspaper this morning about some journalist who'd never played before. Are you that guy?' I confirmed that I was. 'Well, good luck,' said Kirk. 'Just play your natural game.' Before adding with a chuckle: 'On second thoughts, maybe best not to play your natural game.'

I had begun with a pile of 20,000 chips (paid for with Betfair's £10,000) and amazingly enough, by the end of the three sessions on day one, I had somehow not only survived to play another day, but increased my chip stack slightly to around 22,000. The theory about the game being 30 per cent luck and 70 per cent skill might, I thought, have to be reappraised, especially after an oldish man in a Stetson wandered past our table and said to Phil, 'Twenty minutes, and I'm busted out of here.' 'Amazing,' said Phil, to the table in general. 'Who would have thought it?' 'Do you know that chap?' I asked him. Phil gave me another of those looks. 'Know him? Everyone knows Doyle Brunson. He's called the Godfather. Got eleven bracelets.' At the first interval, back in the Betfair lounge, I inquired about the bracelets, wondering whether I should have worn one instead of the sunglasses. 'You don't wear them; you win them,' someone said. 'Apart from the money, that's what you get for winning. An inscribed bracelet. And Doyle Brunson's won eleven of them.' But Doyle Brunson was out of there, I thought. So too was Phil, and I was slightly disappointed to learn he'd already left the building before I could ask him if he'd be interested in buying one of my instructional DVDs. 'It's called *Texas Show 'Em Phil*, I badly wanted to tell him. Always let your opponent know what you've got in your hand. A couple of viewings of this and I guarantee you'll at least last longer than the first day.'

Surviving for the whole day was almost as surprising as discovering how tiring poker can be – having to concentrate through four two-hour sessions, and in my own case using up double the mental energy of anyone else by basically not knowing what was going on around me. I'd by now lost count of the times the silence had been broken by someone looking at me and saying: 'Well, you going to just sit there, or do something?' And me replying: 'Oh, sorry, is it me? Er, how much is it to call?' By the end of the day I was even too tired to play silly buggers with the electric bed, and I was grateful for the following day being a rest day before getting back to the tables for the next round.

Some of my play, I had to report back to the office, was beginning to attract serious interest from the other players, not least when I mentally destroyed an American early in the opening session. With two turns remaining, he had two chances to make a flush, and apparently I was being totally dim by calling his extremely large bet. When his flush cards didn't appear, and he snorted: 'What did you think I had in my hand man?' I was able to tell him perfectly truthfully that not only did I have no idea what was in his hand, I didn't have much of a clue as to what was in my own either. His mood was already a touch on the dark side, and this comment did not do much to lighten it – neither indeed did the sight of the dealer shovelling a large pile of chips over in my direction. The next top poker player to feel the pain of being outplayed by a half-wit (although by now no one was entirely sure whether it was someone pretending to be a halfwit) was a Norwegian by the name of Johnny Lodden. He was a big enough name to be referred to in the online tournament report as the 'famous online player', and had placed so many chips in the middle with one turnover remaining that it required all of my own chips to see the final card. He was showing two pairs to my Ace high, but when the last card was turned, it gave me a club flush. Lodden shot out of his seat as though someone had just shoved 10,000 volts through it, made a kind of howling noise, and beat his head against his hands. Once again a dumb bet, or so I was told, had won the money.

After twelve hours at the table I had 92,000 in chips and was lying seventh out of 362 first-day starters, and was even beginning to learn some of the jargon. An American by the name of Jamie Gold said to me after one hand, 'I wasn't sure whether you had a flush draw or a set.' 'What's a set?' I asked. 'You're having me on, right?' he said. 'No, really, I'm not,' I replied. 'It's three of a kind,' he sighed. At the end of the day, I'd gone a fair way backwards, but was still there after sixteen hours of poker, and ready for anyone wanting to have a conversation about sets. I was even beginning to think about a nickname – Godfather II perhaps. I stepped out into the night, or early morning, with an Irishman called Brendan, who said: 'I've played with you off and on for two days, and I have no idea what you have in your hand. Everyone's scared to play with you.' It was neither meant as a criticism nor a compliment, merely a confirmation that poker players don't feel comfortable against opponents they can't read.

I'd realized this after the opening day, when a faintly ludicrous-looking middle-aged man wearing 1950s rocker gear was being interviewed by a TV crew. He also had a ludicrous stage name, 'Devilfish', and he was fuming about being knocked out of the tournament by inferior and incompetent poker players. 'I tell you man, as soon as I looked round that table I knew I was in trouble. Amateurs, all amateurs. Spare me from those guys. If *they* don't know what the hell they're doin', *I* sure as hell don't. If I'd been on a table full of pros, I'd still be here now. Jeez man. Amateurs.' Listening to this perked me up quite a bit. Partly because it's always amusing listening to a bad loser, but also because it confirmed I was the one kind of poker player that everyone feared. The one who hadn't the faintest idea of how to play the game.

Next day, I found myself sitting next to a more or less expressionless young Oriental plugged into an Ipod. I picked up a pair of Jacks, found myself going head to head with him, and when I went all-in, he folded. He stared at me for quite a while as I arranged my chips into different-coloured piles. 'I wasn't going to call against pocket Kings,' he said. I looked at him, and said: 'Sorry, were you talking to me?' 'You had pocket Kings, right?' I hadn't really exchanged more than a few words here and there in the entire time I'd been playing, so a conversation was more than welcome. 'If,' I said, 'you're thinking I had a pair of something, you'd be right.' 'Yeah, Kings for sure,' he said. 'If you think so,' I said. 'I know so,' he said. 'What if I told you I had a pair of Jacks?' I said. 'C'mon man,' he said. 'I know you had Kings.' 'Actually, I had Jacks,' I said. He smiled, albeit not with a great deal of warmth, and said: 'I think you may not be telling the truth.'

I looked him in the eye and wondered, given that he looked mean enough to have been an enforcer for one of those Triad gangs, whether it was a good idea to upset him. But, by now, I was a dyed-in-the-wool gambler. 'It was,' I said, 'Jacks.' Pause for effect before adding: 'As you could have seen for yourself had you been brave enough to pay for the privilege. But as it is,' I removed my shades to show him who he was dealing with, 'you'll just have to take my word for it.' All of a sudden, the air turned a little chilly. 'Man,' he said, 'now you've got me on tilt.' The guy on my left let out a quiet chuckle, which gave me the chance to ask him what my new Oriental chum was on about. 'Tilt?' I whispered. 'What's he mean by tilt?' He spoke, as many players in the tournament did, in a flat monotone, with neither eye contact nor change of expression. 'He's letting you know that you've upset him,' he said, which was precisely what I'd been hoping to hear. Soon afterwards I picked up a pair of Nines, and we were at it once more. The flop turned up an Ace and two smaller cards, and I decided to shove some chips into the middle. He folded. 'You paired the Ace, right?' 'No, I had two Nines.' 'You're lying again man. How could you bet without the Ace?' I looked at him with what I hoped was an expression that told him he was beginning to get up my pipe. 'I can tell you precisely why I bet without the Ace,' I said. 'It's because I'm stupid.' He gave me another of those Medusa-type stares, before deciding upon another line of inquiry. 'You play on the internet?' he asked. 'No,' I said.

'Tournaments, then?' 'No, never played a tournament before this one,' I replied. 'I get it. A cash player.' 'No.' 'Listen my friend,' he said, 'you've got to be one of those.' 'No, really, I'm not,' I said. 'I actually don't play at all. Unless you count playing for matchsticks at Christmas.' He pondered this information for a while, before breaking into a smile for the first time. 'Hey!' he beamed. 'Good joke. I'm beginning to like you.'

By now, I was two sessions into my third day at the table, and, amazingly, was one of only forty-six players left. At the break, I bumped into Kirk, the American from day one who'd been unfailingly kind when I accidentally kept infringing the various forms of etiquette. He'd been eliminated, but was sticking around for the rest of the tournament, and wanted to offer me a few tips. 'These are mean guys that are left, and I don't want them to run you over. The top thirty-six all get paid, and you're nearly there.' I told him about the Oriental, and how we were getting on famously. 'Oh no!' said Kirk. 'That's Kenny Tran. You don't mess with him. Just don't talk to him. Don't say anything to him at all, you hear? He's trying to get a read on you, and if you've got him as baffled as you got me on the first day – and it sounds as though you have – we want to keep it that way.' It sounded like a smart piece of coaching, but it was one I found impossible to pull off. Soon after the interval, everyone folded after the deal bar me and Kenny, who promptly bet 5,000. I had King–Five, unsuited, which even I could work out by now was pretty useless, but something told me to at least pay to see the next three cards. None of them helped, but I just had this nagging feeling that Kenny had an overwhelming urge to nail me, and wasn't necessarily prepared to wait for a big hand. So I stayed with him until all five table cards were showing, and he bet 10,000. I called with nothing, when the smart play, apparently, would have been to raise and steal the pot by scaring him off. 'You got me, man,' said Kenny. 'If you can call, you got me.' 'Other way round I fancy,' I said, flipping over my King–Five, at which point the entire table let out a collective gasp. Apparently I'd won, quickly confirmed by the dealer pushing all the chips in my direction rather than Kenny's, but I had no idea how. And still don't, despite Sky, who were televising the tournament, later giving me a video of the hand.

In any event, it kept me afloat, and I still had chips in front of me when the MC announced: 'Okay, congratulations everyone. We're down to the final thirty-six, so time for a break.' Kirk was beside himself with glee, and Sky hooked us up for an interview together. 'Listen,' he said 'we're in the money, but we're not settling for that. We're going to win this thing. We're after the million pounds.' Kirk advised aggression from now on – 'Balls to the walls' was how he phrased it – but I was about to have a long-overdue vasectomy. I was holding Queen–Jack, unsuited, but it didn't cost a lot to see the three-card flop against a single opponent, and three clubs came up. My own Queen was a club, so when my opponent lobbed in a few thousand, I stayed with him. No club. One card left, and he went 'all-in', meaning I had to gamble every last chip. All 150,000 of them. We turned over our cards, and for the second time in the tournament there was a collective gasp from the table. He had held two clubs, meaning he'd had a flush all along. But another club would have given me a higher flush, and cleaned him out. He grabbed his head with both hands, as though it was in danger of falling off, and said 'No club, no club, please, no club.' And he got his wish. Over came a red one, and I finally got a piece of etiquette correct by shaking hands with everyone still left at the table.

The next thing I knew I was being escorted to the cashier's desk, and the bloke behind the counter asking 'How would you like it?' 'Pardon?' I said. 'Cash or cheque?' 'Er, how much did I win?', I asked, knowing it was quite a lot, but not entirely certain how much. 'Twenty-seven thousand, one hundred and fifty,' he said. 'What, pounds?' I gulped. 'Pounds,' he confirmed. 'Bloody hell,' I said. I thought about going for the cash, on the grounds that I'd never seen that much in one pile, but it was gone midnight, and walking back to the hotel through central London with twenty-seven grand in a carrier bag didn't seem too clever. 'Better make it a cheque,' I said. I joined Kirk at the bar, who had slightly mixed emotions. 'After everything I told you, you bet Queen–Jack unsuited? You know who that was? It was Tino. He's a big time gambler from Australia. Broke a casino in Canberra one time. But hey, well done. You made me feel like Rocky Balboa's trainer.' We shook hands. 'Thanks Kirk,' I said. 'Sorry I didn't go all the way, but at least I went out, like you told me to, with my balls to the walls. And anyway,' I said. 'What's a million quid compared to taking out Kenny Tran with a King–Five?'

13

SINGULAR SPORTSMEN

Encounters with Colin Montgomerie, Joe Bugner, Gary Wolstenholme, Nick Faldo, Sir Alex Ferguson, Severiano Ballesteros, Luis Suárez

Colin Montgomerie

He can be charm personified, or else appear to be suffering from a virulent case of BSE. Or to give it its full medical title, Boiling Scotsman Eruptus. One minute a captivating ambassador for his native country, the next, a more than plausible solution to the Loch Ness Monster mystery. Namely, are those grainy black and white photos, upon closer examination, a large and frightening denizen of the deep? Or Colin Montgomerie taking an afternoon dip? Which one of the two Montys you came across was mostly dependent on how many times he'd hit his golf ball during the course of a round. When he emerged from the recorder's hut having just signed for a 65, you'd get a beaming smile, first–name recognition, and a kindly answer for even the daftest question. But when the 65 turned into a 75, you first made sure that you warned any mothers with toddlers to fling a protective arm around their offspring, before ensuring that you yourself had enough space around you to take evasive action. Otherwise you ran the risk of being flattened, and having to be peeled – Tom and Jerry-like – from the turf, complete with imprints of a large pair of Footjoys. He never won a major championship, perhaps because of his temperament, perhaps not. However, not only was he a terrifically good player (still is, in fact, and making even more money on the Seniors Tour) but as far as the golfing press were concerned, a tournament without Monty was barely worth getting out of bed for.

There's a limit to the amount of fun to be had from watching golfers playing golf, even when they're playing it very well, but you can never get bored when there is the ever-present prospect of one of the on-course marshals being taken to the St John Ambulance tent for the removal of a 'Quiet Please' sign from a delicate part of his anatomy. Most professional golfers, not to put too fine a point on it, are exceedingly boring. Beginning with how long it takes them merely to select a club for their next shot. This is something your average club golfer will work out in something approximating to five seconds, but as far as your average pro is concerned, *War and Peace* was written in less time than they take to decide whether to pluck a five iron from the bag, or a six. First of all, a piece of grass is thrown up. Then, just in case they don't quite believe which way the grass has blown, even if it has flown straight back into their face and is now firmly lodged in both nostrils, they throw up another clump to double check. Then they fish a small booklet from their back pocket which tells them precisely how far it is to their target, even though they employ a servant, known as a caddie, to pace it off for them. Then he will pluck a pencil from behind his ear and write the calculation down, just in case verbal confirmation alone is not sufficient for the boss to go ahead and hit his ball with an uncluttered head. There will then be a further delay while the player asks the caddie for more information, such as the exact alignment of the Milky Way and the Great Bear, his morning newspaper horoscope, and what the weather is doing in sea areas Viking and Cromarty. Only at this point will the player remove a club from his bag, but with no serious intention of hitting his ball with it until the completion of yet another sequence of rituals. He now addresses the ball, looks up to check his intended target several times, and after a period in which he appears to have contracted rigor mortis, will disengage himself from the ready-to-go position to call for another board meeting with his caddie. It is entirely possible for a spectator happening upon a professional golfer arriving at his golf ball, to wander back to the clubhouse to attend a call of nature, stop for a hot dog on the way back, and return to discover that they haven't missed a thing.

Following Monty around, on the other hand, is a guarantee of anything between four and six hours – given the funereal pace of modern-day play – of pure pleasure, whatever course he happens to be on. Should it be Augusta for the US Masters, for example, you never know whether those pretty azaleas will end up looking as though they've been in the path of a category-five tornado, or whether

Monty's approaching tread will send the turtles around Rae's Creek diving for the sanctuary of the bottom. My first encounter with the great man was in 1996, at the British Masters at Collingtree Park in Northampton. It was a first-time venue for the European Tour, and not a huge success, given that some catastrophe with the course preparation had left the putting surfaces so devoid of grass they had to paint them green, and so bumpy it was like putting over a sleeping policeman.

The first of many irate golfers I came across during a routine stroll around the course on the first morning was Howard Clark, known among the caddie fraternity as Hannibal (as in Lecter rather than the bloke with the elephants), and the subject of a memorable quote from David Feherty. After being partnered in a tournament with Clark and Montgomerie, Feherty said afterwards: 'It was like playing with Dame Edna Everage.' Another of Collingtree's drawbacks was that it ran through the middle of a housing estate, which wouldn't have been so bad had it been a completed housing estate rather than one they'd not quite finished yet. Ergo, when Clark hit a wayward tee shot into the left-hand rough, and found his ball close to a garden fence, his mood – slightly less than chipper already – was not improved by a trio of builders knocking up a garden pergola about ten yards away. Clark waited for a very long time for the banging and hammering to stop, but after failing to get their attention with long glares and muttered oaths, was finally forced into taking his shot. Sadly, just as he began his downswing, there was a loud bang from one of the builders hammering in a nail, and Clark's ball shot off into another thicket of long grass.

Before leaving the scene, however, Clark felt obliged to inform the builders, in fairly blunt language, that he hadn't been over-impressed. At that point, he only had one hole left before reaching the halfway point of his round, and that's as far as he got. Arriving back at the clubhouse, Clark made a beeline for his car, flung his clubs into the boot, and his exit was marked by plumes of smoke and about fifty yards of burned rubber.

Having scribbled this into my notebook, I wandered past an impromptu press conference in which Ian Woosnam was being asked: 'Are you saying, then, that these are the worst greens you've putted on for quite some time?' Woosnam replied that he was saying no such thing. What he was, in fact, saying was that they were the worst greens he'd putted on, period. Anywhere. In his entire life. Everywhere you looked there were irascible golfers, which made it imperative to find Monty, and I came across him on the par three eighth. Putting. Not once, but three times. On a green so lumpy that one of his missed putts didn't go wide of the hole, it went over the top of it. Crossing the bridge en route to the ninth tee Monty hurled his ball into the stream, and shouted 'Pathetic!', which some spectators might have construed as a reference to his own golf, but was in fact a comment on what he thought of the golf course.

I was getting a bit peckish by now, but something told me that lunch would have to wait as long as Monty was still on the course, and sure enough, my dedication was rewarded. Monty hit his tee shot at the tenth, and then turned sharp left to head towards two stationary Portakabins. One was marked 'Players Creche' and the other 'Tournament Director' – both of them a possible destination, I thought, for someone intent on throwing a few toys out of the pram. Monty, though, chose the latter, the door hinges only just managing to survive his entrance, and while it was impossible to hear what was being said, the sight of the tournament director cowering behind his desk suggested that Monty had not popped in to compliment him on the European Tour's choice of venue. My only regret, when Monty finally re-emerged, was that he didn't bump into the head green-keeper. The explosion would have made Krakatoa sound like a car backfiring.

Our next encounter was at the Lancome Trophy in Paris, which I was attending with the dual purpose of covering the event and also securing an interview ahead of the following tournament, of which he was the holder. I caught up with him during the Wednesday pro-am, which he almost always plays in, never failing to show the utmost patience with his amateur partners. This was the kind of patience you rarely saw when he was playing seriously, and I remember reading, before an Open Championship, about a fiery and eccentric American pro called Mac O'Grady, who tried to cure his temper by taking his car out, driving up behind some dithering old lady in the American equivalent of a Morris Minor, and seeing how long he could go without either parping the horn or making rude hand signals out of the window. I mentioned this to Monty's coach, Dennis Pugh, and put it forward as a potential tantrum-curer, but far from giving it serious consideration, Dennis suddenly began wheezing uncontrollably, clutching his stomach and gasping: 'Oh no, stop it. Stop it!' When he finally regained a grip of himself, which was quite some time, he told me he'd had this mental picture of Monty doing an O'Grady in his sponsored Lexus, and scattering school crocodiles and lollipop ladies. It was, we both agreed, something you could sell tickets for.

On pro-am day at the Lancome, though, Monty greeted me as though we were lifelong buddies. 'Of course,' he said. 'Love to do an interview. Absolute pleasure. Let's see now. I'm out early tomorrow, so how about after the round. Say one o'clock? We can have a pot of tea on the terrace. Now then Bill,' he said, turning to one of his amateur partners. 'Let's see about that slice of yours. I think I can see what you're doing wrong.' Next day, in the press tent, I looked at the master scoreboard and the numbers going up alongside Monty. Par, par, bogey, par, bogey, par. It didn't bode well for his mood, and as I headed for our date on the lawn there was a loud crash as he emerged from the recorder's hut, steam pouring from both ears, and a face the colour of freshly boiled beetroot. I suspected that the pot of tea idea perhaps had less appeal for him than it had the previous day, and sure enough, when I found him on the practice putting green, he confirmed – with extreme politeness it has to be said – that the interview was off. 'Tomorrow perhaps?' I ventured. 'Yes, tomorrow, much better. Thank you,' he said. Next day, I looked at the scores. Par, bogey, par, par . . .' Not good again. Once more I found him on the practice putting green, this time with his faithful caddie, Alastair McLean, sitting on the bag waiting for instructions. 'Afternoon, Alastair,' I said. 'How's your man today? Do you think he's okay to approach?' He looked at me. 'Sure,' he said. 'Go right ahead.' Followed by, after I'd taken a couple of steps towards his boss, 'But only if you're tired of living.' 'What do you think I am?' I asked Alastair. 'Man or mouse?' But I already knew the answer to that, and my next call to the office began: 'Er, you know that Monty interview? Well, I've got a much better idea . . .'

I used to particularly look forward to following Monty at the Masters, a course that favours right-to-left players, and the opposite of what he did best. Monty's idea of paradise was a left-to-right course with enough rough to feed a herd of goats. Augusta was a hooker's heaven, where the rough was barely more than designer stubble. On top of which, Monty regarded the greens as only marginally less of a joke than putting through the mouth of a Humpty Dumpty at a seaside crazy golf course. In short, he hated the place, although, along with every other player interviewed before the Masters, he was gushing in his reverence. Special place, hallowed turf, unique aura, that kind of tosh. It's a wonder he didn't grow an extra nose.

He rarely played well round Augusta, and the pace of play was always pitiful. Monty was one of those golfers who likes to get on with it, and this particular year he found himself immediately behind a group featuring Arnold Palmer, by this time getting on a bit, and a complete no-hoper. Arnie was all over the course, but it wasn't so much the fact that he had to wait for him to find his ball all the time that got Monty foaming at the mouth; it was the fact that the popular Palmer had so many old chums in the crowd. A typical scenario was for Arnie to slice his ball into the pine trees, and find it underneath a folding chair belonging to some old buffer he knew from the Latrobe Rotary Club, or the PGA Tour Museum. 'Why, I'll be blowed! Hey, Hiram. How yah keeping?' 'Gee, Arnie, just swell. By the way, how's the new hearing aid?' 'Pardon, Hiram?' 'I said, how's the new hearing aid?' 'We don't have a maid, Hiram, but we got an ironing lady. Well, I better get on and play this shot. Give my best to the lady wife.' And while all this was going on, Monty was quietly steaming on the tee behind, telling his playing partners precisely what he thought about the Augusta rule (as it then was) allowing former Masters winners to carry on playing until they were 150 if they lived that long.

One year at Augusta, I came into the press centre one morning, pretty early as usual owing to the time difference and first-edition deadlines, and one of the English golf writers, Derek Lawrensen, said: 'I see Monty's off at 8.40. No prizes for guessing who you'll be following today.' I replied: 'Ah, but that's where you're wrong. I'm going out with Woosnam and Daly at 8.20.' I couldn't do Monty every day, I thought, even though you were guaranteed a story, but after four holes of Woosnam and Daly, I was already beginning to realize how addicts feel when they're trying to come off the drugs. I looked at my watch, and worked out roughly where Monty would be on the course, and I found him walking down the fifth fairway. 'You just can't live without him, can you?' came a voice behind me. It was Derek. 'I'm beginning to think you're right,' I said. 'So much for the Woosnam and Daly idea. All they do is hit the ball, walk after it, and hit it again. How boring it that? Anyway, have I missed anything?' I asked. Derek replied: 'No, nothing. Very un-Monty like. But now you're here I'm sure he'll oblige.' And blow me down, he did.

The man on his bag – for the first time in years – was not Alastair McLean, who had been forced to fly home for an operation after putting his back out during practice. Monty had opted to use one of the local black caddies, Joe Collins, who'd been recommended to him by the head caddie-master, and Joe's initial delight at earning a bit more than his customary fifty dollars lasted precisely four and a half holes. Out there in the middle of the fifth fairway, after long deliberation with the new man and much tossing up of bits of grass, Monty let out a croon of pleasure as his iron shot flew straight at the flagstick. It never left the flagstick. Straight at it, and then, straight over it. On and on it went, finally coming to rest in a deep swale at the back of the green. I watched Monty's expression change from delight, to puzzlement, to bewilderment, and finally to what might described as not best pleased. There was a collective groan from the spectators around the green as Monty's ball ended up in bogey country, and it was then that I realized that experience counts for everything in the caddie–master relationship. Alastair would have summed it up in a trice, and been long gone, pausing only to collect the divot in the primary objective of putting as much distance between himself and the boss as possible. Joe, on the other hand, had failed to remove himself from the scene of the crime, a schoolboy error which cost him a full half-minute of verbal haranguing, and a prolonged, arms-outstretched, how-could-you-do-this-to-me gesture of irritation. Joe looked at the offending club, and then looked at Monty. Whether or not Joe momentarily thought about employing it in such a way as to reunite his man with his regular caddie on the operating table, he thought better of it, and meekly put it back in the bag. He might have thought about saying something too, but was wise to keep his counsel. Besides, not many get the better of Monty in a verbal exchange – an exception being a middle-aged woman at the Open Championship, who decided to put her umbrella up when Monty was lining up a putt. 'Must you do that now?' huffed Monty. 'Yes,' she replied. 'It's raining.'

Some of the best Monty moments came when confronted by a microphone, especially when the interviewer was trying to make Monty feel better by putting some gloss on a bad round. Such as when he went round in 76 on a windy day in the Open at Troon, and the interviewer opened up with: 'Well, Colin. A good finish at least. Three pars on the final three holes.' Monty opened his mouth, but nothing came out, so he closed it again. He opened his mouth again. Still nothing. His face went through a series of strange contortions, and as he pulled off his visor and stared at it I wondered for a moment whether he was contemplating eating it. Finally, he spoke. 'Thank you. Thank you, there. That was delightful,' he said, through teeth more gritted than a Highland trunk road in January. 'I am really thrilled with that finish. I can take that forward and really go from strength to strength. Thank you.' Some people thought afterwards they might have detected the merest hint of irony, but if medals were handed out for verbal bravery, that interviewer came a distant second to Monty's playing partner, Tom Watson. Monty, two under par for his round after seven holes, had managed to shed seven shots between there and the fifteenth, and when there was a hold-up on the seventeenth tee, he folded his arms and gave that familiar piercing stare into outer space. The one which tells you that the 'do not disturb sign' has been illuminated, and to approach only with extreme caution. Tom, however, doubtless aware that Monty's father was once secretary at the Royal Troon Golf Club, took everyone's breath away by walking up to his playing partner, pointing to some imposing building down the coastline, and saying: 'Hey Monty. Who owns that house over there? Do you know?' Watson perhaps didn't realize it at the time, but his reputation as one of the game's great gentlemen, as well as great golfers, probably saved him. A lesser name may not have been so lucky. 'What an interesting question. Here I am, five over bloody par, cold, hungry, miserable, and you want to know who lives in that bloody house over there . . .' But as it was Watson, he got away with a curt but polite: 'Don't know, Tom.'

I'm not sure whether Monty ever owned a cat, but if he did, it would certainly have had a nervous disposition. Whenever it heard the front-door key turning in the lock, it would have had an instant decision to make. Stay in front of the fire, licking double cream off its whiskers, or make a quick dash for safety underneath the sofa. It was much the same for spectators, who were never quite sure whether to give him some encouragement after a bogey, or keep quiet. There was one occasion when Monty stalked off towards the next tee, just coming to the boil after a three-putt, when a member of the gallery tried to lift his spirits with an encouraging comment. 'Keep going, Monty!' he cried, which, far from keeping him going, had the effect of halting Monty in mid-stomp. He rounded on the well-wisher and shot him the kind of look Medusa reserved for her mythological victims. 'Keep going?!' said Monty. 'Keep going?' – the voice going up another octave. 'Keep bloody going? What does that mean? Keep bloody going!'

He always got stick in America, where he was dubbed 'Mrs Doubtfire' after the film starring the late Robin Williams, and with New York crowds in particular rarely taking prisoners, there was one memorable exchange with a spectator when Monty was down on the driving range practising for a US Open. Monty's weight went up and down so spectacularly that he must have had five different wardrobes at home, and this was during one of his jam-roly-poly-with-extra-custard periods. On a hot day, his shirt was clinging unflatteringly to various wobbly areas above the equator, and the comparative silence was broken by one of those American voices capable of cutting through concrete. 'Hey Monty!' Monty declined to look up. 'Hey Monty!' came the same raucous cry. Monty cocked another deaf 'un. 'Hey, Mr Montgomerie!' came the voice again. Monty decided that this at least vaguely polite call perhaps qualified for a cursory acknowledgement, which turned out to be a big mistake. He looked up, and as he did so his tormentor raised both hands to his chest, made a jiggling motion designed to convey that some of the moving parts beneath Monty's shirt would be more comfortably restrained inside a pair of D cups, and delivered the devastating punch-line, 'Great tits!'

When he was in his pomp, Monty was well aware that the press were always keen to hear from him after he'd played, and it wasn't uncommon, after a bad round, for him to sweep through the assembled hacks with a dismissive: 'I'm not the story! Not today thank you.' But he was always the story. Inside the press tent, when the media liaison officer would announce: 'Martin Kaymer is now in the interview room', no one moved. When he said: 'Colin Montgomerie is now in the interview room', it was a stampede. He was often at his best before the start of a tournament, before anything has happened to upset him, and it's then that he'd talk about anything you wanted. The state of the economy? Global warming? High Speed Railways? It was fill your notebook time. He could keep going for hours. He loved the sight of people jostling for a space ('Come in! Come along! Plenty of room at the back . . .') and dished out marks for what he considered to be good questions. 'Yes. Good one. Like that one. Good. Very good.'

He could also poke fun at himself. Monty has incredible hearing – so much so that reincarnation theorists would be fairly confident in the belief that he must have lived out a previous existence as a bat – and it plagued him throughout his career. Mobile phones have played a major part in some of his more memorable on-course explosions, and a particular favourite was the time a phone not only went off on his backswing, but did so to the tune of 'Scotland the Brave'. So when he was asked what he thought about the Open Championship committee deciding to ban mobile phones, which to Monty (while he was on a golf course at any rate) were the instruments of Beelzebub, we sat back half expecting an 'about time too' rant. What we got instead was a mischievous grin and: 'I'm fine with mobile phones. And cameras going off. It's the other players it was brought in for, the people that really get upset about these things. Me? I'm fine.' It was a great

Monty moment, and everyone laughed. Next day, true to form, a BBC camera buggy disturbed him while he lined up a putt, and the driver got a memorable savaging. And that's why, if anyone asks me what Monty was really like, I usually reply: 'Which particular Monty would you be referring to?'

Joe Bugner

I was in Brisbane for the cricket, just ahead of the first Test of the 1998–99 Ashes series, when I was asked to try and get an interview with Joe Bugner, who'd emigrated to Australia in 1986, and, at the age of forty-eight, had just a few months earlier won the almost wholly unrecognized WBF version of the world heavyweight title against another ancient relic, the forty-five-year-old American, James 'Bonecrusher' Smith. The fight had been a total non-event, a grossly overweight Smith retiring with a shoulder injury before the end of the first round, but it was still enough for 'Aussie Joe' – as he'd become known – to start making noises about fighting Mike Tyson, who'd been disqualified the year before in his WBA title rematch with Evander Holyfield after mistaking his opponent's ear for a tasty snack. Bugner was living in Carrara, on Queensland's Gold Coast, and the office wondered whether I'd be able to 'pop up there' and have a chat to him.

'Popping up there' was a quaint way to put it, given that Queensland is seven times the size of Great Britain and two and a half times larger than Texas, but it was a shortish flight, and before long I was talking to him over the phone from my hotel. We'd arranged to interview him at his house, but he'd had a change of heart. 'I'll have to come over to you,' he said. 'I don't want the press knowing where I live. I'll never get any privacy.' I had to fight off an urge to inform Joe that if Britain's media ever got to know the precise location of Chateau Bugner, a twenty-four-hour paparazzi stake-out was unlikely to be the outcome. A polite knock on the door from the sports correspondent of the *Falmouth Packet*, perhaps, but only on a slow news day in Cornwall. I put down the phone, and ordered coffee in the lobby for me and the photographer who'd been diverted from the cricket to accompany me. 'Good to know Joe's lost none of his natural modesty in his old age,' I told him. 'He's worried your telescopic lens will catch him combing his hair in the bathroom, and you'll flog the snaps to *Hello* magazine for a small fortune. So he's coming over here. In about half an hour.'

No sooner had the coffee arrived than a chap from the front desk came over. 'Could you call Mr Bugner on this number, please sir,' and a minute or so later, he was back on the phone. 'I've changed my mind,' said Joe. 'You come over to me. It's about fifteen minutes in a cab.' 'But what about your privacy?' I asked him. 'Oh, I'll trust you to keep the address secret,' he said. I wondered whether I ought to offer to have the cabbie blindfold us, in case we should memorize the route, and was mildly surprised, when we were paying off the taxi, when a beaming Bugner flung open the front door and came down the driveway to greet us. I'd half expected to hear a 'ssshhh' from behind one of the garden bushes, and a whispered invitation to stay low and creep round to the tradesmen's entrance. However, as many people had already discovered from seeing his bit-part movie appearances, Joe wasn't much of an actor, and after all that guff about not wanting the press to bother him, he was shamelessly arranging for the photographer to get lots of pictures of him in his trophy room. 'And then we'll go down to the gym,' he said. 'You can get some shots of me hitting the heavy bag and doing some skipping. And how about' (he was beginning to sound like a film director) 'some walkabout photos of me on the beach and down at the shops. Everyone knows me here,' he said. And they did.

We went to the gym, took some photos, and then walked over to the beachfront, where everyone waved. 'They never loved me in England,' he said, 'but they love me here.' And then he asked: 'How about some photos of me running through the surf? That'd look good with your article.' I said, 'You mean like a variation on Rocky running up all those steps?' 'That's it,' said Joe. 'Just like that, only Aussie style, splashing through the water.' I was beginning to enjoy this assignment, not least because, conceited old show-off that he was, it was impossible not to warm to Joe. We arranged to do the main part of the interview over dinner at an Italian restaurant – 'I don't get bothered for too many autographs there' – myself, the snapper, Joe, and his formidable Australian wife, Marlene. 'For heaven's sake, darling,' she said after getting herself ready and coming downstairs. 'You've got all the lights turned on again.' 'Sorry, hon,' says Joe. 'I'll turn a few off, shall I?' 'And then you can pour me a Martini.' 'Sure thing, hon.'

We got the full movie star treatment arriving at the restaurant, and Joe took it upon himself to greet all the other diners with a personal visit to their table. They looked suitably honoured, and the wine waiter purred with pleasure when Joe put him in charge of choosing the red. It really wasn't hard to see why everyone appeared to love him in Australia. I had this mental picture of Bugner versus Tyson, two boxers well past their sell-by date, and the MC making the introductions. 'Ladieeeeeeeees and gentlemen. From the State of Queensland, Geriatric Joe Bugner. And from the State Penitentiary, Methuselah Mike Tyson!' So I opened up by asking him whether he was getting a bit too old to carry on fighting. 'Look at me,' said Joe. 'I'm still a handsome old bastard, aren't I?' I silently agreed, while wondering whether he'd be quite so pleased with his reflection in the mirror after Tyson had finished eating his body parts.

Given his Hungarian background, Iron Mike could easily mistake one of Joe's earlobes for a goulash. Joe's ears, he confessed, did bother him slightly, but not because he thought Tyson might mistake the first-round bell for the dinner gong. Both his eardrums had been sensitive from birth, and his balance hadn't been so good since both of them were perforated by the American heavyweight, Ron Lyle. Other than that, he was fine, he said. Why, compared to the then fifty-year-old George Foreman, he was still wet behind his ailing ears – and the suspicion that there was nothing much between them (the ears, that is, not him and Foreman) he cheerfully endorsed. 'People say I'm simple,' he chortled. 'And I am.' Tyson, he said, would do for his next fight, but the opponent he really wanted was Foreman. 'I've been trying to get it on with George for twenty-two years,' he said 'but he wants no part of me because he knows I'm too bloody good. The war of the granddads. It would make millions!' Ah, so it's the old story, then, I ventured. He needed the money. Especially after losing a bundle in an ill-fated vineyard venture in New South Wales. 'No, it's nothing to do with the money; we've got plenty,' said Joe. 'He's right,' said Marlene. 'We've got a lovely house in an exclusive area, and I just hate him fighting. I've told him to pack it all in by the time he's forty-nine.' Joe promptly contradicted them both. 'Sure I do it for the money. But when I go to the gym and do things as well as I did twenty-five years before, that makes me happy. The legs are a bit slower, but everything else is still there. Why should I pack up, sit around and drink beer, and end up as a fat old pig?'

Marlene, though, was less concerned about him drinking beer than coffee. 'I had two this morning and she only allows me one,' said Joe, the rebellious streak in him coming out. 'She insists I go to the bloody doctor every week for a check-up. I tell you. I'd sooner get into a ring with Tyson than my missus.' Marlene piped up: 'And you'll keep on going to the doctor. I don't want you having a heart attack in the ring and embarrassing me.' Which makes them both guffaw with laughter. There was a time when Bugner, who met Marlene at one of Joan Collins' Hollywood house parties, would have packed boxing in completely for a career in the movies, but while you get the impression he'd have made a decent mummy in one of those old horror films, in Bugner's own mind, he'd have a spare room full of Oscars given a decent break. 'I met Stanley Baker at one of my early fights, and he told me to get myself to Rome to learn the trade because they were planning to shoot *Zulu 2*, and he wanted to give me the same opportunity they gave Michael Caine in the original *Zulu*. But my manager at the time, Andy Smith, talked me out of it.'

Bugner actually appeared in quite a few movies, although I've never seen any of them, or if I had, I must have dropped a piece of popcorn and missed Joe's appearance. 'I starred [his word] in a couple of films here in Australia, you know. Not just bit parts.' He was particularly proud about the legendary, never to be forgotten, blockbuster *Sher Mountain Killings Mystery*. I shot him a blank look. 'What?' he said incredulously. 'Don't say you've not heard of it. It was a sci-fi thriller, and I played an eighty-year-old bloke who came back as a youth who was once entrusted with a sacred stone which, unbeknown to him at the time, was cursed. Well he went and lost it, and went into hiding until, as an old man, he decided he had to redeem himself. So he went into his spirit and came back as a youthful person in search of this long-lost sacred rock. And then, um, er . . .' At this point, in more ways than one, he lost the plot.

Joe and Marlene seemed perfectly happy with life on the Gold Coast, which is a bit like Torremolinos, only not as tasteful. They were certainly glad to get out of England where, said Joe – who had acquired a notice-able Australian twang – 'the Poms only really like losers. I was never forgiven for beating Henry Cooper, who was a good home-grown fighter but hopelessly out of his class at world level. I was too intelligent for him' (there's the old modesty again) 'despite being only twenty-one at the time. The press all gave the fight to Cooper, but only because he was a national hero. Well, my hero was Bobby Charlton, but I'm not daft enough to think he was better than Pele or Maradona.' Joe was warming to his task now, helped by the fact that the wine waiter remained obligingly in range for refills. And when he wasn't talking about boxing it was celebrities. Tom Jones was best man at their wedding, and when Joe introduced himself to Frank Sinatra, Sinatra said (according to Joe at any rate), 'I know you big fellah. I'm a big fan of yours.' Marlene suddenly shot out a hand and pinned my arm to the table. 'Did you know,' she said, 'that Joe has been offered parts in the next two *Star Wars* movies?' I confessed that I didn't. 'Well he has, but let me tell you. My Joe is no actor.' I guessed she was probably right on that one. 'No, no. I'm telling you. My Joe,' she repeated, 'is no actor. He's a *star*!'

Gary Wolstenholme

People often wonder how on earth Gary Wolstenholme managed to beat Tiger Woods in the 1995 Walker Cup at Royal Porthcawl, especially as Gary was occasionally as much as a hundred yards behind his opponent off the tee. I wasn't at that match, but my own theory is that Woods must have been talked to death. Most golfers at this level like to play in their own personal bubble, and very often the only words exchanged with an opponent between shaking hands at the start and shaking hands at the end are 'Good morning' and 'Thanks for the game.' Gary, though, could start a conversation in a Trappist monastery, and a casual remark about, say, the weather, could keep him going for several hours. 'Hottest summer since 1953 they say . . . you ought to see the state of my lawn . . . hosepipe ban where we are . . .' and on and on he goes. Your only chance of avoiding a natter with him was to keep missing the fairway, which Gary hardly ever did, and there were times when the old undone shoelace ploy had to be invoked, the equivalent of a dazed boxer taking an eight count. Being an amateur, Gary never played with Nick Faldo, but if they had been paired together, you wouldn't have bet much money on Faldo breaking 100. Nick required absolute silence when he went about his business, and only ever spoke when absolutely necessary: to his caddie, when he wanted a yardage; to his golf ball, if it showed any sign of veering off line; and to himself, when his game was off and he needed a good talking to. So when it came down to Great Britain and Ireland winning the 2003 Walker Cup at Ganton by a single point, it was Gary who talked the team across the winning line in the final afternoon singles. The star of the American side was Casey Wittenberg, a rigid disciple of the Faldo school of on-course non-communication, as I discovered when he responded to my request for a few words before the start of the tournament, first by pretending he hadn't heard me, and latterly by confining every answer to a monosyllabic grunt. In short, Wittenberg made it clear that given the choice between standing in front of a microphone and having his teeth pulled without anaesthetic, he'd definitely plump for the latter. Which made him easy meat for Gary when the draw pitted them together on that decisive final afternoon. The poor lad wasn't in the best of moods when he arrived on the first tee, having helped fritter away a three-up lead with four to play in his morning foursome, and bumping into Gary in one of his more loquacious moods was not quite what he was looking for. Gary opened up by remarking how nice it had turned out since the early morning fog, and when Casey showed no inclination to add his own voice to the topic, switched seamlessly to the quality of clubhouse lunch. 'My God!' gasped an American reporter, as Gary now remarked on how well-behaved the spectators had been. 'He's talking to Wittenberg! *No one* talks to Wittenberg!' I explained that, on the contrary, Gary spoke to everyone, and that there wasn't a single topic he considered to be off limits. Wittenberg, it has to be said, put up stoic resistance, as you'd expect from a man who was so devoted to not talking on a golf course that he never once asked Gary why he wore his sunglasses upside down on his head without ever putting them on. Finally, though – having limited his responses to a shrug here, and a nod there – he succumbed. And spoke back. It could have been because he was leading the match, or perhaps it was simply the irresistible nature of Gary's latest subject. Which was Scarborough. The gist of Gary's conversation was that the venue for the golf match was a very nice town – a bit like Blackpool, but not quite so tacky. 'Have you had a decent stay, Casey? Hotel okay for you? Food to your liking?' For whatever reason, possibly worried that unless he said something Gary might suddenly launch into fish and chip shops, or Yorkshire puddings, Casey broke his silence. 'Uh-huh,' he said. It was the turning point of the match as Wittenberg, clearly exhausted by the effort, promptly lost the next two holes and, eventually, the match. After the traditional handshake, Wittenberg walked off in search of a darkened room in which to lie down, while Gary was invited to share his thoughts on the match with a TV interview on the green. Which only concluded when the referee gave a polite cough and reminded them that the players in the match behind were waiting to play their shots.

Nick Faldo

Whenever I get asked what it takes to become a journalist, I have to fight off an urge to give the standard answers – nose for a story, interest in people, inquiring mind, that kind of guff – and hit them with the truth. Which is, a resilient liver, and the ability to churn out a piece – however ordinary – while suffering from the mother of all hangovers. Contrary, however, to the oft peddled myth that journalists are naturally inclined towards permanent inebriation, it has more to do with a devotion to duty unmatched by possibly any other profession. Put a journalist in a room full of famous celebrities, and combine this with a bar that remains open all night, and will he disappear off to bed early when there's a chance he might miss an important story? Of course he won't. Which is why, having been invited to a Steve Redgrave charity golf tournament in La Manga, which required me to mingle with all kinds of famous sports people, I found myself staggering out of the hotel piano bar at 7.55am for an 8am tee-off time.

My partner turned out to be the then England rugby winger Rory Underwood, an understanding sort of a chap, as he needed to be after watching me play the first two holes in a series of tops, shanks and air shots. I then astounded everyone, not least myself, by hitting a drive straight down the middle at the third, and as I stood contemplating my second shot, Rory came over and said: 'What club are you thinking of?' 'Driver, I think Rory,' I said. 'Driver? It's only 140 yards to the front,' he replied. 'I still think it's a driver,' I said. 'If it was me I'd hit an eight iron,' said Rory. 'Well I'm not you, and I think it's a driver,' I said. 'But why?' he asked. 'Because, Rory,' I said, 'a driver is the only club I've got.' I could only put it down to a combination of barely knowing what time of day it was and sheer astonishment at having managed to locate the fairway, but somehow I'd managed to walk all the way to my ball clutching the driver, but forgetting to take my golf bag with me. 'Rory, as England rugby fans will remember, was a pretty fast runner, and I was just about to suggest he might nip back to the tee to fetch my bag when a bloke driving a buggy arrived with it. Now armed with a choice of clubs, I obliged Rory with his suggestion of an eight iron, and took a hideous lunge at the ball, removing a large enough divot to carpet your average lounge, while the ball hobbled all of five feet. I fell to my knees, looked up at Rory, and croaked: 'See? I told you I needed a driver.' I somehow managed to stagger round the eighteen holes, offering profuse apologies to my partner afterwards. 'Well,' said Rory, 'I dare say even Nick Faldo might have struggled had he prepared like you did.' I tried to picture Faldo, the night before an Open Championship, getting increasingly incoherent in the clubhouse bar, but there are some kind of images that are impossible to conjure up.

Of all the sportsmen or women I've seen, Faldo remains – in terms of how he went about his business – the most single-minded, and the most fascinating. Especially on those rare occasions when there was nothing to play for. At the 1995 Open at St Andrews, when Costantino Rocca holed that miracle putt from across the eighteenth green to force a four-hole play-off with John Daly, there was a collective groan from the press tent that could have been heard right across the Bay. It was already bang on first-edition deadline, and another hour at least would now be required to determine the winner, so why, a colleague felt obliged to ask me, was I not looking as pissed off as everyone else. 'I've done for the day,' I replied. 'Filed around mid-afternoon as it happens.' 'What on?' he asked. 'Faldo,' I said. 'Faldo? He was so far out of the tournament he was in the first group off.' Which was, I said, precisely why I'd chosen to see how he would handle a round of a golf that, to all intents and purposes, was totally meaning-less. Daly himself, who went on to win the play-off with Rocca, had once been first out in an Open, paired with a marker, and waltzed round in something like an hour and a half. Faldo, though, didn't know the meaning of not caring. On the second tee, he hit his drive too far right, and watched it disappear into a bunker. There was no one watching, apart from half a dozen spectators, a couple of caddies and a bunker raker, but Nick responded as though he'd just played the shot that might have cost him the championship itself. He stared into the distance and said, to himself but out loud, 'I don't believe it.' And then he said it again. 'I don't believe it.' And several times more. He really didn't believe it. His ball had been swallowed by a hazard known as Cheape's bunker, which had been there, in the same place, for centuries, but as far as Nick was concerned, his ball had only ended up in it thanks to some dark, inexplicable, supernatural force. Later on, he had a long shot to the green, which, while perfectly judged for distance, finished about fifteen feet left of the flagstick. Nick surveyed the result with the expression of a man who'd just shanked one into the car park, and stood motionless for so long rigor mortis couldn't have been far away. 'C'mon Nick!' came a voice from the small band of followers, and you found yourself thinking – not for the first time with Faldo – 'Yes Nick. Do come on.' At another hole, there was a long discussion with his caddie over the wind before he played, and more exasperation when the crosswind he'd calculated failed to move his ball even a centimetre sideways. 'How can it just bloomin' well *stay* there? It's a joke.' Followed by yet another, 'I don't believe it.' However, once Nick had finally persuaded himself to believe it, he went on and did what no golfer has ever done better. Blocked out the last shot, and got on with the next one. It was a curling twenty-five-foot putt, and it went straight in the middle.

Time didn't fly when you were watching Faldo in his pomp, neither was there much evidence of someone having fun, and there were days when you half expected the referee to drive up in his cart and re-classify him from competitor to immovable obstruction. Faldo won six majors, but it might have been sixteen had the important nature of these events not attracted the awful imposition of people wanting to watch him. Not only were they allowed on the course, but very often to get quite close to him. Making distracting noises, on occasion, such as breathing. 'Thank you. I'm ready,' he said to one poor wretch, not realizing that one of the hardest things in golf was knowing when Nick was ready. One of his favourite ruses was to pretend he's just about to hit the ball, then take a couple of steps back to make sure that his left elbow is properly lined up with the clubhouse clock, and receive one final assurance from his caddie that that bloke with his right hand in his trouser pocket is not about to jingle any loose change.

When Rory wondered on that day in La Manga whether Faldo ever prepared for a round of golf with an all-night session in a resort piano bar, my mind went back to an Open at Troon, when Nick was warming up for a practice round in one of the practice bunkers. He'd not long before changed club manufacturer, and he was alternating between two sand wedges – peering at both after every shot, in much the same way as an antiques dealer squints at a vase to establish whether it's an original or not. Finally, Nick deemed his game ready for the course itself, and spent the first three holes throwing an assortment of balls into various greenside bunkers and proceeding to remove most of the sand from each of them. Something wasn't right, and by the fourth hole Faldo had considered the situation serious enough to call in his swing doctor. David Leadbetter gave the two sand wedges a close inspection, and promptly called over one of Nick's practice partners for an opinion. Finally, the Mizuno rep was summoned. He'd been following from a discreet distance, face growing paler by the hole, and all remaining colour drained from his face when Nick reached into his golf bag and produced a felt-tipped pen. That's it, the Mizuno man must have thought. Contract cancelled. However, it wasn't quite that serious. Faldo made a series of doodles on the bottom of one of clubs – 'shave a bit off here, leave that bit' – and despatched him back to the Mizuno van. If he'd waited a bit longer he could have taken the putter as well, as Nick had about a dozen goes at a ten-footer and never holed it once. Once again Leadbetter was called across for a laying on of hands, or, to be more precise, the laying of his umbrella onto Nick's hands. Faldo tried the next two putts with the brolly handle resting in the V of his wrists, and hey presto, in they both went. Leadbetter's umbrella never went up even when it was raining; it was merely used as one of his training tools. A few holes later, the Mizuno man reappeared, just in time as Nick was now having serious issues with sand wedge no. 2. The rep was invited to compare the merits of Faldo's club with the one belonging to one of his partners, and after another round of design alterations with the felt tip, off he scuttled again. Some people might place the late Severiano Ballesteros ahead of Faldo when it came to demanding perfection on a near obsessive basis, but I have one compelling piece of evidence which gives Faldo the title. It was at a tournament where Ballesteros asked his caddie to get an apple out of the bag, and then, having taken a bite out of it, threw it dismissively into a bush with a glower and mutter. When I finally got a chance to ask the caddie what all that had been about, he replied: 'Not juicy enough, apparently. 'Bout time he made up his mind whether it's a caddie he wants or a bloody greengrocer.' The difference being, of course, that Faldo's apple would have been perfection itself, having been handpicked by the boss – complete with felt-tipped doodles to help the fruit and veg man select the right one. In short, far too important a matter to be left to a mere caddie.

Sir Alex Ferguson

'Have you,' I was once asked, 'ever interviewed Alex Ferguson. 'Well. Yes and no,' I replied. I don't really know if you could call it an interview as such, but an interview was certainly what I'd been briefed to carry out over in Portugal. There was a charity golf tournament being held there under Bobby Robson's name, and Fergie was among the celebrities playing in it. The deal was that I'd fly to Portugal, interview Sir Alex on the day I got there, play golf the following day, and they fly home again. All very agreeable it sounded to me. 'It's all arranged,' said my contact at the office. 'There's a PR girl in charge of everything, and she'll meet you at the airport.' And so she did. As we drove to the golf resort she explained that it was all part of a sponsorship deal, Sir Alex had been briefed, and I was to interview him after his practice round later that afternoon. So when I got to the golf course, I took a seat at one of the tables in the clubhouse lounge and waited for Fergie to appear. Which he duly did, still in his golf gear, and headed to the bar to order some drinks. The PR girl had gone off somewhere, so I thought, 'Might as well introduce myself and get the interview sorted.' I went up to the bar, stretched out a hand, and introduced myself. There was no reciprocal outstretched hand from Sir Alex, just the kind of look he normally reserved for third officials who've added an eight extra minutes when Manchester United were leading by a goal. 'Who did you say you were?' he said. I repeated who I was. 'Which newspaper did you say?' I told him again. 'Sorry, I don't know you. I don't do interviews with people I don't know.' I told him that I'd been assured it was all arranged, and that I wasn't in the habit of spotting celebrities in bars and walking up to them to request an interview. 'Well if I did agree,' he said, 'and I'm not saying I will, I'd need to know what questions you wanted to ask.' I told him that I hadn't got a clue what I wanted to ask him, but would think of things as the interview progressed. 'Well I'm not doing an interview if I don't know the questions,' he said. Suddenly, the trip became a much more attractive proposition. I said: 'Actually, I've no great desire to do an interview with you either. A few drinks at the bar, a nice dinner, a game of golf tomorrow, and no work involved. So if you don't want to do an interview, we're both happy.' He looked at me and smiled. We both smiled. 'Aye, good lad. We'll leave it there then. Enjoy your game tomorrow.' And that was it. If it qualified as an interview at all, it was definitely the shortest one I've ever done.

Severiano Ballesteros

I once had the curious experience of witnessing a golfer's entire career in the course of a single hole. A par five at Saint-Nom-la-Bretèche during the Lancome Trophy. On the tee, Ballesteros selected the driver, and the gallery immediately vanished in a mad stampede to remove their vehicles from the car park before the Spaniard could threaten their no-claims bonuses. Well, no they didn't of course, but there were a few nerves out there in the gallery, and if the Health and Safety laws had been as strict then as they are now, mothers with small children would have been allowed to remove their offspring to the relative safety of the middle of the fairway. Seve let fly, and while he had the ability to miss the short grass either to the left or the right, on this occasion the ball flew left. Miles left. That's what I loved about following Ballesteros for eighteen holes, as I'd elected to do that morning. The certain knowledge that there would be some interesting story to tell, whether it be a round of dazzling brilliance, or interviewing crowd survivors in the waiting room at the local A&E. We located Seve's ball, steering towards its location by a combination of ship's sextant and ordnance survey map, in a spinney of trees. And he pondered for quite some time. Whether to take his medicine, and come out sideways, or attempt something totally outrageous. As ever with Ballesteros, the decision was never really in doubt. The green lay about two hundred and twenty yards away, on the other side of the spinney, and to get there required a shot that first had to fly about forty yards at shin height to avoid the lower branches, and then climb vertically to clear the next set of taller trees. Finally, it needed to turn sharp left to avoid finishing out of bounds right. It was a shot not many would have taken on even in the upright position, but a series of practice swishes had revealed that the only way Seve could make contact with the ball without getting it entangled in the foliage on his backswing was to hit it while kneeling down. Which he then proceeded to do. And sure enough the ball flew low under the first set of branches, then climbed vertically, before eventually turning left to finish about five yards short of the putting surface. It was, by some margin, the single most extraordinary shot I, or anyone else in the gallery that day, have ever witnessed, although when asked about it at his press conference later, Seve wondered what all the fuss was about. It was, he said, something he practised most days, and he was a bit disappointed it finished a tad short of the green. His third shot was a routine little chip, the kind the top pros expect to either knock stone dead or even hole, to a putting surface five yards away, and the pin a further twenty-five feet on. So what does he do? He duffs it. It barely made the putting surface. So now what? He holes it of course. From twenty feet for a birdie. The kind of birdie only Ballesteros ever made.

His was a unique talent, learning how to play with a three iron on the beach near his home town in Pedrena, and I once found myself attending a clinic Seve was holding at his golf school in San Roque. Once again he was holding a three iron, and demonstrating how you could use it to play delicate greenside bunker shots. He casually splashed a couple out to a couple of feet or so, then did it again after deliberately giving himself a plugged lie. And now it was my turn. He gave me a short tutorial, then dropped a ball into the sand, and invited me to have a go. Remarkably, the ball floated out like a piece of confetti, and settled right next to the hole, which had the spectators gathered around the green first gasping, and then applauding. Seve smiled. 'Ees great shot. But I think, ees maybe fluke. You try one more,' he said. I tried once more, and on this occasion it came out with the trajectory of a normal three iron, like a freshly scalded cat, and very nearly performed an instant vasectomy on a stout gentleman perched on a shooting stick. Ballesteros was always incredibly enthusiastic when giving lessons, not least in pro-ams. The moment one of his amateur partners revealed himself to be a serial slicer was when Seve made it his solemn duty to cure him before the end of the round. Which he almost always did, even if it was mostly by turning them from a serial slicer into a serial hooker.

Seve had the reputation of being a difficult employer who would invariably blame the caddie when he hit a bad shot, and when it came to wages, he paid the bare minimum, a bit Tiger Woods in being cautious with his money. His agent once recounted the story of how he flew to a meeting in Spain, where Seve met him at the airport in an old pick-up truck. So he arranged for a sponsor to provide Ballesteros with a brand new Four-by-four, and expected to see it parked outside the terminal on his next visit. Instead, there was the old pick-up again. 'So what happened to the Four-by-four?' he asked. And Seve replied: 'Is okay. But too much miles to the gallon.'

Ballesteros will forever be associated with the Ryder Cup, and how he virtually single-handedly gave Europe the belief that they could beat the Americans. It had a lot to do with the fact that he didn't especially like Americans, and his relationship with one of them, Paul Azinger, got close to nasty at times. Azinger was once asked at a press conference what it took to beat Ballesteros, to which Azinger – having previously advanced the suggestion that Seve's persistent coughing had more to do with tactics than any medical condition – deliberately designed to be offputting – replied: 'I can tell you exactly what you need to beat Ballesteros. A pair of earplugs.' Seve's desire to beat the Americans knew no bounds, and while it rubbed off on most of his team-mates (and you can see the same thing now in Ian Poulter) there were some who didn't get it. One of these was David Gilford, a quiet, self-effacing chap whose experience of the 1995 Ryder Cup at Oak Hill put him off wanting to play in the event ever again, and you've never seen anyone look quite as startled as Gilford on the first tee when he was paired with Ballesteros in one of the fourball matches. Seve grabbed him by the shoulders, shook him hard, fixed him with those flashing eyes of his, and said: 'you. *You* are the best player in the world!' At the time, Ballesteros was in more or less terminal decline, and an appropriate riposte might have been something along the lines of: 'The way you're playing Seve, I'll need to be.' Instead, though, Ballesteros's legendary intensity rubbed off on his diffident partner, who did indeed perform like the best player in the world, and the match was won – with precious little help from Seve – 4&2. There has never been a golfer like Ballesteros. And probably never will be again.

Luis Suárez

Medical science continues to make tremendous advances, and scarcely a weekend passes without picking up your newspaper to read about some breakthrough or other. You know the sort of thing. A laboratory mouse gets injected with anti-Alzheimer's serum, and bingo! All of a sudden it remembers where it left that piece of cheese.

Does it not, therefore, strike you as anything short of remarkable that the best medical brains on the planet have still to discover precisely what it is that makes professional footballers keep falling over? And for no apparent reason.

I, for one, am anxious to discover which way round it is. Do people who fall over a lot become footballers? Or is after becoming a footballer that they find they just can't stop falling over? You wonder whether it might be some kind of unbalancing defect with the inner ear, but it's clearly an issue that needs urgently addressing, and the sooner those boffins trying to cure cancer put that on hold for a minute, and pay more attention to the really serious stuff, the better. And these days, of course, there's the even bigger issue of whether football is turning people into cannibals.

During last summer's World Cup in Brazil, I was down at the pub watching the Uruguay–Italy game when I asked a chum whether he could explain why such an obviously well-built chap like Luis Suárez, with a conspicuously low centre of gravity, should suddenly find himself thrown to the ground by what you couldn't even describe as a passing breeze. A zephyr would be stretching it. More like a draught.

'Well,' he replied. 'You can point the finger at Suárez if you like, but everyone does it. Robben, Ronaldo, everyone.' I had to agree, but what made Suárez the best of all time for me, I argued, was his unrivalled ability to make a meal of it. And a couple of minutes later there he was making a meal of an Italian defender. Literally.

What puzzled me about Luis was that he appeared to have little or no idea that several television cameras would have been pointing at him not only whenever he hurled himself to the ground for no reason, but also whenever he felt like sinking his teeth, Dracula like, into an opponent's flesh.

Suárez is such a hero in Uruguay that it was no great surprise when his country's Football Federation declared that it was all a wicked plot to destabilize their World Cup campaign, an argument which slightly fell by the wayside when their pin-up boy finally coughed. Albeit only in a manner which suggested that his teeth had a life of their own, and that they, rather than him, were very sorry.

The whole business got me wondering, upon the announcement that Suárez was leaving the Premier League for La Liga, whether the Spanish Football Federation might briefly have considered replacing a referee for Barcelona's matches with a waiter. 'So, let's see now, sir. The grilled Ronaldo to start, and fillet of Bale for the entrée. An excellent choice. And may I take the liberty of recommending the Rioja to go with them?'

As for the diving, it was while listening to a World Cup game on the car radio when my eye was caught by a road sign declaring how many fatal accidents had occurred on that stretch of road over the previous twelve months. And it got me wondering whether it wouldn't make sense to apply the same warning at footie matches.

You would, of course, place the sign just inside the penalty area, which is where – purely coincidentally I'm sure – most of the fatal, or near fatal accidents, take place. 'Warning: 257 incidents of players falling over in this area of the field during the last twelve months. Enter at your own risk.'

Until scientists find a cure for the falling-down footballer, my own personal solution would be to make it compulsory for all victims to be instantly flown to hospital by air ambulance, and left to lie on a trolley in a draughty corridor for about eight hours until an NHS doctor finally gets round to examining them.

It's not a new phenomenon, I hear you say, for footballers to fall over more often than usual during World Cups, and I'd have to agree. The 1966 World Cup, which was of course won by England, also had its fair share of players rolling around clutching their legs. The difference, though, was that they had just been tackled by Nobby Stiles, and it was perfectly legitimate for them to be examining their leg, if only to make sure that it was still attached to the body.

However, in fairness, not all footballers at the 2014 World Cup were sneaks and cowards. In fact, I've never seen anything braver in my entire life than the Uruguayan team all hugging and kissing each other when they scored a goal.

Personally, I'd have been terrified that my ear lobes would have resembled a tasty snack – and I've been waking up at night with the same recurring nightmare. I've just scored for Uruguay, and as I look up, there's Luis. Saliva dripping from his mouth, with one hand tying a napkin around his neck, and the other clutching a bottle of tomato ketchup.

14

''OWZAT?' 'THAT'S OUT.' 'I'LL BE OFF THEN'

Cricket as it used to be

I have been working for some time now on inventing a new game, which some might think bears certain resemblances to cricket. Perhaps because it involves a bloke with a bat, a bloke with a ball, a bloke wearing a white coat, someone shouting ''Owzat!', and the bloke in the coat putting up a finger. However, the difference in my game is that the bloke with the bat sees the bloke in the coat raising his finger, and without pausing, looking around, shaking his head, pointing to the edge of his bat, or making a signal to the bloke with the white coat which then involves everyone staring at an electronic screen for several hours, he leaves the field. And here's the really revolutionary part. In my abbreviated form of this new game, which will have its appeal in requiring the attention span of a goldfish, the person with the bat is allowed to leave the field with something approaching dignity, rather than to the sound of: 'Hit the Road Jack', or some similar inanity being piped through the pavilion loudspeakers.

That's how cricket was when I first started reporting on it, and while you can argue whether or not it's a better game now, it's certainly different. Not least in the kind of newspaper coverage that counties get. Years ago, a three-day match between, say, Leicestershire and Derbyshire would fill the press box with reporters ranging from the local news agency to representatives from all the national 'quality' papers, and quite a few of the tabloids as well. Nowadays, by way of contrast, the agency man brings along a good book, on the grounds he may have no one to talk to all day.

When I started out on the evening paper in Leicester, I was actually out of the office all summer chronicling the fortunes of Leicestershire CCC up and down the country. I can claim not only to have fielded at short leg to Ken Higgs, and mid off to Raymond Illingworth, but also, albeit for one fleeting moment, to have captained a team in the County Championship.

It's remarkable to think now that Test players like Illingworth and Higgs would have bothered turning out for a three-day friendly against Oxfordshire – you don't even see them in the County Championship nowadays – but that was certainly the case in 1977, and all you had to do to watch them in action was to wander into The Parks in Oxford and plonk yourself down on one of the wooden benches.

It started out as just a normal sort of day for me, which typically involved coming downstairs to find Illy having an animated discussion with the manager over the springs in his mattress, or complaining about the sausages, but on this occasion he stopped by my table and said: 'We might need you today, kid. Half the team's gone down with food poisoning.' 'Sure thing, Raymond. As long as I get choice of ends with the new ball,' I said, or something similar. But it turned it out he wasn't joking.

Leicestershire spent the morning session with only ten men, and that included borrowing the home team's twelfth man, and when the players came off for lunch Illy popped his head around the door of the press box and that's how I came to end up at short leg sledging some poor undergraduate (Higgs was coaching me from slip) for blocking. The rest of the time I stood at mid off hoping the ball wouldn't come my way, but there was one embarrassing moment when I missed it completely, made a half-hearted jog towards the boundary, and waited for some bloke in a deckchair to throw it back. It was only when he put down whatever he was reading and started waving his arms that I realized the ball had stopped just short of the rope, and by the time I finally got it back to a none-too-happy bowler, Les Taylor, the batsmen had run four.

Les was one of the dressing room characters who'd often have you in stitches with his engagingly dry humour, although he was never more amusing than when he had a bat in his hand and was facing a fast bowler. To describe Les as apprehensive in these circumstances would be something of an understatement, and more often than not, if you watched him through the binoculars, all you could see when the ball was being delivered was an unattended set of stumps.

It was at the Oval, somewhere around the mid-1980s. David Gower was the captain, and with my running copy for the paper over for the day I spent the last session, as I sometimes did, watching from the team balcony. It was the era when Sylvester Clarke was terrorizing batsmen all over the country – fast and mean when he bowled legally, and positively lethal when he chucked it. He'd already that day had Gower caught at slip with a delivery that had ripped the thumb protector clean off his glove, and Leicestershire were still in need of runs when their No. 11, Taylor, went out to bat. Or, in Les's case, try and stay alive. Les liked a roll-up, and I asked Gower whether he'd offered him a blindfold to go with his last cigarette. 'Mmm,' said the skipper. 'Fair point. What do you think?' I watched Les scratching out his guard, and Clarke pawing the ground at the end of his run-up. He was, as ever, expressionless, which somehow made him even more menacing, like Sonny Liston in his pomp. 'Well,' I said. 'He's got a young family, and Sue needs him more than you need the runs. If indeed he gets you any other than four leg byes off the helmet before he's stretchered off.' Whereupon Gower shot out of his chair, leaned over the balcony rail, and declared, bless him. Not for cricketing reasons, but on humanitarian grounds.

Compared to Test matches, county cricket attracted an entirely different type of spectator, many of whom really did wear cloth caps, shout: 'gerrronwithit!', and who wouldn't open their sandwich tins until the umpires took the bails off for the lunch interval. Not a minute before, and not a minute later. Then there was the press box, an apparently endless source of fascination to the spectators, who rarely managed to walk past the windows without having a good old stare at the occupants inside. Derbyshire played at half a dozen different grounds in the 1970s, and their evening paper reporter reckoned they had a different 'mad starer', as he called them, at every one. Spectators at county matches were mostly content just to peer at the inhabitants of the press boxes as they filed past, like a school crocodile on an afternoon tour of Madame Tussauds, but every now and again someone would actually come through the door to either offer you the benefit of their many years of accumulated wisdom, or else assail you with a battery of questions. Of which I offer a not untypical sample.

1. *'Plenty to write about today then!'* Normally through a half-opened door at the end of a game in which side A, chasing 220 to win, has gone from 216 for 0 with ten overs remaining, to 219 all out off the final ball. Inside, half a dozen perspiring hacks – having ripped up their original story – are frantically dashing off a complete re-write with about five minutes to deadline, and – in pre-mobile days – one handset between them. Reply least likely to be heard: 'Yes, jolly good finish wasn't it? That's what makes one-day cricket so exciting.'

2. *'What time do you think it will stop raining?'* Usually heard at one of the more primitive grounds, with no heating in the box, wind whistling through the slats, and rain dripping through

the roof and down the back of your neck. Reply you'd like to give, but rarely do: 'How the bleedin' heck should I know?'

3. *'Do you get to meet all the players?'* Usually timed shortly after you've just bumped into the opening batsman in the car park, and been verbally savaged for the pile of tripe you wrote about his innings yesterday. Usual answer: 'Yes, aren't I lucky?'

4. *'I wish I had your job.'* Again, timing crucial. Could be shortly after your 800-word story has just been mysteriously wiped from your laptop, and the office has just come on to tell you to send it at once because the page is about to go for printing. Answer: 'Don't tell me. Let me guess. You want to know whether I get paid for it as well, right?'

5. *'Have you seen the state of the ladies' toilets?'* Answer: 'Curiously enough, no. But I'm due to have a sex change at the weekend, so can I get back to you on Monday?'

6: *'What time do you think they'll declare then?'* Answer: None. Resist urge to say something along the lines of: 'Hang on a minute, I'll just drop what I'm doing and nip off to ask the captain', and point to watch before picking up telephone for imaginary conversation.

7. *'Which one of you is Martin Johnson?'* Answer (from anyone but Martin Johnson, in that revealing

this person's identity will be followed by an interminable ramble about members' bar prices, or team
selection, and 'Why don't you write something
about it? . . .'): 'Sorry, he's not here. Wasn't feeling
too well, and went home at lunchtime.'

Apart from the fact that people get bowled, caught, and
given out lbw, the county game is a world apart from Test
cricket, as you might expect given its permanently parlous
finances and two-men-and-a-dog attendances. Derbyshire
once offered membership for dogs, and why not? Cricket
has a long tradition of treating its supporters in much the
same way as their canine companions, so it's only right and
proper that they should be able to enjoy a pint and a bone
together in the members' bar. Another difference between
reporting on a county match and a Test match is that at
the former you know most of the supporters by name,
mostly on account of the fact that there aren't very many
of them, but occasionally because they're what's known as
'characters'.

One of Leicestershire's more elderly members in the
1970s was such a one, and popular enough with his fellow
spectators for the club to turn a blind eye to most of his
foibles – the exception being when the combination of his
beer intake and old age proved too much for his plumbing and resulted in him relieving himself all over the tulip
beds. Chris Wright was his name, nicknamed Foghorn on
account of a voice that could strip wallpaper from twenty
paces, and he lived in a terraced house across the road
from one side of the ground. 'I'm on me way!' he'd shout,
just before closing his front door, and about ten minutes

later you'd see him embark on the first of about a dozen circumnavigations of the ground, clutching a pint of mild with which to refresh himself on the way. The ratio of the amount he drank to the amount he spilt being roughly 50:50. He'd stop at regular intervals to offer advice on the state of the game, whether the scoring rate needed picking up, or whether the captain had the right bowlers on. The captain, Illingworth, once confided to me that there were times when he was about to make a bowling change, such as bringing on Jack Birkenshaw, when Foghorn would shout 'Bring Birky on!' And Illingworth would have to do something else. 'I couldn't let it look as though he was captaining the team, could I?'

Illy captained Leicestershire to the County Championship for the first time in their history in 1975, and by common consent he and the club's secretary-manager, Mike Turner, made a formidable team. They did, however, occasionally clash, and the fact that the boundaries were often shortened to accommodate sponsored marquees was a major area of disagreement. 'We've got t'best ruddy spin attack in t'country, and I can't ruddy bowl 'em cos of fifty ruddy yard boundaries.' Followed by his favourite expression when displeased: 'It's a ruddy piss'ole is that.' On one particular afternoon, when Illingworth was bowling from the pavilion end on a pitch far enough across the square to make the legside boundary even shorter than usual, a tail-ender had a bucolic heave at one of his deliveries, and the ball sailed over the rope for six and straight into the Bostik tent. It took a while for the ball to get returned, possibly because it first needed to be wiped clean of salmon mousse, which gave Raymond the opportunity to stride forty yards or so to a spot directly underneath the committee balcony and launch into a long tirade about 't'ruddy boundaries'.

As we touched upon earlier, Illy was a constant source of entertainment when it came to locking horns with hotel managers, although he did meet his match once at the Victoria Hotel in Canterbury, the proprietor of which made Basil Fawlty seem positively normal. We arrived there after a long drive from Leicester, and after checking in, a few of us popped into the residents' bar at around five to eleven for a nightcap. After much ringing of the bell, Basil finally appeared, looked at the clock on the wall, and nearly took the fingertips off our opening batsman's hand when he hauled down the grille. 'Sorry, we're closed,' he said. 'But we're residents,' someone said. 'Don't care. We're closed', he said, and disappeared. Next morning, at the kind of hour employed for police raids, the phone rang in my room. It was Basil. 'What do you want for breakfast?' 'I beg your pardon? Do you know what time it is?' 'Yes, and I've got a lot to get on with, so how do you want your eggs? Fried? Boiled?' I muttered something about having them like my brain – scrambled – which presumably satisfied him as he promptly, without a further word, hung up. Everyone had had the same call, including Illingworth, and an interesting conversation was just developing between them in the breakfast room when Basil suddenly broke off in mid-sentence. 'Oy, you!' Everyone looked up from their pre-ordered eggs, including the left-arm spinner Nick Cook, to whom Basil was now pointing. 'Yes, you!' 'What about me?' enquired Cook, after digesting a mouthful of whatever type of egg Basil had wrung out of him in the middle of the night. 'You can't come in here dressed like that!' said Basil. 'Dressed like what?' said Cook. 'Like that,' said Basil, aiming his pointed finger a little lower down. 'No socks!' Cook was wearing sandals, with indeed, as Basil was claiming, a distinct absence of sock. There was no small print on the breakfast menu stating that eggs, fried, boiled, poached or scrambled, could only be consumed by guests wearing socks, but Basil stood his ground until Cook returned to his room to comply with this unwritten regulation. And so it went on.

One morning, several of the players were sitting in the lobby, waiting for the drivers of the team's sponsored cars to pull up outside for them, whereupon Basil turned up with a vacuum cleaner and started hoovering over their shoes. The last straw for Illingworth was early the following evening, when he decided on an aperitif from the bar well before the sort of time you risked having your fingertips removed by the grille. He rang the bell, several times, and Basil finally arrived with a napkin around his neck. 'Not now,' he said. 'I'm having my dinner.' In his entire career, it was only the second recorded instance of Raymond being rendered speechless – the other one was when I was roped in to be his bridge partner during a long delay for rain, and I managed to go four down in a cast-iron three no trump contract. Cricketers always play cards during rain delays, but it was more of a problem knowing how to amuse yourself in the press box while it was hammering down outside. Crossword puzzles and catching up on getting your records and averages up to date were the favourite, although occasionally we'd invent things like coming up with your Ugly or Thick XI. Just occasionally we'd think of something a bit more novel, and on one soggy day at Leicester, Terry Cooper, of the Press Association, suggested a competition involving movie clichés. It was nearly forty years ago now, but I've still kept the list of some of the phrases we came up with:

'You'll never take me alive, copper.'

'Listen, and listen good. Because I'm only going to say this once.'

'Nobody calls me Sonny. Leastways, not twice.'

'Get yourself another boy. I'm through.'

'Drink this. It will make you strong.'

'All right, I did kill him. And I'm glad. Glad, glad, glad, d'you hear.'

'Police! Open up!'

'Come in Inspector. I've been expecting you.'

'There's a stage at noon. Be on it.'

'Blackmail's an ugly word, inspector.'

'Don't be a fool, Johnny. Throw down your gun and come out with your hands up.'

'A man could settle down here. Raise kids.'

'Call yourself a father? I never had a father!'

'Let's not play games, shall we?'

'Are you people gonna let him get away with this?'

'Get a doctor. Quick.'

'You can't fire me. I quit.'

If it hadn't stopped raining we'd still be going, but the most memorable rain interruption I can remember involved a Sunday League forty-over match between Gloucestershire and Leicestershire at Cheltenham College. It had started raining on Saturday afternoon, and rarely has rain been more richly deserving of the description 'stair rods'. It was still rodding it down at bedtime, and still bouncing off the pavements when the players came down for breakfast. And given that it was still persisting at around 11am, three hours before the scheduled start, two of the players, Ian Butcher and Paddy Clift, decided a lunchtime-ish Sunday pint might be in order. And with no chance of either of them having to play cricket, or me having to write about it, would I care to join them? Anyway, one pint became three, and in the absence of a passing gondola, we eventually hailed a cab – windscreen wipers on full speed – to the ground. Which was, predictably, devoid of all spectators.

I squelched over to the press box at around 1.30, half an hour before we were due to start play, and found that the local agency man had already given up all prospects of play and gone home. Soon after that, Butcher put his head around the door to inform me that the players and press had been invited into one of the hospitality tents if I fancied joining them, and by half past four everyone was spectacularly pissed. It came, therefore, as something of a shock when one of the umpires, Merv Kitchen, poked his head around the tent flap, caught the attention of the respective captains – David Graveney and David Gower – and informed everyone that the rain had stopped, and the ground was fit enough to squeeze in a ten-over-a-side

272

slog before the cut-off point. Which met with hoots of derision, and invitations for Merv to pull the other one. However, shock horror, it transpired that Merv was deadly serious, and the players dashed off – wobbled would be more accurate – to get changed.

The Leicestershire captain, Gower, relieved himself of coin-tossing duties on the grounds that he wouldn't be able to recognize a head from a tail, and the job was entrusted to one of the more sober players. Or to be more accurate, less inebriated. There was one change to the Leicestershire side, with Butcher being ruled out with a broken nose, sustained while popping his head around the home dressing room door at the precise moment one of the Gloucestershire players, Paul Romaines, was practising his golf swing. With a bat. And somehow, the game got played. Gower set the fielding tone very early on by diving the wrong way, like a goalie trying to guess a penalty. Batsmen either flailed away at fresh air, or removed very large divots, while bowlers aimed at a target they knew from experience was roughly twenty-two yards away, but that they were unable to see. It was a shame the game took place in front of an empty press box, as it would have been interesting to see some of the match reports.

It certainly qualified as one of the more interesting Sunday League games, as the forty-over format – introduced in 1969 – had by that time become deadly dull. Side A makes cautious start, trying not to lose wickets, and with ten overs to go, and wickets in hand, starts slogging. Side B makes cautious start, trying not to lose wickets, and with ten overs to go, and wickets in hand, starts slogging. One team wins in the final over, and the spectator goes home under the deluded impression he's seen something exciting. Inside the press box, however, no one would even look up until about six o'clock in the evening, and the real joy about travelling to these matches was to have some banter with old chums. Each press box had a character of its own, often the agency man. At Sussex it was Jack Arlidge, who was forever quoting Shakespeare, and who hired out two telephones. 'Which one Jack?' you'd ask when you wanted to use one. 'The one nearest Middlesbrough,' he'd say, pointing to the one furthest away. Then there was Dudley Moore down in Kent, who couldn't pronounce his THs, the scoreline of 33 for 3 thus becoming, when he phoned the score through to the press association, 'firty free for free'.

In Yorkshire, it was Dick Williamson, who was virtually blind, and couldn't read the scoreboard without the assistance of a pair of Second World War Navy binoculars. One day, during a match at Bradford, he still couldn't see the scoreboard, and wandered onto the field to get a bit closer. 'Hey!' one of the fielders shouted. 'Get off the field.' To which Dick retorted: 'And you get on with your daft silly game. Take a look around you. See many people? One day you'll realize that no one wants to watch you. All they want is the score.' Dick would chat away all day, about all manner of subjects, and on one occasion it happened to be why milometers on cars didn't register anything when you were driving backwards. 'Just think,' said Dick. 'If you drove it everywhere in reverse, you could sell it in about ten years with only three miles on the clock.' At which point, a voice from the back of the box was heard to say: 'Bloody hell. Is that right?' The voice belonged to a Northern cricket writer, and the acknowledged master when it came to claiming on expenses. In fact, I never sat through a day's cricket with him in the box when he didn't spend at least nine-tenths of it doing his expenses. 'Bloody hell,' he repeated. 'I've got the longest front drive in Yorkshire, and I've reversed out of it every day for the past twenty-five years. Let's work this out, now.' And about three hours later he proudly announced that he had travelled about two hundred miles backwards over the course of the previous quarter of a century, without claiming for them, and he duly put in his bill (for 'reverse mileage') to the paper. And, by all accounts, they paid it.

Press boxes in Yorkshire and Derbyshire were the equivalent, for those entering them for the first time, of an initiation ceremony. The door would open, some fresh-faced youth would enter, and the general hubbub would give way to a sudden silence – like the piano player stopping when a stranger enters the saloon in a Western. The gnarled old veterans who'd sat in these press boxes since the days of Hutton and Compton didn't take pris-oners. They were working out what sport might be had from this new boy, looking him over so intensely that he'd feel obliged to look and check whether his flies were undone. Then they set the trap by way of a seemingly casual conversation. 'Interesting story behind Derbyshire's new signing, don't you think?' 'I'll say. Son of a Japanese basketball player. Doesn't come more unusual than that.' 'Plus being the first openly gay fast bowler on the county's books.' 'Yup. Quite a tale to be sure.' And the newcomer would earwig all this, and write it into his match report.

They weren't so cruel at Leicester, where the agency man was a dear old chap called Billy King, who never attended a match without his wife Celia. Quite why he felt the need to bring her along was a bit of a mystery, as she didn't offer any practical assistance, and mostly seemed to irritate him with daft questions. In one game involving Surrey's Pakistani batsman Younis Ahmed, Billy put down the phone after reading over the teams, and Celia said: 'I didn't know some teams had women players, Billy.' 'They don't,' he snorted. 'Oh,' said Celia. 'In that case, who's this Eunice Ahmed?' Her real forte was in pouring the tea every afternoon, and serving the buttered scones. Billy would be halfway through his report and get a sudden tap on the shoulder from Celia. 'Do you want jam on your scone Billy? Or just butter.' Billy wasn't the most patient of men, and would invariably fire back with: 'For goodness sake, can't you see I'm on the phone . . .' and back he'd go to his report, with Celia muttering, 'Well don't blame me if they've eaten all the jam when you're finished.'

Eventually, Billy became a bit too old for the job, and on one occasion, when Northamptonshire were the visitors, the two Watts brothers, PJ and PD, each took five of Leicestershire's ten wickets. Billy started to phone over the scorecard, and was interrupted by a tap on the shoulder by the reporter from the *Daily Mail*. 'Billy,' he said. 'You've got them the wrong way round. You've given all of PJ's wickets to PD, and all of PDs to PJ.' Billy waved a dismissive arm and carried on. 'But Billy—' 'Look, I'm on the phone here.' 'But I'm just trying—' 'Will you stop interrupting!' And finally, after he'd finished, a long silence was ended by the *Daily Mail* man picking up the phone to call his sports desk. 'You will,' he said, 'shortly be receiving the agency scorecard for Leicestershire's first innings against Northants. Do not print it. It is wrong. In its entirety. Every single wicket is wrong. Put me on to a copytaker, and I will dictate the correct scorecard.' And he did. Five minutes passed, with no one saying a word, whereupon Billy picked up his phone. 'Hello old chap,' he said. 'Leicester here. I'm afraid the scorers have got into a frightful muddle here, so I've got an official correction to the scorecard.'

Saturdays were always different, in that the Sunday papers, like *The Times* and the *Observer*, were in the habit of employing non-journalists to write their cricket reports. Usually schoolmasters on their day off, who'd written in offering their services. And being by definition cricket anoraks, a lot of them were frankly a bit odd. There was one genial chap called Michael Booth, who wrote for *The Sunday Times*, who appeared to require at least seventeen different confirmations of an event before he could trust himself to write it down as a fact in his note-book. He also had a habit of sitting outside the press box, and watching from one of the deckchairs, so that when a wicket fell, he'd spring up from his seat and dash up the stairs to the press box. 'Did anyone see that? How was he out?' 'Bowled, Michael.' 'You sure? Not stumped then?' 'Bowled, Michael.' 'It's just that from my angle it wasn't that easy to see, so I need to check. Bowled you say.' 'Bowled, Michael.' 'Right, bowled it is then. Was it off stump, or leg stump?' 'Middle stump, Michael.' 'Ah right. Middle stump. Clean bowled, or played on?' 'Clean bowled, Michael.' 'You sure?' 'Yes Michael. Quite sure.' 'Was he attacking? Defending?' 'He just missed it Michael.' 'Yes, but did it move a bit off the seam do you think?' 'Missed a straight one, Michael.' 'Maybe swung a bit do you think?' 'No Michael.' And after about ten minutes of this, he'd go back down to his deckchair, tap the shoulder of the bloke sitting next to him, and you'd hear him say: 'That last wicket. I think it was bowled. Was it bowled? Did you see it? The ball? Did it do anything? I mean, did he just miss it? Played on? Through the gate? Careless shot? Good ball? Or what?'

15

THEATRES OF SCREAMS

Highly strung at Wimbledon and crackpot potters at the Crucible

Wimbledon

For eleven and a half months of the year, the great British public takes only marginally more interest in tennis than in small bore pistol shooting, or bar billiards. And yet for the other two weeks, Wayne Rooney could dye his hair purple and knock in a double hat-trick while balancing a pint of lager on his head without budging Andy Murray v Aleksandr Nedovyesov from the no. 1 item on the back pages. Wimbledon tennis fortnight is a strange phenomenon, somehow persuading people who would normally prefer to have their toenails removed without anaesthetic rather than watch a Swede and a Croatian biffing a yellow ball back and forth over a net, to camp out on a pavement all night for the privilege of watching them at Wimbledon. Remember Henmania? It was one of those localized viruses which didn't really travel very far – and at places like Roland Garros, Flushing Meadows and Melbourne Park could be treated with half a Junior Disprin. At the All England Club, however, it was more virulent than the Black Death, attacking hitherto normal people and causing them to jump up and down in front of a giant screen on a grassy bank and shout: 'C'mon Tim!' The government was once rumoured to be considering emergency measures, such as ordering crop-spraying planes to hose down every sleeping bag between the All England Club and Southfields Tube station, although most years the most effective control for the virus was when it came into contact with the Pete Sampras strain of antibody.

A no less potent variant of the virus would infect BBC cameramen, who were incapable of letting a point go by without a close-up of Mr and Mrs Tim watching from the competitors' box. I myself broke out into a mild fever as Wimbledon fortnight crept ever closer, usually involving shooting bolt upright in bed, and sobbing: 'No! Please don't send me! I'll do anything. Squash. Archery. Dressage. But please not Wimbledon!' Accompanied by a recurring nightmare in the days, sometimes weeks, building up to the tournament. It involved seeking sanctuary on some remote Scottish island, only to wander past a crofter's cottage to hear Virginia Wade's dirge-like tones coming through the window: '. . . and she's simply got no answer to the Belarusian girl's backhand'. There are few more pretentious places than Wimbledon, where sweets are sold as bon-bons, for heaven's sake, and hot dogs as dutchees. Or for that matter, more predictable. If Andy Murray is playing, we'll have endless close-ups of Andy's mother and girlfriend, and if he's not, the director is fond of cutting to the Royal Box for shots of Terry Wogan or Bruce Forsyth.

The most interesting thing about Wimbledon, in my book, is the interviews, which are normally far more entertaining than the match you've just been watching. There are two main interview rooms at Wimbledon, and I could happily spend all afternoon in either of them, eating popcorn, drinking Kia-Ora, and awarding marks for the most banal interview of the day. And if you miss any, you can always take the transcripts away with you to read on the Tube back to the hotel, or in the pub. One evening, sitting on a bar stool at a pub in Putney, people kept coming up to me and asking if I was all right. It had something to do with tears rolling down my cheeks, and the loud wheezing noises that were being mistaken for some terrible ailment but were in fact the product of help-less laughter. I'd grabbed a handful of transcripts for a spot of light reading over a pint, and laughed so loud on one occasion that I sprayed the poor chap on the next stool with a mouthful of London Pride. Every single transcript involved a woman reporter asking the players what they thought about strawberries, and what tickled me was just how many players tried to give her a serious answer, in the same way as a cabinet minister might have done when invited by John Humprys to explain the unemployment figures on *Today*.

> Q: 'What do you like about strawberries? Why do you think there is a tradition here? A symbol?'
>
> Sergi Bruguera: 'Very good.'

Q: 'What do you think about the traditional strawberries here?'

Lori McNeil: 'What do I think of them? I love them. I eat them.'

Q: 'Why do you think strawberries are a symbol of Wimbledon?'

Martina Hingis: 'I don't know. That's a good question.'

Q: Why do you think . . .?'

Pete Sampras: 'Because they sell them here?'

Q: What is your association with strawberries?'

Sampras: 'I don't like strawberries.'

Q: 'But you like Wimbledon.'

Sampras: 'Yes.'

Q: 'I wouldn't like to let this opportunity go by without asking you if you like strawberries.'

Goran Ivanisevic: 'Why?'

Q: 'Would you care to tell us what you think about strawberries?'

Andre Agassi: 'What the . . .? Are you . . .? Did I

hear that right? We're professionals in this room. Do you realize that? Jeez.' (Agassi, by the way, was such a huge fan of press conferences that he occasionally opted to pay the compulsory fine for giving one a miss.)

Then there were questions that made you think the strawberry ones were verging on the sensible.

Q: 'What did you think of Becker when he went for a toilet break?'

Martina Navratilova: 'I don't know. I didn't go with him.'

Q: 'Do you go sightseeing?'

Sampras: 'I drive past Big Ben every ride home.'

Q: 'Do you have a great fear of being normal?'

Lindsay Davenport: 'I *am* normal.'

Q: 'Are you looking forward to your doubles match with Lori McNeil?'

Bryan Shelton: 'No. We're not playing together.'

Q: 'Do you think it's time to reflect, not about your match, but about your life right now?'

Boris Becker: 'Is he serious?'

And there were other transcripts revealing the emotional strain all those questions must put the players through.

Q: 'Who would you like to play in the next round?'

Ivanisevic: 'Bates.'

Q: 'You've got a mixed record against Brits, haven't you?'

Ivanisevic: 'I don't like to play Brits much.'

Q: 'Why do you want Bates then?'

Ivanisevic: 'I don't know.'

Q: Tough match today.

Todd Martin: 'That was a match I would not have won two years ago.'

Q: 'Why?'

Martin: 'I have no idea.'

Q: 'What part of Wimbledon do you enjoy?'

Bruguera: 'Not one.'

Q: 'Not one?'

Bruguera: 'Not one.'

The worst thing about Wimbledon is never knowing what time to get there, or what time you'd be leaving the place. By comparison, a football match or a rugby game was easy. Get there an hour before kick-off, and leave about an hour after the final whistle. But at Wimbledon, with so many matches on the same day, you were at the mercy of the office, and lived in constant dread of hearing the instruction: 'Your match is third on Court 1.' Which would turn out to be a ladies' singles, scheduled to follow two men's matches that would inevitably be five-set marathons, meaning your own match wouldn't even start until supper time. Leaving you with a report straddling three different deadlines, and sometimes not even getting finished. Suspended in pitch darkness, at one set all, for completion the following day. You'd get to the pub just in time for last orders, with your colleagues having kindly saved you a bag of salted peanuts in lieu of the splendid dinner you were unable, sadly, to join them for. You'd do anything to avoid a late match, desperately pleading down the phone for anything at all that was first on. You find yourself holding the most bizarre conversations with the office. 'But what's wrong with Miss Krstulovic v Miss Strebotnik on Court 17? It's the one everyone's talking about. The match of the championship. If not the decade. I've checked the women players' handbook and it's fascinating stuff. Miss Krstulovic has a pet Chihuahua named "Popsicle", and Miss Strebotnik likes to eat sushi while watching *Home and Away*. Hello. Hello. Are you still there?' Then there were the bad-weather days – long before the Centre Court acquired a roof – which involved the following sorts of conversation. 'What do you mean, you want 800 words? On what exactly? There hasn't been a ball struck all day. It's been pissing down since breakfast time, or hadn't you noticed? Look, can't you give an extra page to the cricket or something? Hello? Hello?'

And so, on one such occasion, I opened my umbrella, gave a Captain Oates-style 'I may be gone for some time' farewell to the Press tent, and wandered off to find out whether A. Gondola was an unseeded Italian on Court 16, or something to be hired for the journey back to Southfields Tube Station. The special of the day at one of Wimbledon's swankier restaurants was half a stuffed lobster – possibly sent round from Billingsgate, but more probably, I thought, caught in a pot hanging from one of the outside court covers. Everywhere you looked there were spectators huddled together in miserable-looking groups, resembling the crew of a North Sea trawler out on deck in a Force Nine, but just in case some of them needed reminding that it was raining, the All England Club was piping Cliff Richard music through the loudspeakers, interrupted from time to time with weather updates. 'Ladies and gentlemen. We *must* remain optimistic!' It wasn't an invitation, it was an instruction. There was, though, little to be optimistic about. There were none of the usual queues outside the 'used championship balls' stall, as there weren't any used balls to sell on account of the rain. And up on Henman Hill, the giant video screen was offering a guided tour of the Wimbledon Museum. 'Every year at the championship, 80,000 half-pints of Pimm's are consumed' boomed the commentary. The spectators digested this fascinating piece of information, and pined all the harder for a mug of Bovril. The screen also showed scenes of the groundstaff putting the covers on, almost as fast as a Formula One pit crew changing a set of tyres. One year, I recalled, they were so fast that a large bulge underneath the tarpaulin turned out to be a member of the workforce, who was on the verge of asphyxiation when someone noticed he was missing and pulled him out. The Hillites would probably have preferred to see some tennis up on the screen, or last year's re-runs of themselves jumping up and down and waving perhaps. It's a strange business, but whenever the people on the Hill realize that the camera is on them, they abandon their picnic, or whatever it is they're doing, and start cheering and waving to themselves.

Then, just when you thought it couldn't possibly get any more interesting, there was a short feature about a day in the life of a Wimbledon woman tennis player. It began with here telephoning the All England Club's courtesy car hotline – 'Can you send a car round in ten minutes please?' – and continued with a cheery conversation with her chauffeur on the way to the Club. 'Lovely day isn't it?' she said, giving the sodden spectators a clue as to the fact that this wasn't going out live. 'Certainly is. Are you ready for your match?' 'Yes. I'm looking forward to it.' That was enough for me, and it was back to the press centre, where the BBC director was filling a day with no tennis with much more exciting stuff than the Hillites had been getting. The Beeb had pressed Greg Rusedski's wife Lucy into action as a roving television reporter, and had sent her off to a letting agency to find out what kind of property the superstars had been renting this year. 'Do you leave food for them?' Lucy wanted to know. 'What about the microwave oven? Do you take it away?' Riveting or what? It was enough to make you stop fretting that Jeremy Paxman can't go on forever, and will need replacing one day. After that it was a visit to the players' restaurant, where a Swede by the name of Thomas Johansson told us that rainy days made it tough for the players to stay focused and relaxed. 'As you can see,' said Thomas, 'the weather is not good.' In actual fact, all we could see at that precise moment was a player in the queue taking possession of a plate of pasta, but Thomas was certainly right about the weather, despite a series of announcements trying to convince the fans that brighter skies were just around the corner. Which indeed they might have been had we been in Melbourne or Paris, but not in SW19, and the inevitable abandonment announcement finally had everyone streaming for the exits. Apart, that is, from those poor hacks such as myself, who'd by then managed around four hundred words of waffle, and with four hundred more still required, were wondering whether to use that interview with the catering manager about what effect the rain had had on strawberry sales.

People occasionally ask me who my favourite tennis players are, and the entirely truthful answer is always: 'The ones who win the first set of the match I've been asked to write about.' On the grounds that only that particular player could possibly go on to win in straight sets, and thereby ensure you get away reasonably early. Some, of course, are more watchable than others, and it was always a regret that I never saw much of John McEnroe. I'm told that it was worth a night on the pavement just to see one of his backhands, and having seen on TV the backhand that destroyed an entire table of glasses and water jugs in a

Davis Cup tie in Stockholm – almost drowning the King of Sweden in the process – I can well believe it.

Mostly, though, while managing to appreciate that some-one like Federer has an attractive way of playing, I always found a player's quirks and foibles far more interesting than whether they had an aesthetically pleasing forehand, or a well-disguised drop shot. Which made Greg Rusedski my first real tennis hero, mostly for his peculiar mannerisms during a match. Especially during changeovers. With most players, those TV close-ups of them sitting in their chairs more often than not involve someone in trance-like medi-tation, staring blankly ahead while plotting their strategy for the next game. Greg, on the other hand, had far too much to cram into his sixty seconds to waste any time thinking about strategy. In fact, Greg was the one player at Wimbledon, or any tournament come to that, who needed a break after a break. When Greg sat down, his table looked more like something you'd find on the Duchess of Arundel's back lawn just before the neighbours popped round for afternoon tiffin. Towels, paper cups, water, all manner of different-coloured liquids, bananas, and a pile of energy bars. First, he'd towel himself down, then work his way through the water and coloured liquids in what appeared to be a strict order of preference. It would go something like: swig of water – bite of banana – swig of orange stuff – bite of banana – swig of blue stuff – bite of banana – swig of water. All of this while untying his shoelaces half a dozen times, and then tying them back up again. He also liked to pluck at his racket strings every five seconds, possibly to check whether they were more tightly strung than he was. Then there were his endearing attempts to convert from being Canadian to British, which only just stopped short of him walking onto court wearing a Noel Coward smoking jacket, and calling the umpire: 'old chap'. For my money, though, he only finally became a fully-fledged Brit during a match against the American Andy Roddick at the Australian Open, when he called the umpire a 'wanker'. The agency reporter dealing with the transcript for North American consumption called across to his colleague: 'Say, they'll never understand this British word back home' and altered 'wanker' to 'jerk'.

Is Roger Federer the best player ever? Don't ask me, ask someone who knows about tennis, although you'd have to say that all these different-era comparisons are nigh on impossible. Look at motor racing. The cars these days more or less drive themselves, while Fangio whizzed around wearing a swimming cap, half blinded by oil running down his goggles, and losing a filling from his teeth every time one his pneumatic tyres clipped a kerb. And how would Federer have got on with Rod Laver's old tennis racket? Used it for straining spaghetti most likely. Besides which, modern tennis players aren't built how they used to be. Ken Rosewall was nicknamed 'Muscles' in the same way that bald men are called 'Curly', and if Ken were playing today, he'd be blown off court in the ladies' singles. However, there is one measure of Federer's greatness that may have been slightly overlooked, and for me it just tips the balance in favour of him being regarded as the greatest of all time. It is one thing to dominate men's tennis over a considerable period, but quite another to do so while forever having to fiddle with your coiffeur. Laver came on court looking as though he'd just spent five minutes with an inebriated Australian sheep shearer, but Federer had to grapple with three different eras of awkward hairstyle.

First there was the pony-tail, when the band holding it in place required adjustment after every point. Then there was the Ena Sharples bun. The grand old lady of Coronation Street managed to cope by encasing it in a hair net, but no such luxury for Roger, whose own bun invariably involved a rogue, flyaway strand, not dissimilar to Bobby Charlton's towards the end of his career. And next up we had the almost sensible haircut, but not sensible enough to prevent bits of it from having to be constantly tucked back inside his headband. He also, lest historians forget when they come to weigh these things, had to combine his tennis with a modelling career, what with his monogrammed designer cardies, jackets and handbags. On one occasion, when he dipped into the handbag before the knock-up, you wondered whether he might be rummaging around for a silk cravat, and the crowd clearly shared that thought too, judging from the sigh of disappointment when all he came up with was a pair of sweatbands. He reminded me a bit of the old comic-book footballer Gorgeous Gus, aka the Earl of Boote, who used to play centre forward for Redburn Rovers. Gus was a member of the aristocracy, who would hand his silk dressing gown to his butler before the kick-off, score a first-half hat-trick, and leave to open a village fete. News would then reach him that Rovers had now been pegged back to 3–3 with five minutes left to play, at which point his chauffeur would drive him back to the ground in his Bentley, and Gus, pausing only to receive a mouth spray from the butler (lest he come into contact with any germs from the *hoi polloi* he was forced to share a pitch with) would go out and score a last-minute winner.

Gus never did anything remotely as vulgar as running, or perspiring, instead demanding that the ball be delivered precisely to the point of his boot before shooting – the similarity extending to Federer in his pomp, who only ever appeared to break sweat when absolutely necessary. I don't recall Gus ever giving a press conference, but if he had, it couldn't possibly have been as excruciatingly dull as one of Federer's. He might have been a magician on court, but Federer was almost as boring in the interview room as Pete Sampras, although in fairness to both of them, almost all of the questions in a men's tennis interview – apart from the year of the strawberries – are about, er, tennis. There are only so many ways you can tell people how you managed to save those break points in the second set. Who knows, Federer might even have had something interesting to say if he'd been quizzed more often about his fashion accessories. The Williams sisters, by contrast, usually get the tennis questions (if there are any) over and done with quickly, before the interview moves on to the really exciting stuff, like earrings and handbags.

It's an odd business, but while men's tennis is mainly exciting on the court and tedious off it, the reverse is true of the women's game. Five minutes after the No. 1 seed has dusted off some Ova or other from the Eastern Bloc, in she comes to the interview room to a barrage of questions about her choice of knicker colour, whether she intends to spend her rest day being photographed with the giraffes at

Whipsnade Zoo, or whether she's missing her pet dog. All women tennis players seem to have dogs, hence the way you end up with interviews that are appropriately barking. Where else, other than the Wimbledon interview room after a couple of ladies' singles matches, could you find the following post-match dialogue?

Q: (to Venus Williams) 'Is your dog Bobby your lucky charm?'

A: 'Well, Bobby has been having some discipline problems lately.'

Q: 'Really?'

A: 'Yeah.'

Q: 'Is that why your game is fluctuating?'

A: 'As a mom (of the dog, this is) you have to worry.'

Q: 'If Bobby were here?'

A: 'He'd be a joy every day. He's a feel-good dog.'

Which was followed later in the day by a press conference involving sister Serena.

Q: 'Do you have a dog problem like your sister?'

A: 'What type of problem does she have?'

Q: 'She was missing Bobby a lot.'

A: 'I have pictures of my dogs in my purse. I look
at them every day. I don't want to talk about it.'

Martina Navratilova once decided that she was missing her
pet dog so much during an extended stay in Australia that
she had to go out and buy one. She bought it during a tournament in Sydney, and when she then flew to Melbourne
for the Australian Open, she had the pooch driven down
by car to join her. Perhaps in one of those stretch limos
with a cocktail cabinet and a TV, and the chauffeur under
strict instructions to stop at all available lamp-posts. But
for the return journey to America, the animal went with
her on the same plane. Possibly in an adjoining seat in first
class. 'Would sir like an aperitif before dinner, or should
I serve the marrowbone now?' On occasions, when the
questioning strayed away from dogs and into areas like
gay rights, Navratilova press conferences could be heavy
going, but generally speaking, if there were ever a case
for equal prize money for women tennis players, it's the
entertainment value they provide in the interview room.
And in this area, the Williams sisters are definitely the best
of all time.

Venus once spent most of an interview after a match
at Wimbledon talking about her male hitting partner's
coiffeur. 'He has, like, really great hair, so I told him, your
hair is great. I hate it. It's not fair.' And within seconds
we'd seamlessly moved onto her love of reading. And the
novel she was currently reading. 'It's called *Who Moved
My Cheese?* My dad told me to read it. I was, like, praying

for some inspiration, so then I read the book, and I was, like, okay, God answered my prayers.' Serena once sat through a press conference fielding one question about the match she'd just played, and the next twenty-four questions about the size of her bottom. It was at the Australian Open, and an unflattering photograph in one of the morning newspapers had been printed, along with a pretty uncomplimentary article, only just stopping short of suggesting that if she felt like taking a dip off one of Melbourne's beaches, she'd need to be accompanied by Greenpeace to protect her from Japanese whalers.

Nevertheless, Serena not only cheerfully answered all posterior-related questions, but somehow turned the entire body-shape question into how God made all creatures different. And started banging on about Genesis. The Old Testament version, as opposed to the rock group. 'Genesis is so much fun, you know; all about the creation. You get to read about how God made the earth in seven days, but there's parts of it that make you wonder. Like about the dinosaurs. I don't get it. God made part of the earth on the first day, so maybe that's when the dinosaurs lived.' Thought provoking, you have to admit. Clearly, tennis is the kind of sport that has a strange effect on everyone involved in it, including the commentators.

The Australian Open was a perfectly normal tournament until they decided to ask Jim Courier to do the post-match interviews, and a more oleaginous chump you'd have to go a long way to find. When Federer was in his pomp, Jim nearly drowned in his own saliva. 'Tell me, can you cook? Do you make your own bed? Is there anything the Fed can't do?' And Andy Roddick was once lost for words when Jim inquired: 'Just what it is that makes you so hot?' Which is why Wimbledon will always be the superior Slam. No one gets carried away in front of the microphone (although Virginia Wade sounding like the Speaking Clock may be too big a step in the opposite direction) and even bad behaviour has a tradition of commentators giving their own slant on the old Dan Maskell technique of a mildly disapproving, 'Oh, I say.'

I remember a match involving Goran Ivanisevic walking back to his chair in a boiling rage – a condition not uncommon in the volatile Croatian – and it was clear that he was giving serious thought to turning his tennis racket into the equivalent of a box of cocktail sticks. An option he finally decided to exercise. John Barrett was commentating, and immediately sprung to the player's defence. 'Perfectly controlled, that,' said John, as though talking about a backhand winner down the line. 'Not an uncontrolled outburst at all. Just annoyance, really.' And Wimbledon is also the Slam where you find the real tennis fans. Sure, you get your debenture holders, and the VIPs up in the Royal Box who never take their seats for the early afternoon play until luncheon has gone past the port and brandy course, but just take a look out there in the boondocks. It was some remote outpost like Court 7 where I once sat shivering with so much cold that when a voice called out 'new balls, please' I looked around to see whether the request had come from the umpire or a brass monkey. It is here that you find the true tennis aficionado. It's here where the fans are fighting off aches and pains from having spent the previous night on a pavement, and fatigue from being kept awake by a hooting owl. And it's here where, above all, a reverential hush descends as the umpire leans over in his or her high chair and addresses the microphone. 'Quiet please. Miss Papadopoulos to serve. Play.'

The Crucible

The two big sporting events of the spring are the London Marathon, and the World Snooker Championship, one of which takes two hours to find a winner, and the other no less than seventeen days. Plus, around a hundred hours of television coverage. The daffodils have been and gone by the time the pasty-faced champion is finally crowned, and during this time there will be a special prize for anyone who doesn't hear the word 'Crucible' uttered in the same sentence – either by player or commentator – as 'pressure', 'atmosphere' or 'unique'. To listen to the BBC's commentary team, the Crucible is up there alongside Wembley Stadium, Royal Ascot and Wimbledon in the list of iconic British sporting venues, but when you actually get to the place, you find yourself wondering whether you'd be marginally more awestruck on your first sighting of Wolverhampton Town Hall. The Crucible is, for those who've never been, a poky city-centre theatre, and its reputation for generating atmosphere is predominantly down to cramming 950 people into a space barely large enough to accommodate a meeting of the Sheffield Chamber of Commerce. Front-row spectators can reach out and take a sip from Ronnie O'Sullivan's glass of water, or even, perhaps with the assistance of the extension, pot one of the reds while Ronnie is chalking his cue.

Sure there's pressure, although to listen to the commentary team, it's a miracle a ball is potted at all given that the players' cue arms are vibrating like pneumatic drills. If anyone's under pressure at the Crucible it's the spectators, who are forever having to suppress a cough, and run the constant risk of the embarrassment of being shaken awake and told – on live television – to stop snoring. Backstage, the Crucible is a labyrinth of passages barely wide enough to accommodate a bow-tie, or Dennis Taylor's glasses, and the press room gets regular visits from the players, whiling away the time before their own match is due to go on.

As at all provincial theatres, the general peace and quiet is sometimes interrupted by a loud voice conducting a last-minute rehearsal. For most of the year it will be someone running through the first few lines of *Oliver Twist*, or *Separate Tables*, but during the snooker it's the MC practising his introductions. Snooker once used to be associated with the hushed reverence of Whispering Ted Lowe, but nowadays its some bloke in a shiny suit with a voice capable of stripping the plaster from every wall inside the Crucible. You'd think it was a couple of heavyweight boxers waiting behind the curtain, rather than two blokes wearing waistcoats and shiny shoes, and the guy sweats more profusely than a Grand National runner returning to the unsaddling enclosure as he churns out his catchphrase: 'Let's get the boys on the baize!'

The other thing that's changed is that everyone now has a nickname. It's a comparatively recent phenomenon, otherwise we'd have had matches between Fred 'Methuselah' Davis, and, as a former bus conductor, Terry 'the Clippie' Griffiths. There was a player (still might be) by the name of Anthony Hamilton who was introduced as the 'Robin Hood of Snooker' for no other reason than the fact that he lived in Nottingham. He should actually have been re-labelled the 'Friar Tuck of Snooker', on the grounds that he was so slow that Maid Marian would have been drawing her pension by the time he got round to springing her from the Sheriff's castle. Fast players are Rockets, Whirlwinds and Hurricanes, but why is it that slow players (i.e. the majority) are not given nicknames involving weather patterns at the other end of the scale. 'Ladies and gentlemen, would you please welcome Graeme 'The Draught' Dott.' Mind you, leaving aside the fact that Ronnie O'Sullivan once sat through a Peter Ebdon break with a towel over his head, nearly every modern player plays quickly compared to the old timers. Cliff Thorburn and Terry Griffiths once finished a match at the Crucible at 3.51am, and the likes of Eddie Charlton and Ray Reardon relied so heavily on safety that they didn't so much apply chalk to the tip as a condom. By God, they were boring, taking so long to finish a frame that the key to success was not so much cue ball control, as bladder control. The modern players, though, will have a pot from anywhere. Maybe it's because they're generally a lot younger – over the hill and past it by the time the acne is starting to fade. Joe Davis was still winning the world championship at the age of forty-eight, and his brother Fred was sixty-four when he made it to the semi-finals, in an era when the main purpose of putting water jugs on the tables must have been to give the players somewhere to put their false teeth in.

The one thing that's never changed about snooker is that it has serious claims to be the sport carrying the least risk of injury. You could make out a case for darts, perhaps, but there's always the risk of an arrow bouncing off the rubber tyre and doing a King Harold on the bloke doing the chalking. Or croquet perhaps, although here again, if you're a fraction out with your aim and drill the mallet onto the side of your foot it would make the eyes water a bit. But in snooker, you can't conceivably come to any harm. There has never been a recorded case of anyone overdosing on Perrier water, and the only obvious reason for an ambulance to be despatched from Sheffield Royal Infirmary to the front door of the Crucible would be for loss of circulation in both buttocks.

By its very nature this is a sport that requires a player to sit in a chair for very long periods, although not quite as long as they used to do in billiards, when, in the 1907 world championship, an unfinished break of 499,135 lasted for five weeks. Clearly, though, if you listen to the commentators banging on about the pressures of the Crucible, the real risk is not so much physical damage, as going potty. Of ending up dribbling down a bib, and thinking you're Napoleon Bonaparte, or two poached eggs on toast. It would be a good deal less pressured if the game's etiquette allowed you to bury yourself in a magazine, or plug yourself into an Ipad, while your opponent was racking up a century break, and with so much time to get lost in your own thoughts, all manner of demons can get released. So the next time you tune into the Beeb's Crucible coverage, don't focus on the player who's doing the potting. Take a close look at the bloke sitting in the chair, chewing lumps out of his fingernails, and constantly fiddling with his cue-wiping towel. And ask yourself this.

Is he thinking: 'Shall I go for a Chinese tonight?' or: 'Can I make it through to the interval without biting the tip off my cue?'

16

CAN'T BAT, CAN'T BOWL, CAN'T FIELD

Well, you can't get them all right

Life, when you come to think about it, is more or less a series of accidents. You know the kind of thing. If you'd been walking past a greengrocer's when it suddenly started to rain, for instance, and you'd nipped inside for ten minutes' shelter, you'd have come home with a bag of Cox's orange pippins. If, on the other hand, you'd been passing a newsagents instead, you'd have come home with the lottery ticket which ended up buying you the Scottish castle and the ocean-going yacht. Which made me wonder, as I boarded an aeroplane at Heathrow for the flight to Australia for the 1986–87 Ashes cricket tour, about the strange sequence of events that resulted in me being there at all. It started with a job at the *Leicester Mercury*, which wouldn't have been a job at all had it not been for the fact that telephone lines in 1974 were not quite as crystal clear as they are nowadays.

The interview – for the position of junior sports reporter – had gone well enough, until the editor informed me that my previous boss, the editor of the *South Wales Argus*, happened to be a personal friend, and would I mind just popping to the canteen for a cup of tea while he phoned him for a reference? 'Not at all,' I replied cheerily, while at the same time suppressing an inward groan. The editor he was phoning had come close to giving me the sack when I was a district reporter in the *Argus*'s Abertillery office, deservedly so as well. My old jalopy had broken down in a thunderstorm, and a friend and colleague Will, who worked in the *Argus* office at Ebbw Vale, about five miles away, had driven out to give me a tow. In the process we both got soaked, and decided to give the two night jobs we were assigned to that day a miss. His was the Ebbw Vale Sports and Recreations Committee, and mine was the Abercarn District Council monthly meeting. 'Nothing ever happens at either of them,' I said after changing into some dry clothes, and after having a couple of pints in one of our locals, we called it a night.

Next morning, I arrived at the office, picked up the *Western Mail*, and read the front-page heading. 'Multi Million Pound Sports Centre for Ebbw Vale', it read. I gulped, flipped to page 3, and the headline on top of it was equally disturbing: 'Abercarn Mothers Storm Council Meeting in Killer Crossing Row'. The phone rang. It was Will. 'Have you seen the *Western Mail*?' 'Yes.' 'Okay, see you in the editor's office later.' Which is exactly where we ended up, and though we somehow avoided the sack, we were both relocated and placed in the last-chance saloon. So when the editor of the *Leicester Mercury* informed me that he was phoning that very same person for a reference, I suspected I'd do well to land a job as a tea boy never mind a sports reporter. Which made the beaming smile on his face a little difficult to work out when I was summoned back into his office and received the startling announcement that I'd been given a 'terrific' reference. Just at that moment, a glancing blow with a feather would definitely have rendered me horizontal.

He then went on to ask why I hadn't mentioned having worked for a motor magazine, and whether I'd managed to overcome the natural shyness that my previous editor felt might hold me back in a career like journalism. At which point, all became clear. He'd mistaken me for another Martin on the paper, who was both a vintage-car anorak and a serial stammerer in female company. But, to my own good fortune, he was an exceptionally dedicated reporter, and a firm favourite of the editor. And so, thanks to a dodgy phone line, I found myself working on the *Leicester Mercury*, where the new boy traditionally faced a long apprenticeship of sitting by a desk for several years putting headlines on senior journalists' stories, and phoning around the district offices in late afternoon so that readers in places like Hinckley and Market Harborough could locate the result of the 4.45 at Uttoxeter in the stop press. My only role outside the office was that of boxing correspondent, which mostly involved the occasional visit to one of the two main amateur clubs in Leicester, both of which were run by secretaries called Shirley. Shirley Withers, and Shirley Dakin. Which would have been unusual enough in itself, but in this case they were both male.

Fate, though, took another hand just a few months into the job when the cricket correspondent informed the sports editor that he was away from home so often in the summer that his wife had given him a choice between herself and cricket. Amazingly, it seemed to me, he chose her, and before I knew it, I was sitting in press boxes in places like Canterbury and Scarborough chronicling the fortunes of Leicestershire County Cricket Club. And then came another break. Every season, the deputy sports editor of the *Guardian*, Charlie Burgess, put himself down to cover a cricket match, and the one he chose this particular summer was Surrey versus Leicestershire at the Oval. At the same time, he'd been offered the job of sports editor at a new, yet to be launched, national daily, the *Independent*. We got chatting, he told me he was looking for a rugby correspondent, and would I be interested? Sorry about the cricket job not being available, he said, but cricket was too high profile to entrust to someone the readers had never heard of. The ex-England bowler and *Guardian* cricket writer Mike Selvey had been lined up for the position.

With double the wages, and a company car thrown in, I'd have taken the tiddlywinks job if that had been the offer, but when the then *Guardian* cricket correspondent Matthew Engel decided he'd had enough of the job, and the position was offered to Selvey, Charlie phoned me and asked me if I'd mind switching to cricket. I ummed and ahhed a bit, for no other reason than the fact that cricket was one of the more important sports to be entrusted with, and also because my first assignment was to involve three and a half months away from home with a wife scheduled to give birth halfway through it. 'I, um, don't really know whether I can, Charlie,' I said. 'I mean, I'm quite happy with the rugby, and, um, surely there's someone you can get for the cricket who'll um, er, what's that? Another grand a year? Say no more. I'm your man.'

Two days after the launch I was touching down in Brisbane, and a day or so later found myself checking into a motel in Bundaberg, where the manager greeted us with complimentary plates of freshly boiled local crab, followed by bowls of ice cream smothered in the local rum. Followed by a couple of hours on a sunbed by the side of the motel swimming pool, with the *Daily Telegraph*'s Peter West lying there next to me. Westy put a match to his pipe, and suddenly burst into a chuckle as he lit his pipe. 'Just think,' said a man who was also on his first ever cricket tour, 'we're actually getting paid for this.' It did seem a bit too good to be true, and in Westy's case, it all went downhill from that moment onwards. It had always been his ambition to cover a cricket tour for the *Telegraph*, and with the paper in between correspondents at the time, he was given the assignment. However, the toughest part about touring Australia is the time difference, and the fact that you can be working both sides of the clock. Namely, when the people in the sports department are in bed, you're working, and when you're in bed, they're working. And the mixture can be fairly volatile at times, especially if, like Westy, you were in the habit of sending your piece before anyone had arrived at the office in London, having a nice early dinner with a bottle of wine, taking a couple of sleeping pills and putting out the light at 8pm. And at 8.30pm, the sports editor would read his copy in London, and either decide he didn't like it, or wanted more of it.

Or something different. Or something extra. Whatever, Westy spent the entire three-and-a-half-month tour redoing his pieces at about 1am and it was a regular event to come down to breakfast, and spot him face down in his cornflakes. He'd groan quietly, mutter something about those 'bastards on the sports desk', and go through the entire daily ritual again. For three and a half months.

He occasionally rebelled, as when the receptionist informed the caller from the *Telegraph* that she was unable to put him through to Mr West's room as she had a 'do not disturb' instruction. 'Oh, you can ignore that,' came the voice at the other end. 'This is his office calling.' The receptionist said: 'Just a moment, I've just seen a note here. Ah,' she continued. 'It says do not disturb – *especially* if it's the office.' The other thing which plagued dear old Peter was that he never got to grips with the time difference, which meant that it was impossible to project ahead in an article on the grounds that, to an English reader, it would already have happened. Another, more minor difficulty, I'd already been warned about. It involved the common practice in Australia of using 'quotebacks' in their newspapers, which involved informing their readers what the English cricket reporters were sending to their own newspapers. The first quoteback of the tour was an intro Peter had written shortly after we'd arrived from England. 'The hot news from Brisbane', read the quoteback, 'is that there is no news.'

This was, as it happened, perfectly accurate, but the Cardus era had long gone, and newspaper offices didn't want to hear that there was no news. If there wasn't any news on a particular day, you had to go out and find some. I too was quoted back pretty early on that tour, although it was for something I'd said rather than written. As I wandered around the outfield along with the other journalists the day before England's opening game in Bundaberg, some bloke wandered across and asked me if I was, as he put it, 'part of the Pommy press corps'. When I confirmed that I was, he asked me if Ian Botham, who had recently been involved in stories involving cannabis and alleged hotel romps with beauty queens, was, as he put it, 'behaving himself'. I told him that Beefy had thus far been a story-free zone, before adding: 'Mind you, if he so much as farts, half of Fleet Street will suddenly be parachuted in.' Next morning, I idly flicked to the back page of the morning paper. And there, under a headline which read something like 'Poms On Botham Fart Alert', was my quote, although it didn't cause as much of a stir as my next one just before the first Test in Brisbane.

England's performances in the warm-up games suggested that while they might be able to give a half-decent game to the Toowoomba Girl Guides' XI, anything stronger in the way of opposition would wipe the floor with them. There were only two ways to go for the English media out there: give it the full 'Send 'Em All to the Tower Of London' treatment, or go down, as we often do in times of distress, the black humour route. I went for the latter, urging everyone back at home not to worry too much, as there were only three real areas of England's game that required attention. Batting, bowling and fielding. I wasn't quite, though, prepared for the mileage that the Australian newspapers were to make out of that. Next morning, one of the tabloids had devoted their entire front page to it.

Not back page; front page. 'Can't Bat, Can't Bowl, Can't Field' was the giant headline, and underneath, in marginally smaller print: 'Latest on Pathetic Poms. See Page 12.' And there on page 12 was a selection of uncomplimentary comments from various publications, but the 'Can't Bat' reference appeared to provide the best soundbite, and it became the tour catchphrase. Especially after England won the first Test at a canter, and the players' celebrations included turning up to the next game, in Newcastle, New South Wales all wearing 'Can't Bat, Bowl, or Field' T-shirts.

In those days, the players and press mingled together on a more or less daily basis, which is not the case now. You would just as likely find yourself sitting next to, say, David Gower or Mike Gatting on a plane as to a newspaper colleague, and with thirty-one internal flights on that tour, you sat next to most of them at least once. It was the same at hotels. These days players tend to confine themselves to the team room, but in those days everyone mixed together at the bar, and so it was on the first night in Newcastle. Which led, after the Can't Bat victory, to a couple of awkward moments. The first had nothing to do with the Test match, but was the result of me buying a round at the bar. One of the drinks was a whisky for the Independent Radio News reporter, a Scotsman who liked a tipple, and who became more and more irascible as the tipple count mounted. And on this occasion, the barman, as barmen tend to do in Australia unless instructed otherwise, had put a large quantity of ice in his malt whisky. He considered the barman blameless in this atrocity, his colonial background meaning he knew no better, but I was verbally lacerated for some time on the subject, and was still recovering when I got a tap on the shoulder. It was Neil Foster, the Essex player, and he said something like: 'I gather you've been writing some not very nice things about us.' I had to admit that I hadn't been especially complimentary, but at that point he broke into a broad smile and pulled up the sweater he was wearing to reveal a T-shirt underneath. 'Can't **** Write', it said. Which gives you some idea of player–press relations in those days, now long since consigned, sadly, to history.

My one regret from Newcastle was that when England lost to New South Wales with a day and three-quarters of the scheduled four days to spare, the flight out to the next venue was brought forward twenty-four hours. Which meant that the consignment of T-shirts I'd ordered from a local shop, with 'As I Was Saying' on the front of them, and 'Can't Bat etc.' on the back, weren't ready by the time we left. Another difference is that the modern cricket tour is almost a weekend break compared to what they used to be like. We were away for a hundred and thirty-odd days, and it was the norm to find yourself flying to remote places in the Outback for matches, with players and journalists sandwiched together in three or four single-propeller aircraft. Those times were good fun, even when flights were delayed. We got stuck at Perth airport once waiting for a delayed flight to Kalgoorlie, and Botham decided to pass the time by hosting a drinking school for Leicestershire players and journalists only. Which was Gower, Phillip DeFreitas, James Whitaker, and me. It was only about a two-hour wait, but it was plenty long enough at the rate with which Botham ordered drinks to render the

Leicestershire contingent half out of it. There was one last-minute request from a small boy for Gower's autograph when boarding was finally called, which he finally got after Gower's initial attempts to make the tip of the biro connect with the paper resulted in three air shots.

The up-country games were great fun, played on small grounds upon which internationally famous players like Gower, and Allan Lamb, would come in to bat by politely asking the people queuing for the Portaloo (or the Dragaway Dunny as they call it in Australia) if they wouldn't mind letting them through. There was a dramatic start to one of these matches, against a Western Australian Country XI, when the home side's opening bowler ran in to bowl the first ball to the accompaniment of the MC cheering him on. 'And here comes Stormy Gale!' shouted the announcer, as Stormy raced to the wicket . . ., 'hoping to put the wind up the Poms!' Alas, the build-up was all too much for Stormy, who, with the announcer still in full cry, lost his undercarriage in his delivery stride, and was stretchered from the field. Every couple of weeks, or so it seemed, we'd find ourselves in Crocodile Dundee country, watching bowlers running in from directions known as the 'Piggery End', and unable to eat your hot dog without consuming, at the same time, a sizeable number of the 500 flies attached to it.

The hardest part of the tour was actually getting your words back to England. There was no Wifi, or Broadband, or anything as sophisticated as that, but we all carried something called a Tandy, which was nothing much more than a glorified typewriter. It did, though, come with an attachment resembling a pair of swimming goggles, into which you plugged both ends of the telephone receiver in your hotel room before dialling what seemed like forty-five digits designed to connect you to England. What it actually did, after first making a dialling noise and then falling silent, was connect you to an engaged tone. This would go on for at least half an hour, until, joy of joys, the engaged tone was replaced by high-pitched noise like one of those old primus-stove whistling kettles, followed by a slightly lower pitched tone, followed by a noise which sounded a bit like a hiccup. And then you'd get a tele-printer-type effect on your laptop screen, with rows of words being flashed up on the screen. Your words. The ones you'd composed at the close of play, and which were now on their way to your newspaper in London.

The trouble was, it took almost as long to transmit those words as it had taken to type them in the first place, and the phone line rarely survived for as long as you needed it. And so, roughly halfway through the thousand or so words being sent, the screen would change from transmitting in English to a cross between Japanese and the kind of ancient hieroglyphics you'd find on the walls of an Egyptian pharaoh's tomb. Then the English would come back. Then some more gibberish. And then you'd get properly cut off. So you'd have another go, and another, and then give up and head off to the pub to swap hard-luck stories with your fellow journalists, none of whom had managed to get their stories across in one piece. The only exception was Jack Bannister, transmitting to his newspaper in Birmingham, who would regularly ruin your evening by announcing, in his distinctive Brummie accent, that he'd sent fifteen stories with no trouble at all, and had never had so much as a single garbled word since leaving England five weeks before. His equally Brummie wife Pauline would be with him, and her eyes would glaze over as Jack talked everyone through that night's Tandy experience. 'Jack, Jack,' Pauline would say with her Birmingham twang. 'You're so boreeng, Jack.' But Jack couldn't be stopped on the subject of Tandys. 'Have you tried flicking that switch just to the side of the couplers?' Or, 'If you put the couplers on a pillow they never work. They've got to be on the bedside table, or the carpet.'

And, armed with this information, you'd return to your room at one, two or three o'clock in the morning, usually in a state of inebriation, and try all over again. You kept at it for so long because, when it worked, it saved you from having to go through the tiresome business of dictating it to a human typist, but eventually, usually at around 4am, and by now late afternoon back in the office, you'd give up the unequal struggle, and dial the number for a copytaker. Most nights in Australia, and don't forget this was in the era of a hundred and thirty or so nights of sending stories, I'd get John. Who was a very nice chap, but clearly a frustrated journalist. So you'd dictate a paragraph, which would perhaps finish up with some sentence like: 'But just when England were starting to wobble, Botham saved the day with an extraordinary innings.' At which point you'd say: 'New paragraph.' Then you'd become aware that John had stopped saying: 'yep' after each pause, to tell you he was still with you. So you'd say: 'Hello? John? You still there?' Then you'd hear: 'Yes, still here. I was just wondering, with that last para. Very nice, don't get me wrong, but when you said "extraordinary" innings, do you think "amazing" innings might read better? Up to you of course, it's just that . . .' And you'd have this after every paragraph. At four in the morning. Half pissed. Totally pissed off. Knackered. Fed up. And ready for bed. By the end of the tour, I'd lost the will to resist, and every story I sent back was more or less written by John. And probably read a lot better too.

Before the age of the Tandy, it was almost impossible to miss a deadline in Australia, where you're mostly ten hours ahead on the eastern side, but my very first Test match report for the *Independent* actually made the paper with about three minutes to spare. I'd gone through the Tandy ritual after the first day's play in Brisbane, but instead of giving up on it at 4 o'clock in the morning, I'd fallen asleep with the thing still connected to the bedroom phone. With the result that, when the office started getting worried as the first-edition deadline approached, my room number registered engaged when they phoned the hotel and asked to be put through. Eventually, I woke up to find the Tandy on my lap and still connected to the phone, and two security guards at the bottom of the bed. 'Streuth, mate. Glad yer still alive. Your office is having kittens. They want you to phone. Pronto.' We were a month and a half through the tour by then, which is about the full distance nowadays, but on this one we were still well short of halfway. Christmas was still a month away, and I was looking forward to my first yuletide season outside England, despite the disappointment of not seeing my two brothers.

They both lived (still do) in Belgium, and when I got the job on the Indy they said they planned to come over to

Australia for Christmas. However, I got a phone call in early December to say that they couldn't come after all, and on the 23 December, having just flown in from Canberra, I was checking into our hotel in Melbourne when the bloke behind the desk pointed to the bar across the passage and said there was something behind the bar for me. I couldn't think what, but went across and was presented with three bottles of Belgian beer, and a note in an envelope which read: 'Sorry we couldn't make it; have these on us. Merry Xmas.' A nice touch from the brothers, I thought, but I still had to write my piece from Canberra, and I said to the barman: 'Keep them in the chiller, I'll have them later.' Which is when I heard a voice behind me say: 'Open 'em now if you don't mind. We've got a bit of a thirst on here.' I turned round to see two newspapers slowly being lowered by the occupants of two leather chairs, revealing my brothers. It was a nice surprise, and made Christmas away from home that much more enjoyable, or at least I think it was, because there's not much of it I remember. The Can't Bat thing had continued to follow us around, so much so that when we came to start organizing the Christmas-morning panto, a long-standing tradition and attended by almost all the players, it was the obvious theme for the script. Loosely based around *A Christmas Carol*, and mostly written, with a bit of help from me, by the *News of the World* cricket correspondent David Norrie, it involved the England captain Mike Gatting being visited in his bed by the three ghosts of Christmas. Can't Bat, Can't Bowl, and Can't Field.

We didn't finish writing it until around 5am on Christmas morning, by which time we'd made a pretty decent dent in the champagne supplies, and after a Christmas-morning reception, followed by the panto itself, I got a note from one of the hotel staff asking me to phone home at once. Which is when I discovered that sometime during the panto I had acquired a daughter, who had decided to arrive earlier than expected, just after midnight on Christmas Day UK time, and around late morning Melbourne time. Out came more champagne, and what should have been a ten-minute walk from the hotel to the restaurant that was hosting us for lunch, turned – thanks to us being unable to travel in a completely straight line – into something closer to half an hour. I'm not sure what time it finished, although you can get some idea from the fact that when I rose to invite the assembled hacks, wives, girlfriends and guests to raise a glass to the Norrie for organizing the day, I heard him hiss: 'We're the only ones left, you daft pillock.'

It was dark when we set off back to the hotel, which I'd never have found without Norrie's assistance, and as soon as we made it back there I was handed a note by a member of the hotel staff. 'Phone Radio Leicester urgently', it said, and I suddenly remembered that I'd promised them an interview on how the players had spent Christmas Day. I made it up to my room at the appointed time, whereupon the phone rang, and I heard the familiar voice of Jonathan Agnew. I'd known Aggers for eight years or so, he as a Leicestershire player and me as the evening paper cricket reporter, and he was spending his winters doing a bit of work for the local BBC radio station. It was a good relationship by and large, which had only once been tested, after I'd been none too complimentary about his bowling during a match against Warwickshire at Edgbaston. 'So tell us, Martin,' he chirruped. 'It's a cold old day here in Leicester. What's it like seeing people dressed up as Santa Claus when it's 40 degrees centigrade?' To which he got a reply something along the lines of: 'Well, itsshh, um, er, hic, letshfaysitAggersholdboy, I haven't sheen many people throwing shnowballs today, letsh puttit thatway. Hic.' 'Well listeners, they're a few hours ahead in Australia, and it sounds like Martin's been having a good day, but tell us Martin, how have the players spent Christmas Day with a Test match starting in the morning?' 'Hic. Well I hope they're not as pisshed aszzIam Aggersholdshtick, otherwizh we'll be all out for buggerall, ha ha, hic, er, I, um, we're not live are we?' Fortunately we weren't, and Aggers later told me the Radio Leicester boffins had worked for hours trying to splice occasional moments of coherence together to be able to broadcast something, but eventually had had to give it up as a bad job. He later revealed that they'd kept the tape, and that it was occasionally given a private airing along with other car-crash interviews.

On that particular Christmas Day, it wouldn't have been a bad idea, once back in the room, to have stayed there, but there were still people downstairs anxious to buy me a drink on the birth of my daughter, and, as with most people who've had a few, the prospect of another one was pretty inviting. All of which meant that to this day I have little recollection of the opening day of the Boxing Day Test, most of which – I was informed later – I managed to sleep through. However, I still had to write about it, which would have been quite a challenge had I not been able to phone various colleagues' rooms to ask questions. 'Er, who won the toss?' being one of them. Somehow, the euphoria of managing to send a thousand words back to England on a day's play that had totally passed me by seemed to warrant a celebratory drink, which is how I found myself back in the hotel bar on Boxing Day evening. 'Hello again', said a barmaid, which puzzled me a little as I was pretty certain I'd never seen her before in my life. 'How's your daughter?' she inquired. 'How do you know I've got a daughter?' I said. 'You mentioned her last night,' she said. 'Did I?' I said. 'Yes,' she said. 'About four hundred and fifty times.' Oh dear, I thought. And not wanting to put the poor girl through another evening of incoherent ramblings, I retired to bed. England went on to win the match, and with it the Ashes, in only three of the scheduled five days, and also went on to win both their one-day tournaments in Australia. Which left me to try and find a way out of the 'Can't Bat' story that was still doing the rounds at the end of one of the most successful cricket tours in England history. I sat in my room on the last night, counting myself a tad unlucky in that no one had actually realized at the time how completely useless Australia would turn out to be. Which gave me the get-out clause I'd been looking for. 'Right quote', I typed. 'Wrong team.'

17

YOMPING TO MOSCOW

Napoleon never made it, but our intrepid hack sees off Polish serial killer and Rosa Klebb en route to Champions League final

There was a time, in the world of sports journalism, when you'd be at a golf tournament, the phone would ring, and someone senior on the desk would ask: 'Any idea what you're writing about today?' And you'd say something like: 'Probably walk round with Monty. Maybe Faldo, not sure yet.' Whereupon the conversation would end with: 'Righto. Can you give us 800 words. By about 6.30. Thanks.' These days, though, someone phones up and tells you what they want you to write – usually after several people have exchanged ideas at what's known as an editorial conference. The phone will go at a Test match, and some-one will say: 'The editor's wife was asking him the other day why everyone at the match is dressed as a Viking, or a banana. Could we have a piece on that please?' Same with tennis. I was at Wimbledon one day, and phoned the office to see what they wanted, and was told: 'We've got you down for Court 1 today. There are a couple of Frenchmen playing each other.' 'Yes,' I said. 'And?' 'Well, we thought it might be interesting.' 'You thought *what* might be interesting, exactly?' 'The match.' 'You mean a match between two Frenchmen?' 'Yes.' I could have understood it had it been a match between two players from Tierra del Fuego, or Baffin Island, but two Frenchmen? However, that's what I ended up doing, and I can only hope that the readers, in the unlikely event that any of the readers had made it past paragraph one, were equally puzzled.

Just occasionally, though, you get a call asking you to do something, and you think 'What a good idea. That sounds like fun.' As happened to me when Manchester United and Chelsea had made it through to the Champions League final in Moscow, and the build-up to the match was already under way three weeks before the event. 'We'd like you to go to Moscow,' said the voice down the phone. 'Fancy it?' 'Well,' I replied, 'won't we have enough football people there already?' 'No this is different. I've just come out of conference . . .' (cue small inward groan) '. . . and the editor is keen on a series of pieces from someone simply on travelling to the match. Apparently they're charging about four thousand quid for a seat on a private charter, and a grand just for a normal return. Not to mention the hotel prices in Moscow. He thought we might find a way to do the trip more cheaply, and then write about it. So what do you think?' Sounded good, I thought. The Eurostar to Brussels, maybe. A high-speed train to Germany, followed by the overnight sleeper to Moscow. Nice and relaxing, plenty of gourmet dining, a glass of wine or two, and we should still be on the right side of a grand. 'Sure,' I said, and briefly outlined my plan. 'Yes, well, that's not quite what the editor had in mind,' he said. 'He wants you to imagine you're just an average footie fan, a bit strapped for cash, and willing to yomp across there with just a knapsack on your back. Catching the bus, hitch-hiking, and staying on the cheap in hostels. That kind of thing. We worked it out. You could set off about a fortnight before the game, and it could probably be done on around £30 a day. Hello. Hello. You still there?' Indeed I was still there, albeit in a mild state of shock. All of a sudden, I had re-filed this latest idea in the folder marked 'Bonkers', containing inspired brainwaves such as two Frenchmen playing tennis. 'Knapsack?' I said. 'I maybe should have told you my back's been playing me up a bit, and those hostel beds won't improve it any. Besides which I'd have to get over there on a cross-channel ferry, and I get seasick on a pedalo. I'm a bit hopeless with public transport as well. Chances are I wouldn't get much further than Belgium in a fortnight, and all you'd get would be a series of pieces about honking over the side of a P&O ferry, and that statue of the boy in Brussels peeing into a fountain. Great idea, though. Perhaps someone a bit younger and fitter.' 'No, no,' he replied. 'We think it's right up your street.'

Various plans churned around in my head, including doing a Donald Crowhurst. Back in the 1960s, I'd read a book about an eccentric English yachtsman who had set off to sail single-handed around the world, but instead of battling the Southern Ocean, Crowhurst decided to anchor himself somewhere less dangerous, and, in the days of less sophisticated communications, sent out bogus radio messages about his position. I could, I thought, find myself a little B&B on the south coast, buy myself an Eastern European guidebook, and send back stories of authentic-sounding coach journeys in Moldova, and what was on the menu at that modest little café in Belarus. But I was also aware that Crowhurst had leapt overboard when he realized his ship's logs wouldn't stand up to scrutiny when he eventually sailed back into Plymouth, and while I doubted whether getting rumbled would have ended in suicide, I fancied it wouldn't have done much for my career prospects. Which is how I came to find myself boarding a train at Liverpool Street Station, armed only with a backpack, a map, a set of waterproofs and a guidebook.

The night before setting off, the guy coordinating the trip had phoned me at home to wish me *bon voyage*, and asked where I was setting off from. 'I'm getting the ferry from Harwich to Rotterdam,' I told him. 'Oh,' he said, the long pause indicating that maybe this was not what he'd wanted to hear. 'Any chance of starting off from Calais instead?' 'A bit late now,' I told him. 'Anyway, why Calais?' 'It's just that we wanted to organize a photo to go with your first piece, and I thought we could get a snap of you setting off from a French field. Give it a bit of continental atmosphere.' I paused for a moment to consider this, and waited for the sound of a chuckle at the other end. None came, so I had to assume this was a serious suggestion. 'Um,' I said, wondering whether there was any way of replying that wouldn't cause too much offence. 'Look, I don't want to sound too negative here, and I can see where you're coming from, but I've been to France once or twice, driving through the countryside and all that, but I can't recall ever thinking, or anyone ever saying: 'Ooh, look at that field. It looks really French.' I also deliberated about pointing out that the reader would be unlikely to be able to tell the difference between a field in Rotterdam and a field in Calais, unless we got lucky and managed to arrive there at the same time as a bloke on a bicycle wearing a beret and a striped jersey, smoking a Gitanes, and with a string of onions draped over his handlebars. But it wasn't necessary. He kind of got the point. And Rotterdam it was.

As it turned out, I could indeed have provided a French flavour to a photograph within a few hours of setting off, merely by the fact that even that early into the trip my posture bore a close resemblance to that of the hunchback of Notre Dame. A few hours of wearing my knapsack and Charles Laughton would never have needed a fake hump for the part, the problem being the weight of the guidebook inside it. It ran to 1,284 pages, and if I'd dropped it on my foot, I'd never have made it to Liverpool Street Station, never mind Moscow. It was called *Europe on a Shoestring*, which was basically the object of the exercise, but while it was full of tips on how to travel light, I could have travelled even lighter with the complete volume of the *Encyclopaedia Britannia* inside the knapsack. The author could have saved some weight by dispensing with the first chapter, which was all about European history. Very informative, and it passed a bit of time on the cross-channel ferry, but learning a bit more about Alexander the Great and the fall of the Berlin Wall didn't seem to me to be indispensable information for the budget-conscious traveller.

There were also some glaring omissions, including one which would have been seriously helpful for the budget-conscious suicide traveller. Instead of forking out large sums of money to a Swiss doctor in one of those Dignitas clinics, I discovered after leaving Rotterdam and arriving at Enschede that all you had to do to put yourself in with a decent chance of ringing St Peter's doorbell was to take a stroll down a Dutch pavement, and then change direction without looking behind you. In which case, death by bicycle came more or less with a written guarantee. The things were everywhere, and they came at you in squadrons. And if you'd ended up in the local infirmary being treated for spoke lacerations, it wouldn't have been one of those sleek, streamlined modern machines that got you. Every Dutch bicycle I saw appeared to be of Second World War vintage, the kind ridden by resistance fighters during the occupation, and one false step sideways onto the vast network of dedicated cycling tracks meant that the very best you could hope for was a free lift inside a Halfords shopping basket.

Next stop was Dortmund, which, when I arrived on a warm Sunday afternoon, appeared to be closed. I finally found some signs of human habitation down in the city square, and with my main objective being to find a bar screening the English Premier League games involving Chelsea and Manchester United, I established that the Bar Hasselhof was the place to pitch up to later. First, though, I needed a room for the night, and ended up at a hostel with the not especially welcoming name of 'Jugendgastehaus

Adolf Kolping'. Forty-four euros seemed a bit steep for a child's bunkroom, on top of which you had to make your own bed from a pile of sheets in the lobby. Then there was a towel, which, being not much bigger than my handkerchief, I originally mistook for a flannel. The lady at reception spoke good enough English for me to inquire whether I was supposed to dry myself with it or use it for blowing my nose, and she said, deadpan, 'For after shower.'

The Germans, as everyone knows, are not renowned for their sense of humour, which I reckon is largely down to foreigners poking fun at them over the War. This had occurred to me while reading my *Europe on a Shoestring* on the train. It gave every country a listing under the heading 'Famous for . . .' and sure enough, there under Germany was '. . . Beer, BMWs and Invading Poland'. Returning to the Bar Hasselhof, having got into the shower to find no soap, and then got out of it to dry off with my hanky, the landlord's prediction of a throbbing establishment was spot on, but not for the footie. The outside tables were full of people enjoying a drink in the sunshine, but inside, where Chelsea and Man U were playing their respective matches, the place was practically deserted. Eventually I retired to my room to – given its childlike proportions – crèche out so to speak, and I fell asleep at last knowing why the Germans pinch all the towels when they go on holiday.

From Dortmund, to Berlin, by which time I was beginning to wonder whether the moment had arrived to invoke the office's kind offer to 'Pay a bit more if you really have to' before I'd set off. As I stood in the dingy reception area of the 'Three Little Pigs Hostel' in central

Berlin, the notice informed me that while it was seventeen euros for an eight-person dormitory, for forty-five euros I could have had a private single with en suite toilet and shower. Tempting to say the least, but in the spirit of the assignment I resisted, and before setting out for a mid-afternoon exploration, I popped up to the dorm to dump my bag and found one of my sleeping companions sitting on the edge of his bed. He had a strange, vacant look, and when I ventured a cheery 'Guten Abend' his reply consisted only of a strange whistling noise through his teeth. A set of teeth, incidentally, which made it perfectly clear that whatever he'd spent all his money on before being reduced to sleeping in hostels, it certainly wasn't toothpaste.

Wandering outside into the city, I saw a newspaper billboard. I had no idea what it said, but after the dormitory experience I wondered whether it might be: 'Police Uncover More Bodies in Hostel Serial Killer Horror'. If only, I thought, I had decided to stay the night in Hannover instead, which had been my original intention after leaving Dortmund. However, upon alighting from the train, I found that, just like the place I'd just come from, Hannover was closed. I roamed the town searching for any kind of local attraction, but was enticed neither by Happy Hour at 'Jack the Ripper's London Tavern' nor by that night's variety show at the Hannover Hippodrome: 'Rockabilly – mit Max und Willie'. Neither did Hannover appear to have any culinary appeal, as I once again encountered a 'wurst'-dispensing vending machine containing long dark objects which appeared best retrieved by a pooper scooper. So I hopped back onto the train to Berlin and to my date with the escaped inmate from the asylum.

Looking out of the carriage window I'd been struck by the large number of wind turbines, and got to wondering why a country with a national dish of boiled cabbage would need to go in for artificial wind production – and the same thought occurred again while searching for something to eat before returning to my dorm to become a meal myself for Berlin's equivalent of Hannibal Lecter. I'd had sauerkraut before, and wasn't desperately keen to repeat the experience, so when the guidebook told me that the Restaurant Romana in the Potsdamer Platz gave out free baskets of bread when you bought a beer, I decided to push the boat out there. Especially if this was to be my last supper. However, when I got back I discovered that Hannibal had checked out, and that my only prospect of being eaten that night came not from a fellow inmate, but from the bed mites.

I had some time to kill next morning, so plumped for a guided tour of the city, opting, given the low-budget nature of my trip, for the on-foot freebie rather than the bus ride (fifteen euros) or the pony and trap tour (seventy euros). Our guide was a girl called Maria, who, considering she probably did this every day, was amazingly enthusiastic. 'And now we're going to do something you couldn't have done twenty years ago!' she yelled, pointing at the Brandenburg Gate. 'Walk through there without being shot!' Walking past Marlene Dietrich Platz automatically triggered a series of microphones to pipe through a chorus of 'falleenk in luff again', and it was a relief when the phone rang.

'You're not,' came the voice at the other end, 'sending us much stuff about football.' I concurred. That was my reading of the situation also. 'Well, could you try and give us more of a football flavour?' My reply was something along the lines of my not being entirely surprised, with over a week to go before a game being played in Moscow, not to have encountered hordes of Manchester and Chelsea fans rampaging through the streets of Enschede, or drinking the bars dry in Dortmund. 'Well we've got an idea for you. It's not far from Berlin, so we'd like you to go to Michael Bonallack's home town and do a bit of vox pop with the people living there. See who remembers him, and what they think about him.' 'Pardon?' I replied, wondering what an earth he meant. The line was a bit crackly, and I'd misheard. It wasn't the former secretary of the Royal and Ancient Golf Club he was talking about, but Michael Ballack, the Chelsea midfield player.

Even so, it seemed a pointless exercise, not to mention squandering quite a few unnecessary euros on train travel, but if that's what they wanted, fine. Gorlitz was the town of his birth, in former East Germany, and so close to the border I was able to walk over a bridge and have a cheap lunch in Poland. It was a pretty little town, but after a brief wander around the shops I took myself off to the tourist office to get directions to Ballack's old family house. It was closed, though. I didn't see any monument, or statue, in his honour, so maybe a Michael's Hotel? Nope. MichaelBallackstrasse? Not that I could see. Café Ballack? No sign of one. A sports shop then, selling replica Chelsea shirts? 'Fraid not. There was a Micha's Bistro, but it was boarded up and covered in graffiti. No, the grim facts had to be faced. Gorlitz was a Ballack-free zone. Or so I thought, until walking back to the station.

Two youths were having a kickabout on a corner of a park close to the street, and having established that they spoke English, I asked them if they'd heard of Ballack. One of them replied: 'Yes, Ballack. I know. He play for Englisch futball team. But how can you tell,' he asked, 'that he iss German and not Englisch? Just by watching him play.' 'Tell me,' I said. 'Becoss,' said the youth, 'he never miss a penalty.' And with that he laughed so loud I worried he might rupture something. Please. Don't let anyone tell you again that Germans have no sense of humour.

Having wasted an entire day in Gorlitz, next stop was Poznan – en route to Warsaw – via the overnight bus from Berlin. We were due to leave at 11pm and arrive at 3am, but left at 11.30pm and finally staggered off at 4.55am. By which time Poznan, unlike myself, was just coming to life. It's actually quite hard to come to life after an overnight trip on a Eurolines bus. You might consider putting your dog onto one, but if you do, the next knock on your door will more than likely be from the RSPCA. On the upside, though, the Poles were so friendly that when I asked inside a small shop for directions to the railway station, the woman running it locked up and escorted me there personally. Arriving at the Nathan Villa's Hostel in Warsaw, I was allocated a bunk in one of the dormitories, and then went out to look for the 'Bar Below', which, according to one of the posters in the hostel reception, was offering 'two for the price of one' vodkas and also screening a match between Leeds United and Carlisle. Aha, I thought, I can include a bit more football in my next piece, which should keep them happy back at the office.

Sadly, though, despite being seated only a few yards from the screen I couldn't see anything of the game, on account of the fact that the Bar Below was apparently hosting the world smoking championships. I'd previously thought that Japan were unbeatable when it came to per capita fag consumption, but I fancy that a Cup final against Poland would be too close to call. Probably go to penalties. My stay in Warsaw was about as comfortable as I'd experienced all trip, and the price of the hostel even included washing and drying your laundry overnight. The challenge there, though, was in trying to find your laundry again in the random pile dumped in the corridor, and I had visions of some Polish lorry driver rummaging through his backpack at the next venue to find it full of bras and knickers. Warsaw was also the easiest place to stay under budget, and I could have had lunch just across the road from the hostel for 50p. However, with a starter of duck's blood soup, and main course of fried lard with bread, I decided to pass – stocking up instead on Kit Kats, a perfect complement for the on-board sump oil disingenuously advertised as coffee for the eleven-hour overnight trip to Vilnius.

It was a bone-jarring journey, with sleep consisting of five-minute cat naps in between visits to potholes the size of bomb craters, and the grumpy disposition acquired as a result was not improved by the discovery that Lithuania was no improvement on the culinary front. I decided to skip lunch after perusing the specials board outside a downtown café offering smoked pig's ears with mayonnaise and cheese, figuring that there'd be hot dogs and meat pies on sale at the rugby match I'd been invited to by one of the town's ex-pats. Instead, the only snacks on offer were pieces of rock-hard fried bread and dried salted fish, although better news came with the discovery that rugby in Lithuania – in terms of drinking vast amounts of beer in the clubhouse after the game – is much the same as anywhere else. Three weeks earlier, by all accounts, after an 'international' against Austria, the Austrian Rugby Federation had felt obliged to issue an apology after their players had taken to the streets to treat their hosts to a traditional post-match dance. It wouldn't normally have caused any offence, but several hours on the clubhouse ale had persuaded the Austrians to perform without any clothes. Apart from those hats with the feathers in. Personally, I figured that they were entitled to let their hair down if they'd travelled all the way from Vienna on a Eurolines coach.

As dusk fell, I was back on a bus to Riga, peering out of the window at all the traditional and historical landmarks. KFC, McDonalds and Ikea to name but a few. Unlike the TV and the overhead light, the radio worked, pumping out not very Eastern-European-type songs like 'Eye of the Tiger' and what I figured ought to have been the Eurolines signature tune, 'I Will Survive'. The ex-pat who'd invited me to the rugger match told me I'd have more chance of bumping into some Man U or Chelsea fans in Latvia than Lithuania, where all they were interested in was basketball, and sure enough, Riga was positively teeming with English people, all of them male, nearly all of them wearing replica football shirts, and most of them head-ing for Paddy Whelan's Irish pub. Riga, with its cheap drinks and striptease joints, had apparently become the in-place for British stag parties, and Paddy's was heaving with extremely pissed Brits. Or 'pigs', as a Latvian cabinet minister had recently described them.

Mind you, none of them was half as inebriated as the youth who attempted to board the morning bus to Tallinn. His attempt to board would have been difficult even if he'd had both hands available to cling to the rails, but in using them instead to try to light a fag while mounting the steps, he set fire to his beard and fell backwards onto the tarmac. He was informed by the bloke checking the tickets that he wouldn't be allowed on until he was capable of responding to questions with something more coherent than a belch, or at least that was my guestimate of what he shouted at him shortly before the electronic doors slammed shut. Tallinn turned out to be a bit like Riga, with slightly fewer pissheads, and a few hours there made the prospect of yet another Eurolines overnighter – this time to St Petersburg – seem almost appealing. I even fell asleep for once, but we'd only been going a couple of hours when I was awoken by a soldier carrying a rifle and demanding to see my passport. I maybe should have guessed that crossing the Russian border wouldn't be quite the same as the Severn Bridge, and shortly afterwards, my long-held belief that Rosa Klebb was a totally unbelievable fictional invention of Ian Fleming, who worked for some sinister organization such as Smersh, or Spectre, was shaken by the arrival of a female shot putter who'd joined the Russian army after failing a sex test. Or at least that's what she, if indeed it was a she, looked like. While Rosa scrutinized passports, her chums emptied all the bags onto the road, and a soldier with a torch climbed into the luggage hold. If a hay wagon had come along, they'd have speared it with pitchforks, as they did in the old war films. Another soldier walked up and down the aisle counting heads, even though no one had been allowed off, and after an hour or so of this, they sent us on our way again.

We were now in Russia, and at six in the morning we arrived at our destination. The guidebook told me that St Petersburg had a 'taste of Tsarist splendour', but they couldn't have been referring to the bus station, which was full of alcoholics on benches, and packs of wild dogs roaming around looking for dustbins. St Petersburg itself was a bit more like the guidebook description, but with the football match now only a day away, I was soon on a train for Moscow. For an eight-hour journey you'd have thought they might have provided a buffet car, but all we had on board were a couple of old boilers – contraptions dispensing hot water for those who'd remembered to pack a mug and a tea bag, although the description could equally well have applied to the two uniformed harridans examining the tickets, Otherwise, in terms of culinary sustenance, niet. The journey would have been even more depressing had I not met Fyodor, who came to my attention via the loud voice of the woman sitting next to him, a few seats down the carriage. Her name, I later discovered, was Irene, and a glance at my watch confirmed that she had been talking, very loudly, for as long as the train had been moving. Which was precisely an hour. Fyodor caught me looking in their direction, gave me a broad grin, and drew an imaginary knife across his throat. I gave him a smile back and a thumbs up, which he interpreted as an invitation to join me – and we bonded in seconds. Fyodor spoke about a dozen words of English, which was quite a few more than I could manage in Russian, but we were brought closer by the beautiful game. 'Chelsea!' he said. 'Rooney!' he exclaimed. 'La, la, la . . .' he stuttered. 'Lampard?' I ventured. 'Da!' he cried, almost crushing me with a bear hug, and preventing me rocking backwards to avoid the lethal combination of vodka and Russian cigarettes on his breath.

Thus, the journey passed relatively quickly. By the time we finally chugged into Moscow, I'd somehow managed to convey to him that I'd like to see Red Square before heading off to my hostel, and Fyodor took it upon himself to personally escort me to the Metro. Irene wasn't happy, but he escorted her to some dark corner of the station, grabbed my arm, jumped a queue and bought a ticket. It was only one ticket, but he clearly knew how to beat the system, and we both went through a turnstile together. 'Irene,' I said, pointing at his abandoned companion. 'What about Irene?' He wagged a finger in a 'don't you worry about her' kind of gesture, and before long we were sitting in one of the cheaper bars alongside Red Square having forked out about twelve quid for two small bottles of beer. The prices were horrendous, and when you got out of a taxi you felt entitled to remove the keys from the ignition on the assumption that you'd bought it, rather than had a ride in it. The only remaining connection, I thought, between Lenin and revolutions was the number of times he would have turned in his grave every night since the arrival of capitalism. And I pictured the bloke in charge of his tomb having to turn the old boy face up again before opening up for the tourists. I gave Fyodor the address of my digs, and he escorted me past a line of taxis before flagging down an old Trabant in the middle of the road. A conversation took place, and he told me he'd agreed on a very reasonable 400 roubles for the driver.

I wasn't too worried, as the guidebook actually recommended this practice to hard-up travellers, on top of which, I was game for a bit of adventure. Three hours later, I was slightly less game for a bit of adventure, as the driver slowed down for the umpteenth time on an eerie unlit road, peered at the street sign, and then drove off again. Eventually he pulled over, turned off the engine, pointed at the needle on the petrol gauge, and emitted a quiet sobbing noise. I hadn't a clue what to do, but a miracle then took place in the form of a passing pedestrian, who turned out to be not only Swedish, but multilingual. He hopped into the back seat, barked out some instructions in Russian, and within about a minute and a half we pulled up outside my sleeping quarters.

I went along to the stadium on the night of the match, with the intention of interviewing supporters on how they'd made their own way to Moscow, when a couple of Chelsea fans in a hot dog queue asked me if I'd like one of the two spare tickets they'd got. For nothing.

And so, after two weeks of rarely being very far away from a park bench wrapped in an old copy of the *Moscow Advertiser*, I wasn't totally surprised when it all ended in drink.

It would never have happened if the office had allowed me to return home the same way. 'No, no!' I protested when they told me they were flying me back. I wanted the open road again, the rucksack on my back, and the exhilarating heightening of the senses that only sharing a youth hostel dormitory with a Polish axe murderer can provide.

'It's in my blood now,' I said. 'You can have the company car back. I'm down for the Test match next Thursday and I'll be thumbing a lift down to Lord's. None of those overpriced hotel bills and expensive dinner receipts either. I'll find a nice bench in Regents Park, and grab a piece of sandwich from anything the pigeons leave behind.'

Nevertheless, while the office were adamant that I return in some degree of comfort, they did at least meet me halfway with my new found wish to slum it by booking me back on Aeroflot. And not only did Aeroflot turn out to be not much of an upgrade from Eurolines Coaches, they also managed to break my vodka bottle.

I only discovered this when I strapped my backpack on again in transit in Düsseldorf, and the contents of the bottle I'd bought in Moscow seeped through and soaked my shirt. At least, I thought, as I sat there ponging in the departure lounge, I smell so badly of hooch no-one will guess I need a bath as well.

There'd been no time for a kip or a wash after the game, as I'd needed to be at the airport by 4am, and the two large swigs I'd taken from my vodka bottle before Aeroflot destroyed it were mostly for medicinal purposes.

The anaesthetic was required for my right arm, which was purple with bruises, and giving me a lot of gyp. This was the result of finding myself seated next to a spectacularly inebriated local, in his mid-twenties or thereabouts, who quickly made it apparent that he'd managed to get around the Stadium alcohol ban by taking on large quantities of fluid – camel like – in order to get through a match which might easily, and indeed did, stretch to extra time and penalties.

He spoke fairly good English, or would have done had he not parted company with the majority of his brain cells earlier in the day, This much I'd managed to work out when he decided to introduce himself by thumping his fist into my arm, and shouting 'Da!'

I might have expected something like this had it followed hard on the heels of some piece of brilliance from Ronaldo, or Drogba, but at the time they were still releasing balloons in what passed for pre-match entertainment. And when the game finally kicked off, my companion continued his assault on my arm, even for such mundane events as the ref blowing for a goal kick.

Half time was the worst. 'English?' he slurred. I shook my head. 'Yes, English,' he asserted. '*Niet*,' I said. 'No fool me' he said. 'I know England. It is, it is, is place of, place of . . .' I wondered what was coming. Winston Churchill? Bowler hats? Fish and chips? Finally, he remembered. 'It is place of . . . many ships!' At which point he broke into a huge laugh, and launched another right hander into the piece of rare steak that was now my upper arm.

'Er, not any more,' I told him. 'More?' he said. 'Ships. Not many ships any more.' He thought about this for a while, before deciding to change tack. 'What you think of Russian cinema?' Shamefully, I had to tell him that Russian cinema wasn't my strong suit. 'Hollywood!' he shouted. 'No good!' It was probably no different to watching the game back at home in Wetherspoons. Bloody hell, I thought. If I'd wanted to watch the Champions League final listening to gibberish like this I could have stayed at home and gone to the pub.

I was consoling myself with the thought that it was probably no different to watching the match back at home in Wetherspoons, when, early in the second half he punched me again. This time with a cry of 'No!' At which point he somehow hauled himself upright, let out another cry of 'No!', and was off down the exit. Cannoning off various spectators as he went.

The smell of vodka has finally gone, but the nightmares still return from time to time, and if ever someone asks me now 'can I carry your bags?' I trot out the trip to Moscow story. The moral of which is: 'be careful what you wish for'.